MW00713462

Cornel West and the Politics of Prophetic Pragmatism

Cornel West and the Politics of Prophetic Pragmatism

MARK DAVID WOOD

University of Illinois Press
URBANA AND CHICAGO

Manufactured in the United States of America
∞ This book is printed on acid-free paper.

Library of Congress Cataloging-in-Publication Data
Wood, Mark David, 1959–
Cornel West and the politics of prophetic pragmatism / Mark David Wood.
p. cm.
Includes bibliographical references and index.
ISBN 0-252-02578-4 (alk. paper)
1. Social classes—United States. 2. Racism—United States.
3. United States—Race relations. 4. Communism and Christianity.
5. Liberation theology. 6. Pragmatism. 7. West, Cornel. I. Title.
HN90.S6W66 2000
305.5'0973—dc21 99-050749

C 5 4 3 2 1

To my students

Contents

Acknowledgments

I want to acknowledge Professors Charles Long, Laurence Thomas, Jim Wiggins, Charles Winquist, and Mas'ud Zavarzadeh for their generous support of my intellectual development as a graduate student at Syracuse University. I especially want to thank Charles Winquist for nourishing my passion for intellectual work. I also want to acknowledge Professors Njeri Jackson, chair of the African American Studies program at Virginia Commonwealth University, and Cliff Edwards, chair of the Religious Studies program at Virginia Commonwealth University. Dr. Jackson's tireless efforts to illuminate the truth regarding race, class, and gender oppression and her many contributions to overcoming these maladies have been an endless source of intellectual and existential sustenance. Dr. Edwards's remarkable commitment to teaching, his graciousness as a human being, and his encouraging words have been soulfully refreshing. I also want to acknowledge Jonathon Jones, Judith Poxon, Pam Stockman, Kristi Swenson, and Jon Waybright for their rejuvenating friendship. They have been lifeblood for me. I also want to thank my brother, Greg Wood, for walking strongly by my side and my mother, Debbie, for her loving belief in me. I also want to thank several persons at the University of Illinois Press for their generous assistance. The anonymous readers provided many helpful comments and suggestions. Bruce Bethell's meticulously critical editing, which he described as being akin to the "rantings of some English teacher from hell," substantially improved this manuscript. University of Illinois Press executive editor Richard Martin confidently guided this book from early drafts through several major revisions to completion. I also want to acknowledge Maria Christina Ramos. She spent a good portion of her summer proofreading the manuscript and consistently urged me on to the finish line during those moments when my spirit was low. Finally, I want to acknowledge my students, whose energetic dedication to justice eternally inspires me.

Cornel West and the Politics of Prophetic Pragmatism

Introduction: Prophetic Pragmatism and the Future of Revolutionary Democratic Politics

CORNEL WEST AND Henry Louis Gates Jr. appear on the cover of the March 1999 issue of *Emerge*. The cover reads, "Dream Team: Harvard Scholars Race for the Future." Jacqueline Trescott opens her article about the "Dream Team" with a vivid portrait of one of its major stars:

> Cornel West is pacing the floor of the Lowell Lecture Hall auditorium at Harvard University. Wielding a dog-eared copy of Toni Morrison's *Beloved* and moving his head from side to side, he looks as if he is spinning. His students, packed to the balcony's last row, are captivated. Some have even brought their parents to his introductory course on Afro-American Studies, now the fifth most popular class in the undergraduate curriculum. Waiting for it to begin is like waiting for a movie you've heard a lot about to burst onto the scene. "Take a risk, exercise your critical imagination," he says, as he talks about a writing assignment. He uses the novel to discuss the dehumanization and the African-American struggle for identity, the desire for protection, for family. One second he is quoting Keats, another it's funkmeister George Clinton. "Can the people of African descent in America ever feel they can be protected from violence, physical violence, psychic violence?" he asks, letting the trained philosopher slide in front of the pop-savvy professor. (Trescott 1999:38)

When West is not lecturing in the classroom or writing another book to add to the fourteen already published, he is presenting his ideas to thousands of individuals each year in churches, synagogues, temples, and mosques; civic association and labor assembly halls; nationally syndicated radio and television shows; and, most recently, in the streets advocating for former presidential candidate Bill Bradley. At Faneuil Hall Marketplace in Boston, several hundred citizens heard West's argument as to why they ought to support Bradley's run for the presidency: "Let the word go forth from this historic place here and now that Bill Bradley is on the *move,* he is on the *move!* And that we are there *with* him, be*side* him, a*round* him, because we are fundamentally dedicated to keeping alive the best of the democratic tradition and Bill Bradley *is* the president who best em*bod*ies that, he en*acts* that, he in fact provides the presidential *gra*vitas necessary to take this nation into the 21st century! Let me say that again: presidential *gra*vitas!" (in Goldberg 2000:A7).

Indeed, in the eighteen years that have passed since West published *Prophesy Deliverance,* in which he boldly elaborated an Afro-American revolutionary Christian perspective to advance "the cause of human freedom," West has become one of the most widely recognized and publicly influential academic intellectuals in the United States (West 1982:11). His critical theory of *prophetic pragmatism* and dedicated practice as a *critical organic catalyst* have contributed considerably to American progressivism. West has theoretically and practically engaged many of society's most challenging cultural, political, and economic problems and articulated concrete proposals to build a more democratic, just, and humane society. Unlike those who seek little more than to lessen the cruelty of capitalist-controlled development, West is motivated by a concern to create a genuine "alternative to an unnecessary and unacceptable fate" (Unger and West 1998:58). Not only is West inspired by the possibility that "class, race, and gender hierarchy" will not "have the last word on how far democracy will go in our time"; he also inspires other individuals to join him in the fight for social justice and human rights (1999b:xx). As the Alphonse Fletcher Jr. University Professor at Harvard University, a key member of the Democratic Socialists of America and President Clinton's National Conversation on Race advisory council, a cochair of the National Parenting Association's Task Force on Parent Empowerment, an ardent supporter of Bill Bradley, a lay Baptist preacher, an eloquent orator, and a prolific scholar, West remains as deeply committed to the task of constructing "a more free and democratic world" today as he was when he began his career, and by his own account he is just now "begin[ning] a whole new wave of work and texts" (ibid.:562, 563).

West's impact as a scholar, teacher, and activist was widely recognized within academic and theological circles by the end of the 1980s. By the early 1990s West had achieved national recognition as one of America's most important intellectuals (Boynton 1991). Academic colleagues and extra-academic commentators alike noted his exceptional ability to connect his scholarship and teaching to everyday issues of ethical and societal import. The publication of *Race Matters* in 1993 dramatically demonstrated West's ability to write about affirmative action, black politics, leadership, sexuality, Malcolm X, and the future of democracy in America in a style that was at once philosophically challenging and reasonably accessible to nonacademic readers. In fact, *Race Matters,* as Ellen Coughlin observed, moved West "into a different orbit" (1993:8). His name became virtually synonymous with the notion of the scholar as public intellectual. West placed philosophy in the service of democracy and creatively combined Christianity, pragmatism, and Marxism to develop a liberationist "theology of the street" (Sanoff 1992–93). He was "one complex dude: brilliant scholar, political activist, committed Christian and soul brother down to the bone"; in the eyes of many he had become "one of the most insightful and passionate analysts of America's racial dilemma to emerge in recent years, the architect of a post–civil rights philosophy of black liberation that is beginning to be heard across the country" (White 1993:60). West presented his ideas at universities, was interviewed on radio talk shows, and appeared on numerous television programs, including William F. Buckley's *Firing Line.* By the mid-1990s he was "one of the most talked-about academics in the United States" (Anderson 1994:40). In "an era when African American thinkers are drawing greater public recognition than ever before," Gene Seymour observed, "Cornel West may well be the biggest star of all" (1994:33). Harvard Divinity School dean Ronald Theimann compared West to Reinhold Niebuhr, New School for Social Research Philosophy Department chairperson Richard Bernstein likened him to John Dewey, and Harvard University Afro-American Studies Department chair Henry Louis Gates Jr. simply declared that West is "the preeminent African American intellectual of our generation," adding in concert with Bill Bradley that "for anyone concerned about the crisis of contemporary America, Cornel West matters" (*Race Matters* cover material).

Through his prolific scholarly writing and unmistakable oratory, West has become a major source of inspiration for individuals committed to social justice (Dyson 1993; Wallis 1994). In his introduction to a series of articles published in *Monthly Review* on "the ethical dimensions of Marxist thought," John Bellamy Foster writes that West's work constitutes the kind of "resource of hope [that] enable[s] socialists to continue the 'shared search' for human emancipation in spite of all the obstacles posed by the reality of capitalism and of the first attempts to create socialism" (1993:8). West's efforts to illuminate the ethical dimensions of Marxist thought by discussing his religious identity, Samir Amin argues, are invaluable, for they allow others to identify the ethical core of their own commitment to social justice (1993:56).

Whereas *Race Matters* catapulted West into the national spotlight, the 1998 publication of both *The Future of American Progressivism* and *The War against Parents,* as well as his participation on the National Parenting Association's Task Force on Parent Empowerment and President Clinton's National Conversation on Race advisory council, guarantees West even greater recognition and influence within and beyond academic circles. Psychologists, sociologists, politicians, CEOs, religious representatives, and community activists applaud *The War against Parents* as, according to William Julius Wilson, "the book we have been waiting for" (*War against Parents* cover material). Hewlett and West propose a parents' "Bill of Rights" that, as Carol Gilligan indicates, amounts to a "Marshall Plan to rebuild families devastated by social and economic policies and by the racial and gender divisions which this book symbolically ends" (ibid.). When Maya Angelou says that "Cornel West thinks like a sage, acts like a warrior, and writes like a poetical prophet," she voices a sentiment shared among academics and nonacademics alike (in Hewlett and West 1998:i). Kweisi Mfume, president and CEO of the NAACP, says *The War against Parents* "presents an insightful social analysis that examines the parent's role in American society and how it vastly affects our children. This important discourse creates a powerful case for uniting parents and healing the nation across the racial divide" (ibid.).

With each new scholarly publication, public lecture, and political engagement, West's place within the unfolding development of American intellectual, cultural, and political history is looking increasingly similar to that of John Dewey. West's philosophical and political affinities with Dewey are especially evident in *Race Matters, The War against Parents,* and *The Future of American Progressivism.* All these works, especially the last, outline a post–New Deal compact that "rejects the simple contrast between governmental activism and free enterprise, not because it wants to have a little of each, but because it insists upon having more of both" (Unger and West 1998:57). Unger and West's project in fact constitutes one of the first serious attempts to elaborate a progressive alternative to the neoconservative orthodoxy that has dominated capitalist politics over the past twenty-five years. Perhaps this explains why Edward Said christens West "the authentic teacher of hope and freedom" (*The Cornel West Reader* cover material).

Like all figures who are widely praised, West has also been widely criticized. Indeed, West's scholarship, pedagogy, and activism have been criticized from a range of political perspectives. Leon Wieseltier criticizes West's work as "sectarian, humorless, pedantic and self-endeared" (1995:31). Adolph Reed (1995) adds that the problem with black public intellectuals such as West is that they are in large measure "hand-picked" by white elites and consigned the task of communicating the reality of black life to predominantly white audiences in a manner that does not significantly challenge the status quo. Manning Marable, director of the Institute for Research in African-American Studies at Columbia University, agrees that "a significant number of black scholars speak primarily to white elites, rather than addressing the specific problems of the African-American community," adding that "few black intellectuals today maintain an authentic, organic relationship with multi-class, black formations which have significant constituencies among working class and poor people" (1995:168, 170). West, Marable notes, is, however, one of the few intellectuals who has maintained such alliances even as many scholars have criticized him for embracing traditional liberalism (170).

Among those to advance such criticisms are Stephen Steinberg and Kofi Buenor Hadjor. In *Turning Back: The Retreat from Racial Justice in American Thought and Policy* (1995), Steinberg suggests that because West "presents social breakdown and cultural disintegration as a problem *sui generis,*" his analysis "comes dangerously close to the prevailing view of ghetto youth as driven by aberrant and anti-social tendencies" (130, 127). West's synthesis of liberal structuralist and conservative behaviorist positions leaves him "in a political never-never land where, as Du Bois once said in his critique of historiography, 'nobody seems to have done wrong and everybody was right.' And nothing changes" (133). Although he criticizes the conservative "blame the victim" perspective, his own emphasis on personal morality and spiritual conversion, writes Hadjor in *Another America,* conforms closely to this perspective (1995:165). Other scholars contend that West persuasively enjoins people of goodwill to build a more democratic society and yet says little about how to achieve this goal (Sanders 1994:647; Bowman 1994:7; White 1993:62). When West has elaborated what must be done to build such a society, his proposals have been criticized as inadequate and confused. In the online magazine *Salon,* Joan Walsh concludes her review of *The War against Parents* by stating that the book "is a case study of what happens when reformers attempt to please everybody: West and Hewlett's moral diagnosis will enrage liberals, their policy prescription will drive away conservatives and the book leaves us no closer to a family agenda than before they began" (1998:3). Still others argue that because West's prophetic pragmatism combines progressive government interventions and market-friendly reforms, it lacks sufficient coherence to advance genuinely radical democratic politics.

Whether criticized or praised, discommended or celebrated, West's scholarship, pedagogy, and activism have consistently energized, provoked, and inspired individuals both inside and beyond the academy to think more critically and participate more fully in the struggle for human freedom.

West's work has generated a range of sympathetic and critical responses and will no doubt continue to do so. Whether or not West assumes the mantel of Neibuhr, Du Bois, Dewey, or some combination thereof remains to be seen. What can be said with relative certainty, however, is that West has contributed significantly to the development of progressive pragmatist theory and practice. Regardless of whether one agrees with all, some, or none of West's philosophical views, theoretical concepts, pedagogical strategies, rhetorical tactics, or policy proposals, his work is, as he says of Emerson's, James's, and Dewey's work, provocative, inspiring, and energizing for scholars and students within the academy and for tens of thousands more outside the academy who read his work and hear him speak. Although he may think of himself as "just a brother who comes out of the black church on the block, trying to make sense of the world, and making a blow for freedom," West has already made substantial contributions to progressive politics, and as we begin the new millennium, he optimistically declares that he has "only just begun" (in Yancy 1999:47; West 1999b:562).

The Central Project of This Work

This book critiques West's theory of prophetic pragmatism and his concept of the critical organic catalyst. To the extent that West is profoundly informed by and significantly contributes to the progressive pragmatist tradition, my work is equally a critique of this tradition. My critique of prophetic pragmatism is thus a minor contribution to the task of criticizing progressivist politics, a task that in turn constitutes an important component in the project of developing a political theory that supports the work of democratizing global productive and consumptive relations.

My interpretation of prophetic pragmatism is based on three interrelated sociological, philosophical, and political premises that function as methodological guideposts throughout. First, individual self-creation depends on satisfying basic needs and having access to the resources required to engage in creative work. Second, building a society in which all human beings may enjoy creative work—the basis of individuation—in a manner that is responsible to and empowering of society as a whole can be accomplished only on the basis of public ownership of productive property and democratic planning of societal development. Third, capitalism, as the dominant mode of global socioeconomic organization, is *structurally* incapable of achieving these goals. At best capitalism realizes them haphazardly and for only a small minority. At worst it destroys the natural and social resources required to achieve these goals for most human beings.[1]

Although many on the left will agree with this last premise, most would no doubt add that "really existing" socialism has proven itself little or no better than capitalism with regard to accomplishing these goals. In many respects they would be correct, even though it is also true that the cold war mantra "socialism was tried and failed" erases postcapitalist states' successes in establishing more humane conditions of life. That socialist societies have so far fallen short of ensuring satisfaction of basic needs and rich individual development indicates only that these goods have yet to be achieved. In this respect I agree with Brian Lloyd when he claims "that we are witnessing, not the death of Marxism [and socialism], but the end of the first period during which Marxists [socialists] managed to seize and, for a time, wield state power" (1997:3). Just as capitalism did not come into the world with one great revolution, so it will not pass out of existence with one mass strike. Nor, for that matter, will a genuinely socialist society be created overnight. The abolition of private ownership of productive property would merely liberate the resources to build such a society.

Capitalism is structurally incapable of lifting all boats. Competition among private property owners to increase their share of naturally existing and socially generated wealth inescapably results in socioeconomic inequalities. Attempts to mix capitalist and socialist principles of production and distribution have met with little success, for they represent incompatible modes of organizing and orienting societal development. This is not to say that attempts to restrict corporate power and distribute wealth more equitably—that is, to introduce "socialist" principles into the market economy—are not important. Rather, it is "to underline that the struggle must be for working-class power" (Tabb 1999:6). Only by constructing the U.S. political economy on the basis of democratic control of productive property can the ideals of liberty, equality, and fraternity be fully realized.

Although I assume that workers and their allies can achieve these ideals, I do not assume that an awareness of the need to abolish private property mechanically, spontaneously, or inevitably results from capitalist exploitation and resistance to it. To paraphrase Marx, capitalism may produce its own gravediggers, but no metaphysical or teleological necessity compels workers to execute this task. Diverse ideological and institutional forces contain revolutionary potentials within the boundaries of capitalist property relations. Although resistance to oppression and exploitation is dramatically expanding around the world, this resistance does not inevitably develop into a self-consciously revolutionary movement. To paraphrase Lenin, no such movement develops without the development of revolutionary theory. Developing such a theory requires discerning the extent to which competing theories accurately grasp the social, political, and economic conditions of subjection and liberation. Deconstructionist caveats aside, to change the world, we must acquire an accurate understanding of the world we seek to change. Thus, my critique of prophetic pragmatism is finally a critique of West's claims regarding the causes of human suffering and what can and ought to be done to alleviate this suffering.

Throughout this work I engage in both an *immanent* reading of the philosophical and conceptual development of prophetic pragmatism and a *contextual* reading that explores this development in the light of the social forces that presently inform intellectual production. The first task involves excavating, explicating, and evaluating the theological, philosophical, sociological, and methodological assumptions and concepts from which West draws to articulate prophetic pragmatism. At this juncture I am less concerned with West's positions on specific issues and more with examining the assumptions that provide his metatheoretical foundations. To move beyond an immanent reading of prophetic pragmatism and examine how prophetic pragmatism is shaped by and shapes present efforts either to maintain and expand capitalist property relations (relations that produce and are reproduced by racist, sexist, and nationalist relations of authority and power) or to maintain and expand democratic property relations (relations whose realization depends on the abolition of capitalist as well as racist, sexist, and nationalist relations of authority and power), we must have at least a general understanding of the society that informs prophetic pragmatism and that prophetic pragmatism seeks to change. Thus, throughout this work I describe some of the principal cultural, social, political, and economic features of transnational capitalism. The description I present bears the stamp of my theoretical and political commitments and provides the empirical and theoretical point of reference for my investigation and evaluation of prophetic pragmatism.

I begin my critique in chapter 1, "The Christian-Marxist Dialogue and the End of Liberation Theology," by examining the impact of West's Christian identity on his theoretical articulation of prophetic pragmatism. I begin here because, as West clarifies, his vocation as an advocate for the wretched of the earth derives from his identification with prophetic Christianity. Whereas Marx, following in Feuerbach's footsteps, assumed that the criticism of religion is "the premise of all criticism," West premises his social criticism on his faith in God. In *The Ethical Dimensions of Marxist Thought* West explains, "I am a non-Marxist socialist in that as a Christian, I recognize certain irreconcilable differences between Marxists of whatever sort and Christians of whatever sort" (1991:xxvii). West's belief in God was nurtured by his family, friends, and community. *Prophesy Deliverance* is dedicated to his grandfather, Rev. Clifton West Sr., a Baptist preacher who awakened West to the power and value of the prophetic Christian tradition. For West, Christianity provides personal sustenance and "a way to demand that service and sacrifice, care and love sit at the center of what it means to be human" (West 1991:53). Prophetic pragmatism, says West, represents a critical synthesis of the existentialist issues of dread, despair, and death and the political concerns of democracy, equality, and justice. West's Christocentric orientation vigorously animates his belief that class, race, and gender oppression will not "have the last word on how far democracy can go" and existentially sustains his tireless efforts to foster the development of more just, democratic, and equitable conditions of existence (1999b:xx).

My interpretation of West's religious identity focuses on the way his theological assumptions regarding human nature, historical development, social transformation, and human liberation inform not only his interpretation of Marxist theory and politics but also his analyses of and solutions to social, political, and economic problems. I also explore his arguments regarding the tragic nature of existence to discern their implications for the struggle to create a democratic, just, and humane society. What are the consequences of translating social and political problems into theological and existential ones? Is a tragic sense of life really necessary to fuel radical democratic struggles, as West argues, or might this and other theological/existentialist categories discourage such struggles? In the last section of this chapter I consider West's contributions to liberation theology and the meaning of liberation theology in relationship to international anticapitalist politics. I argue that liberation theology may be to capitalism what the Protestant Reformation was to feudalism—namely, its death knell sounded in the categories of theological discourse and revolutionary religious practice.

In chapter 2, "Race, Class, Power," I begin to investigate West's interpretation and reworking of Marxist presuppositions and categories, a project I continue throughout the book. Unlike many on the left who rejected Marxism with the "collapse of communism," West has developed his own theory and practice through a critical engagement with the Marxist tradition.[2] Like C. R. L. James, Cedric Robinson, Henry Winston, and Manning Marable, West develops Marxism to advance the cause of black liberation. As a research program, Marxism emphasizes the need to investigate, analyze, and explain the relationships between various aspects of specific modes of production. Without investigating these relationships, says West, it is impossible to grasp the "totalizing forces in the world," and without comprehending these forces, "our politics become emaciated, our politics become dispersed, our politics become nothing but existential rebellion" (1993c:82).[3] Although West "somewhat hesitant[ly]" rejects what he calls the "linchpin" of the Marxist view, which maintains that "the economic sphere is the ultimate determining explanatory factor for grasping the role and function of racism in modern societies," and although in *The Future of American Progressivism* he calls Marxism a European theory that is paralyzing inasmuch as it presupposes "the existence of a system out there" (Unger and West 1998:29), he maintains that we cannot understand "the market forces around the world and the fundamental role of transnational corporations . . . without understanding some of the insights of the Marxist tradition" (in Yancy 1998:41). West's engagement with Marxism continues the exchange between pragmatists and Marxists initiated a century ago. Like his pragmatist predecessors, West contends that Marx shares much in common with James, Dewey, and the father of American pragmatism, Ralph Waldo Emerson. Indeed, West's development of the thesis that pragmatism and Marxism share much in common constitutes one of his principal contributions to the elaboration of a post-Marxist politics. My criticism of West's interpretation and reworking of Marxism in chapter 2 focuses on his development of a "genealogical materialist analysis." West grafts Foucault's concepts of discourse, power, and knowledge onto Marx's concepts of property, politics, and class struggle to explain the "discursive" variable in the racial formation of racial identitics, relations, and inequalities. Although I focus specifically on West's synthesis of Foucauldian and Marxist theories, I also draw conclusions regarding the consequences of theoretical eclecticism for radical democratic politics.

In chapter 3, "Racism and the Struggle for Working-Class Democracy," I elaborate on West's Marxist critique of racism as articulated in *Prophesy Deliverance* and in many of the essays in *Prophetic Fragments.*[4] In these earlier works West explicated a general theory regarding the relationship between race and class and argued that efforts to combat racism must be advanced as part of an international working-class-based movement against capitalism. He contended that class is more significant than race in determining who possesses and who lacks power, that capitalism is an antidemocratic mode of social organization, and that only public control of societal planning constitutes the basis of genuine democracy. In agreement with West, I describe some of the ways in which the relationship between racism and exploitation has changed since the end of the civil rights era and how these changes have in turn altered the ways in which race and class reproduce each other. Among the most notable of changes to occur since the end of the civil rights era is the emergence of a socially significant and politically influential black middle class and business elite. Meanwhile, conditions of life for a majority of black citizens remain very much the same as they were prior to the passage of civil rights legislation. The deepening and increasingly visible class divisions within black America have in turn affected the formation of capitalist ideology, resulting in a discourse of ethnic and cultural diversity that supports transnational processes of capital accumulation just as the discourse of biological racism supported capital accumulation under slavery and segregation. After describing this discourse, I conclude by arguing, as West argued prior to the publication of *The American Evasion of Philosophy* (a period hereafter referred to as pre-*Evasion*), that the struggle to abolish racism is most progressively advanced as an integral aspect of the struggle for working-class democracy. This claim cuts both ways in the sense that the "only hope for unifying the overwhelming majority of people of various races, ethnic groups, and people of both sexes in the United Sates, in a movement for a just, equitable society, is by placing the principle of racial [and ethnic and sexual] egalitarianism on the top furl of our marching banner" (Goldfield 1997:362).[5] The struggle against racism is thus a key to abolishing class divisions and building a society in which every person may enjoy labor, leisure, and life in the context of peace, community, and fraternity. In this regard West was exactly right when he contended that "class politics must be the prism through which black politics are elaborated" and that workers across the color spectrum must act together to defeat imperialism and "common capitalist foes" (1988a:137, 77).

In chapter 4, "The Pragmatic Concepts of Truth, Reality, and Politics," I explore the relationships between West's rejection of foundationalist epistemologies and realist ontologies and his conceptions of society and social change. As a pragmatist, West affirms a soft relativism that denies any absolute, universal, and eternal principles on which to ground ethical practices and yet simultaneously affirms that history and the struggle for democracy provide the principal bases for articulating and assessing the practical value of competing truth claims (1989:4).[6] John Bellamy Foster notes that West "has no difficulty in claiming that some moral positions are better than others. [His theory's] criterion of judgment, however, is historical rather than philosophical. It places trust in the messy process of the making of human communities through collective action, rather than relying on abstract philosophic adjudication from above, when faced with competing moral views" (1993: 14–15). I argue that West's antifoundationalist and antirealist arguments do not so much address purely philosophical concerns as provide support for his transition from a predominantly property-based to a non-property-based analysis of race and class relations. Although West remains attentive to the problem of race and class as structural and not merely subjective impediments to the realization of individual freedom within community, in his post-*Evasion* works he increasingly uses cultural, discursive, psychological, and existential categories to interpret societal problems and conceptualizes the problem of class divisions as a matter of creating greater movement within the existing system of socioeconomic relations. Thus, for example, in *Race Matters* West contends that "the major enemy of black survival in America has been and is neither oppression nor exploitation but rather the nihilistic threat, . . . the loss of hope and meaning," and that nihilism can be "tamed [only] by love and care," by "a politics of conversion," by a "turning of one's soul" (1993a:15, 18, 19). In *The War against Parents* he and Hewlett argue that corporate greed is the root cause of social inequalities and that we must reform, rather than replace, capitalism to reestablish a more egalitarian society. In *The Future of American Progressivism* he and Unger argue for a reform program that creates greater class mobility instead of abolishing the division of society into separate, unequal, and hostile classes. I conclude this chapter with a critique of West's post-Marxist response to racism in *Race Matters.*

In chapter 5, "The Past, Present, and Future of American Pragmatism," I begin to examine the politics represented by pragmatism in order to assess West's own claim that the American pragmatist tradition is the best that America has to offer to itself and to the world in terms of supporting both autonomous and allied struggles to create a society based on democratic planning of development (West 1989:8). To accomplish this task, I draw from and summarize West's own genealogy of American pragmatism. I then explicate how West's concept of the critical organic catalyst provides a strategy for breaking with pragmatism's reform-oriented politics. I complete this chapter by examining West's move away from class-struggle to class-coalition formulations of social change and suggest that, as West indicates, pragmatism may prove inadequate as a theoretical guide to help us solve the global social and ecological crises we face.

In chapter 6, "Saving the Nation in the Era of Transnational Capitalism," I examine West's formulation of democracy, freedom, individuality, and the nation-state and argue that whereas in *Prophesy Deliverance* West elaborated these categories in terms of the ways in which they are mediated by class relations, in *The American Evasion of Philosophy* and subsequent works he defines them increasingly in abstraction from these relations. Although West remains concerned about economics and the manner in which class structures inhibit individual mobility and democratic practice, he is less and less concerned with the manner in which wealth is produced—that is, with who controls the processes and means of production—than he is with loosening class structures and distributing income more equitably through institutional reforms. I contend that West's internationalist, anti-imperialist, anticapitalist perspective, as expressed in *Prophesy Deliverance* and *Prophetic Fragments*, remains essential to the struggle for genuine democracy and that his post-*Evasion* work represents a furthering of his turn away from Marxist theory and politics.

In chapter 7, "Prophetic Pragmatism and the American Evasion of Class Struggle," I examine the post-Marxist politics West elaborates with Sylvia Ann Hewlett in *The War against Parents* and Roberto Mangabeira Unger in *The Future of American Progressivism.* These works present West's concrete articulation of prophetic pragmatism and, as such, provide a generative opportunity to evaluate the extent to which prophetic pragmatism accurately comprehends the nature of contemporary capitalist realities. To what extent does prophetic pragmatism challenge why the pie "never gets recut more equally or how it gets baked in the first place" (West 1982:116), and to what extent does it remain primarily concerned with distributing "pie slices" more equitably among American citizens? Is prophetic pragmatism a political philosophy that, in the tradition of Dewey, seeks to create a kinder, gentler capitalism, or does it supersede Dewey's project by advancing the struggle for a genuine alternative to capitalist civilization?

In chapter 8, "The Future of Revolutionary Democratic Politics," I summarize my investigation of prophetic pragmatism in the context of a discussion of the problems that confront those who are committed to progressive change and yet dependent on conservative institutions. West's reflections illuminate "the paradox of earning a living from corporate institutions while attempting to redress many of their oppressive effects" and the ways in which the articulation of theory and practice is situated by larger social forces (Sanders 1994:648). These forces may in no small measure explain West's transition from the explicit internationalist, anti-imperialist, anticapitalist revolutionary politics he advanced in *Prophesy Deliverance* and *Prophetic Fragments* to the American-centered, free-market, left-liberal reform politics he articulates in such works as *Race Matters, The War against Parents,* and *The Future of American Progressivism.* West's defenders would no doubt add that unlike Marxists, West understands that revolutionary politics are not likely to find a readily receptive audience in the U.S. working class and that West's transition is guided by his strategic appreciation of what can be done given prevailing ideological realities. Although I agree that revolutionary theory and practice remain underdeveloped, the protests against the World Trade Organization that took place in Seattle, Washington, and in cities around the world during the last week of November 1999 indicate that forces opposed to corporate domination of planetary life are diverse, organized, and growing—so much so that many left-identified academicians, having long since abandoned the possibility of advancing anything like an anticapitalist politics, find themselves having to rethink their commitments. Although members of national and international labor, environmental, and human rights organizations marched side by side in Seattle, it should be noted that they represented divergent and in many respects fundamentally incompatible political perspectives: from trade union protectionists and liberal democrats to anarchists and revolutionary socialists. There is thus widespread opposition to various aspects of capitalist development and in some cases to capitalism as a totalizing system, but it remains undetermined as to whether this opposition will develop ideologically and organizationally into a coordinated movement to replace capitalist-controlled with democratically controlled globalization. I thus conclude my critique of prophetic pragmatism by describing several projects that left intellectuals may undertake to foster the development of such a movement.

Looking Backward, Looking Forward: Race and Class

In *Left Out* (1977) Brian Lloyd sets out to discern the reasons for American workers' repeated failures to advance a genuine anticapitalist movement. Scholars cite various factors to explain this failure: that the United States was established without having to defeat feudalism; that workers here have enjoyed (albeit unevenly and in large measure on the basis of imperialist exploitation) relatively better standards of life than do other workers around the world; and that racial, ethnic, and religious divisions have repeatedly subverted working-class solidarity. Although all these factors have impeded and continue to impede the development of revolutionary socialist politics, Lloyd contends that a crucial cause of this failure has been pragmatism's repeated ideological transformation of Marxist theory and practice into an eclectic mixture of reformist ideologies and programs. It is not that the working class would not have been served by Marxist theory but rather that either Marxism was never fully developed or, more often than not, whatever theory was developed made little or no distinction between, for example, trade unionism and seizure of state power or between social reform and socialist revolution. Collapsing these differences abetted the preservation and expansion of capitalist social relations. "The failure worth lamenting," writes Lloyd, "is not the absence of a labor or social democratic party" or the absence of movements with explicitly anticapitalist, if not explicitly prosocialist, political agendas. Nor is it the absence of racial solidarity (Lloyd 1997:14; see Aptheker 1992). Rather, the failure that warrants our consideration is the repeated "surrender of the ideological ground upon which a genuinely anticapitalist campaign could even be visualized, let alone actually fought. American and European radicals contributed equally to this defeat" during the late nineteenth and early twentieth century (Lloyd 1997:14).

Almost one hundred years after Du Bois gave the address in which he stated that the problem of the twentieth century is the problem of the color line and almost one hundred years after the revolutionary potentiality of the Populist movements of the late nineteenth and early twentieth centuries were subverted by white supremacy and dissolved into social democratic and liberal reformist politics, capitalism remains alive and, though perhaps not well, powerful enough to continue its forced march of humanity into ecological and social devastation. Assuming the triumph of global capitalism, the question that haunts many of us is whether the earth itself will survive this "triumph" (see Greider 1997:444–45; Quammen 1998; King and Woodyard 1999). In his sobering essay "The Social Immune System and the Cancer Stage of Capitalism," John McMurtry contends that capital is destroying social and natural resources at a terrifying rate (1995:1). We "now confront a situation where the cumulative breakdown of society's structures of life-security and health protection"—a breakdown whose cruel effects are, as always, distributed as unequally as money—"poses a more systemically far-reaching threat to social and planetary well-being than we are yet prepared for" (ibid.).[7] Capitalism is generating grotesque socioeconomic inequalities between and within nations and leaving a growing proportion of humanity jobless, homeless, and desolate.

> All over the world, people are finding themselves reduced from human beings with the right to speak, vote, organize, and act collectively—and entitled to food, housing, healthcare, and job security—to mere flotsam and jetsam of the labor market, surviving only by selling their labor on a short-term, contingent

> basis. Meanwhile, their environment is being destroyed by an unrestrained global economy that poisons the air and water, turns plains into deserts, chops down forests, and disturbs the most basic balance on which all life depends through the uncontrollable emission of greenhouse gasses. (Brecher and Costello 1998:xx)

In addition to fostering socioeconomic inequality and environmental destruction, capitalism is also generating, through the same mechanisms that ensure its "success," structural contradictions that if left unaddressed will create a crisis far worse than the 1930s depression—a possibility already evident in the financial tremors that have shaken and continue to shake economies worldwide. The contradiction at the core of capitalist social relations is that in pursuing profit, each investor seeks to lower production costs primarily by lowering labor costs, and yet in doing so the capacity of workers to purchase the products they produce is simultaneously reduced. This process, William Greider notes, "creates a growing gap between production potential and the market potential to buy all that production, which in turn eventually leads to financial collapse" (1998:46), no matter what stop-gap measures (e.g., government bailouts and corporate alliances) are deployed to postpone such a collapse. Jeffrey E. Garten, a financial investor who spent thirteen years on Wall Street, served as U.S. undersecretary of commerce for international trade, and is now dean of the Yale School of Management, adds that "massive overproduction is creating downward pressure everywhere—not just in Asia but also in the United States. Just pick up this morning's newspaper. In the auto industry, for example, there is tremendous excess capacity" (in ibid.:43), which is to say, underconsumption of the commodities produced. In fact, at current rates of production and consumption, the global overcapacity of cars by the year 2000 is expected to be the "equivalent of the entire North American industry—only larger. To bring supply and demand into balance, the industry would have to discover a new consumer market that was bigger than the United States" (Greider 1997:112), and of course one that possessed the cash to buy these cars. Yet this is precisely the issue; the dominant logic guiding capital investment is to seek out the lowest possible costs, and yet, as Peter Schavoir, IBM's director of strategy before his retirement, points out, "You can't become so efficient that all this stuff is made without any labor content. Because then you have nobody with the money to buy anything" (in ibid.:119). Built into the very structure of global capitalism is a "perverse syllogism," says Greider, "company by company, sector by sector: the burdensome presence of overcapacity quickens the price competition and threatens market shares, but the only obvious response is to create more new capacity—that is, to build new factories that will be more cost-efficient than one's rivals" (103–4). And so it goes, such that, if not addressed on an international scale, this structural contradiction will eventuate in a worldwide financial, social, and political meltdown. Moreover, as diverse social justice, environmental, and human rights organizations increasingly express themselves in the form of both autonomous and unified actions against corporate power, states in wealthier nations will no doubt deploy more repressive means to dissipate and contain this opposition, a tactic already used in poorer nations. The declaration of martial law, deployment of national guard troops, and use of tear gas, pepper spray, and mass arrests against predominantly peaceful protesters in Seattle (as well as the military's use of cities throughout the United States to practice urban assaults and the expansion of domestic security, public surveillance, and prisons) may well signal a new phase in capital's war against those who demand a people's democracy in the realm of economics.

Indeed, the present period is characterized not only by a dramatic extension of capital's control over productive resources, financial assets, and state apparatuses but also by the dramatic growth of resistance to capitalist-controlled development.[8] In fact, opposition to capitalist domination of planetary life is on the rise around the world as students, citizens, church organizations, indigenous peoples, and workers of all faiths, ethnicities, races, and nationalities fight capital to gain control over the material and spiritual conditions of their lives. Nonetheless, a self-consciously anticapitalist movement has yet to develop among workers in the United States. In the light of the relatively privileged position U.S. workers occupy within the international division of labor and the pivotal role that the U.S. state plays in promoting, propping up, and protecting global capitalism, U.S. workers have an immense potential to contribute fundamentally to the project of creating a humane mode of planetary life.[9] Failing to realize this potential has been and would be nothing less than a disaster.

This potential can be realized only if we first recognize the need to realize it and the possibility of doing so. This recognition in no small measure depends on the "class struggle" of theoretical criticism. Interestingly enough, this struggle is presently and increasingly articulated as a response to the problem of the growing gap between the haves and the have-nots and have-too-littles. "The Two Nations of Black America," a documentary produced by Henry Louis Gates Jr. for PBS's *Frontline,* examined the growing divide within black America. Reflecting on the gains of the civil rights movement, Gates explained the working assumption as being that once "we got rid of legal racism all of us would plunge headlong into the middle class. Well, it turned out that that's not the case" (1998). The nature of racism cannot be understood without examining class divisions. Pursuing this thesis with Kathleen Cleaver, Angela Davis, Jesse Jackson, Quincy Jones, and Cornel West, Gates initiated a conversation that he argues is as important to have as the conversation Clinton initiated on race. In fact, the problem of race and class has become central to the project of Harvard's Dream Team. "We study how race and class interact," says Gates, "to delineate what it is to be an African-American" (in Trescott 1999:42). What remains to be determined is the extent to which the conversation will help to foster the development of a political movement for democratic globalization. The present work is written as a contribution to ensuring that the conversation about class does not lead down the social democratic path of seeking only to reform, rather than replace, capitalism. In this sense, this work contributes to recapturing the ideological ground that has been repeatedly surrendered by self-identified leftists who have rejected Marxism, class struggle, and socialism in favor of social democracy, class collaboration, and the "free-market" as the only *realistic* framework within which to advance democracy. My own view is that nothing is more *unrealistic* than the belief that capitalism is capable of solving the considerable social and natural problems facing humanity today. My critique of prophetic pragmatism constitutes a Marxist contribution to the following: first, the Marxist/pragmatist exchange that has been central to the history of American progressive and radical theory; second, the Marxist/Christian exchange that has been central to the international development of liberation theology; and last and most important, the articulation of a theoretical outlook that might prevent us from revisiting the nightmare of the 1930s and 1940s—a nightmare, it should not be forgotten, that never ended for most human beings—and enable U.S. workers to realize their revolutionary potential, or to use Unger and West's own formulation, to realize deeply the "American religion of possibility."[10]

Unlike many on the left, I believe that, seen within the purview of a slightly expanded historical perspective, the present period of capitalist dominance and socialist subjugation is nothing more than the present period (a belief shared with Herbert Aptheker, Jeremy Brecher, Tim Costello, Angela Davis, Cynthia Enloe, Beverly Harrison, Doug Henwood, Brian Lloyd, Harry Magdoff, Manning Marable, Kim Moody, Michael Parenti, John Rosenthal, Paul Sweezy, William K. Tabb, Ellen Meiksins Wood, Behzad Yaghmaian, Michael D. Yates, and Howard Zinn, among others). Lloyd usefully refreshes our memory when he reminds us that the "bourgeoisie rose to dominance not by proceeding smoothly from one quick, painless victory to another but by lurching through states of a protracted contest that saw republics and monarchies savagely leapfrogging, bloodying at each phase of the game participants and bystanders from every social class and nationality in every corner of the globe" (1997:2). Those leftists who, in chorus with the right, proclaim the death of Marxism, class struggle, and socialism have mistaken the time being for being itself. They may even, notes Lloyd, deny the possibility of discerning the difference between the two, if not the very idea that there is a difference. Like "occupants in a stalled vehicle, they mistake the immediate vicinity for the whole picture," supposing that so-called "free enterprise, bourgeois democracy, and U.S. global dominance are and should be eternal" (3, 2–3). Such leftists, says Lloyd, "might as well affix to their late-model imports the SHIT HAPPENS sticker that now adorns the bumpers, mostly, of high-mileage pick-ups" or, in language more acceptable within the academic economy, maintain that we must follow Friedrich Nietzsche in loving our fate and affirming the "eternal return of the same," an accomplishment that is among those of privilege something less than noble (3). Yet the reality of human suffering virtually ensures that capitalism will not escape the fate that has befallen all previous civilizations. Whether it falls sooner or later depends on nothing more extraordinary than what we do.

1. The Christian-Marxist Dialogue and the End of Liberation Theology

I believe the alliance of prophetic Christianity and progressive Marxism provides a last humane hope for humankind.
—Cornel West, *Prophesy Deliverance*

Man cannot save himself, for man is not the measure of all things and humanity is not God. Bound by the chains of his own sin and finiteness, man needs a Saviour.
—Martin Luther King Jr.,
"How Should a Christian View a Communist."

In this chapter I examine West's synthesis of Christian and Marxist concepts of human nature, history, agency, social change, and liberation as an initial step in the larger task of deconstructing the theoretical concepts and presuppositions that constitute prophetic pragmatism. For West, Christianity is the metatheoretical framework informing his commitment to building a more democratic, just, and humane society. "I am," says West, "a Chekhovian Christian with deep democratic commitments" (1999b:xv). Consequently, my investigation of prophetic pragmatism proper starts with an analysis of Christianity's influence on West's prophetic pragmatism. I begin by situating prophetic pragmatism within the development of North American liberation theology.

The Radicalization of North American Liberation Theology

Central and South American liberation theologians were theoretically and politically radicalized through their organic engagements with Marxist theory and revolutionary movements. The Peruvian theologian Gustavo Gutiérrez notes that many, if not most, Latin American liberation theologians "agree with Sartre that 'Marxism, as the formal framework of all contemporary philosophical thought, cannot be superseded'" (1973:9), and in this sense, says

Juan Luis Segundo, "Latin American theology is certainly Marxist" (1976:35). In contrast, the majority of North American theologians have been slower to revolutionize their own theoretical and political practices. There are numerous ideological, political, and economic factors that explain North American theologians' hesitance to develop their theology in the light of Marxist theory. Among the most significant of these factors are the ideology of anticommunism, the middle-class position of theologians, the ideology of American exceptionalism, the fact of working within rather than against the American Empire, and the incompatibility of Marxist philosophy with Christian metaphysics. Both secular and religious thinkers have been neither unaffected nor uninfected by cold war ideology. Indeed, it is difficult and perhaps impossible to appreciate the degree to which intellectuals and their products have been subjected to and shaped by anticommunist ideology (Cook 1989:470).[1] Religious institutions and representatives have been among the most conscientious supporters of anticommunism ideology throughout this century. Even socially progressive black and white religious leaders and theologians have allied their theologies, sermons, and congregations with America's cause to combat world communism in the name of democracy and freedom (see Silk 1988). Although black theologians forged their own theology of liberation, transforming theological categories into ideological weapons in the struggle for civil rights, their desire to be included within existing institutions inhibited most from challenging the legitimacy of these same institutions. Those who identified with the civil rights and black power struggles of the 1960s and 1970s argued that racial discrimination and inequality denied life, liberty, and the pursuit of happiness to most black citizens, yet most defended capitalism, under the banner of democracy, as the best possible social system for realizing these ideals.

There were, of course, notable exceptions. Although King did not publicly promote socialism and was critical of existing communist states, he was critical of capitalist economics as well (see Cone 1991). In *Where Do We Go from Here: Chaos or Community?,* King wrote that blacks "are now advancing to programs that impinge upon the basic system of social and economic control. At this level Negro programs go beyond race and deal with economic inequality, wherever it exists. In the pursuit of these goals, the white poor become involved" (1967a:17). Indeed, King's 1968 Poor People's Campaign was to be a class-based movement unifying poor and working-poor citizens across the racial spectrum to march on Washington and to demand that power and wealth be redistributed along democratic socialist lines so as to make possible the construction of a beloved community. Not only did King argue for "jobs, income, the demolition of the slums, and the rebuilding by the people who live there of new communities in their place . . . , a new economic deal for the poor," but he also asserted that racial oppression and economic exploitation in the United States were linked to oppression and exploitation of workers and the poor around the world: "We in the West must bear in mind that the poor countries are poor primarily because we have exploited them through political and economic colonialism. Americans in particular must help their nation repent of her modern economic imperialism" (1967b:6, 62). At the same time that King publicly protested the U.S. war against the Vietnamese struggle for national independence, he was, notes Manning Marable, "beginning to articulate a democratic socialist vision for American society: the nationalization of basic industries; massive federal expenditures to revive central cities and to provide jobs for ghetto residents; a guaranteed income for every adult American" (1991:103).[2]

Following his pilgrimage to Mecca, El-Hajj Malik El-Shabazz, formerly Malcolm X, overcame the theoretical and practical limitations of the Nation of Islam's essentially color-based analysis of racism and fundamentally separatist politics. Referring to recently liberated African nations, he explained: "None of them are adopting the capitalist system because they realize they can't. You can't operate a capitalistic system unless you are vulturistic; you have to have someone else's blood to suck to be a capitalist" (X 1965:121). Postcolonial nations do not have this option. They must either develop along noncapitalist lines or risk being resubordinated to foreign capitalist powers. In response to a question about the kind of social system that would best facilitate African American liberation, Malcolm noted that the current "system in this country cannot produce freedom for an Afro-American," adding: "It's impossible for a white person to believe in capitalism and not believe in racism. You can't have capitalism without racism. And if you find one and you happen to get that person into a conversation and they have a philosophy that makes you sure they don't have this racism in their outlook, usually they're socialists or their political philosophy is socialism" (69).[3] Like King's, Malcolm X's criticisms of capitalist society, as well as his developing internationalist and anti-imperialist perspective, differed markedly from criticisms advanced by the majority of religious leaders during the same period. Both men were moving from the goal of civil rights, a goal that could theoretically be achieved within the framework of bourgeois institutions, to the goal of human rights, a goal that can be achieved only by transforming these institutions.

For the most part, however, other religious leaders did not follow suit, for doing so meant risking not only their metaphysical security but also their financial status and even their physical existence. Like their white counterparts, even the most socially progressive black ministers were "not prepared to repudiate the system which rewards their own political accommodation at the expense of the continued exploitation of the Black working class and poor people" (Marable 1983:211). Those who criticized the continuing racial inequalities nonetheless remained reluctant to challenge a system of property relations that inevitably produces social inequalities. Just as they presupposed humanity's inability to save itself without divine grace, so they presupposed the social necessity of capitalist civilization. Thus, whereas Malcolm X and Martin Luther King began to advance democratic socialist politics, most religious and secular leaders articulated their liberationist concerns within the theoretical limits of bourgeois categories and advanced their political agendas within the practical limits of bourgeois institutions.

Meanwhile, many black radicals were quick to caution their fellow travelers that Marx was, after all, a white man whose empirical basis of theoretical production was specifically and therefore nongeneralizably nineteenth-century industrialized England, whose own perspective was uncritically "Eurocentric," and consequently whose theoretical and political work could not be trusted as a productive guide to the African American struggle for self-determination. Although Malcolm X and Martin Luther King were moving toward an economic analysis of racial oppression, most "Black theologians and Marxist thinkers [were and remain] mostly strangers" (Wilmore and Cone 1993:409), as West notes. In *My Soul Looks Back* James Cone adds that "because both the black church and Marxism have been marginal in American society, they have been preoccupied with their own survival and have taken little notice of each other" (1986b:125).

Yet West has suggested that Christian and Marxist concern for liberation constitutes the basis for and necessity of the two groups' coming together to discover "the possibilities of mutually arrived-at political action" while keeping in mind that the "aim of this encounter is to change the world, not each other's faith" (in Wilmore and Cone 1993:409). Several contemporary North American theologians, including Beverly Harrison, James Cone, Rosemary Ruether, and West, have engaged in a serious study of the Marxist tradition because it productively advances the struggle for liberation.[4] West writes:

> Marx was fundamentally concerned about the interlocking relation between corporate, financial, and political elites who had access to a disproportionate amount of resources, power, prestige and status in society. Certainly, that is a starting point for understanding any society that we know of today, especially the United States. Once we lose sight of the very complex relations between those three sets of elites, corporate, financial-banking and political elites, and the reasons why the working people, the working poor and the very poor, find themselves with very little access to resources—once we lose sight of that, which the Marxist tradition, which was not the only but the primary tradition which would analyze this, once we lose sight of this, then we have little or no analytic tools in our freedom fight. (1993c:59)

West, however, has claimed as well that Marxism is underdeveloped in at least two respects. First, Marxism has not adequately explained—and perhaps cannot explain—the existence and persistence of racism, sexism, heterosexism, and ecological degradation without reducing these phenomena to effects of capitalist exploitation. Second, Marxists have not adequately investigated the complexity of culture in general and religion in particular. They have too often assumed that religious consciousness is always "false consciousness," that religious practice is always conservative practice, and that religion thus always supports the interests of the dominant economic class. Rarely, if ever, says West, have Marxists explored culture and religion as sources of political resistance to the status quo.[5] To do so, Marxist theorists must go beyond "European bourgeois attitudes toward the culture of the oppressed, without [at the same time] idealizing or romanticizing these cultures" (West 1988a:20). Radicals should not "simply enact *negative* forms of subversive demystification (and, God forbid, more bourgeois forms of deconstruction!)" (ibid.). Rather, they should also advance "*positive* forms of popular revolutionary construction of new personal meanings, social adjustments, and political struggles for human freedom and democracy" (ibid.). What is needed is a mode of Marxist practice that critically engages cultural forms as sometimes justifying the dominant social relations and at other times providing the raw material for building opposition to the status quo.

Liberation theologians argue that developing such a methodology requires separating Marxism from its philosophical materialism (Boff 1987:224)—a difficult move, as many of them concede, for Marxism's analysis of society presupposes its materialist assumptions regarding humanity's dependence on natural conditions of existence. Indeed, as James Cone admits, it "has always been difficult to separate Marxism as a tool of social analysis from Marxism as an atheistic ideology" (1984:93). It has not been easy to arrive at common political goals without Marxism and Christianity calling into question each other's fundamental philosophical assumptions, or as West describes them, metaphysical "faith claims." To the extent that theologians believe that humanity's fate ultimately rests in God's hands, they must reject the notion that human beings are solely responsible for their own historical destiny. Martin Luther King Jr. explicates this point in "How Should a Christian View Communism?"

> Communism is based on a materialistic and humanistic view of life and history. According to Communist theory, matter, not mind or spirit, speaks the last word in the universe. Such a philosophy is avowedly secularistic and atheistic. . . . At the center of the Christian faith is the affirmation that there is a God in the universe who is the ground and essence of all reality. A Being of infinite love and boundless power, God is the creator, sustainer, and conserver of values. In opposition to Communism's atheistic materialism, Christianity posits a theistic idealism. Reality cannot be explained by matter in motion or the push and pull of economic forces. Christianity affirms that at the heart of reality is a

> Heart, a loving Father who works through history for the salvation of his children. Man cannot save himself, for man is not the measure of all things and humanity is not God. Bound by the chains of his own sin and finiteness, man needs a Saviour. (1981:98)

Separating sociological from philosophical assumptions in Marxism is problematic because to critique conservative theological positions, liberation theologians must accept the materialist claim, incisively formulated by Feuerbach, that "man makes religion, religion does not make man" (in Tucker 1978:53), while simultaneously exempting their own claims from a similar analysis. On the one hand, liberation theologians affirm that theological claims reflect the historical time, social location, and political interests of the particular individuals who make such claims. On the other hand, they also maintain that the real truth revealed in the gospel of Jesus Christ is that God sides with the oppressed in their struggle for justice. On the basis of this theological assumption, liberation theologians use Marxist theory to support this struggle because, as West writes in *Prophesy Deliverance,* it helps to "uncover the systematic misunderstanding of capitalist society by bourgeois thinkers; to show how this misunderstanding, whether deliberate or not, supports and sanctions exploitation and oppression in this society and to put forward the correct understanding of this society in order to change it" (West 1982:110). Thus, Marxism remains, despite its materialism, a vital weapon in the theoretical arsenals of theologians committed to a this-worldly liberation.

Freedom and the Metaphysics of Human Nature

In the first half of *Prophesy Deliverance* West outlines the primary tasks of revolutionary African American thought, describes the social situation of African Americans, develops a genealogy of racism, and delineates four traditions of response to racial oppression. In the second half of *Prophesy Deliverance* he articulates what must be done to advance the struggle for African American self-determination. West explains that his work is not principally concerned with developing a new science or field of study or with establishing or discerning epistemological foundations and ontological grounds for African American liberation. Rather, he is concerned with creating what he describes as a "textuality and distinctive discourse" that, paraphrasing Marx, "can be a material force for Afro-American freedom" (West 1982:15). West draws on theoretical materials from Marxism and Christianity to construct a "demystifying hermeneutic of the Afro-American experience which enhances the cause of human freedom," arguing that "an alliance of prophetic Christianity and progressive Marxism provides a last humane hope for humankind" (11, 95). The first source, which constitutes the metatheoretical structure of his work, is the prophetic Christian tradition as represented by

African American figures such as Denmark Vesey, Gabriel Prosser, Nat Turner, David Walker, Martin Delany, Harriet Tubman, Sojourner Truth, Henry Turner, Ida B. Wells, George Washington Woodbey, Marcus Garvey, Martin Luther King Jr., James Cone, Jacquelyn Grant, and Delores Williams. This tradition, says West, provides the moral norms of individuality and democracy, which hold that "every individual regardless of class, country, caste, race, or sex should have the opportunity to fulfill his or her potentialities" (16). West calls this "radical egalitarian idea *the Christian principle of the self-realization of individuality within community*" (ibid.).[6] West adds to this principle the Christian anthropological conception of humans as being both *dignified* and *depraved.* Our dignified status means that human beings are equally valuable in the eyes of God and that we should work to improve our collective conditions of life as much as we can. Our depraved state, which derives from our fallen nature, means that our efforts to improve our lives will always be circumscribed by our unchangeable imperfection. West describes "the Christian dialectic of human nature and human history" as the "dialectic of imperfect products and transformative practice, of prevailing realities and negation, of human depravity and human dignity, of what is and the not-yet" (17 [emphasis omitted]). Unlike Marxism, the Christian dialectic of human nature and human history presupposes that our nature as human beings remains more or less the same even as we engage with and transform our material conditions of existence and that our path of historical development has more or less already been determined as the story of our fall from paradise and eventual redemption through some combination of human faith and works and divine intervention and grace.

The Christian notion of human nature as being dignified, and therefore deserving of salvation, yet depraved, and therefore in need of salvation, means human beings are responsible for *penultimate liberation*—that is, the building of a beloved community—while God is responsible for *ultimate salvation.* Although human beings ought to work to perfect their relations with one another and with nature, Christians contend that human "power can never cast out evil from the world" (King 1981:129). The radical Enlightenment assumption, shared by Marxists, that humanity has the capacity to create a genuinely human or, in Christian terms, beloved community is "based on too great an optimism concerning the inherent goodness of human nature" (ibid.).

Penultimate or historical liberation and ultimate or spiritual salvation are integrally related to each other. There is no unbridgeable chasm separating these two processes. Rather, they constitute aspects of a unified process. Humanity is, in the words of Gustavo Gutiérrez, the "agent of history, responsible for [its] destiny," and yet salvation is a "total gift" from God that "gives the whole process of liberation its deepest meaning and its complete and unforeseeable fulfillment" (1973:67, x). This-worldly, historical liberation integrally embodies and is ultimately fulfilled through otherworldly, spiritual redemption. What God begins—namely, the drama of salvation—human beings advance through their concrete acts and God completes through divine salvation. The Latina feminist theologian Ada Mariá Isasi-Díaz writes that "salvation refers to having a relationship with God, a relationship that does not exist if we do not love our neighbor. Our relationship with God affects all aspects of our lives, all human reality. As Latinas become increasingly aware of the injustices we suffer, we reject any concept of salvation that does not affect our present and future reality. For us, salvation occurs in history and is intrinsically connected to our liberation. . . . For Latinas to talk about salvation, liberation, and the coming of the kin-dom [*sic*] of God are one and the same thing" (1993:35).

The Christian conception of human nature and history marks one of the most important differences (perhaps the most important difference) between Christian and Marxist theoretical perspectives. The "Christian espouses a dialectical historicism which stresses the dignity and depravity of persons," says West, "whereas the Marxist puts forward a full-blown historicism in which the eventual perfectibility of persons within history is inevitable" (1982:19). The "Christian world view is a clandestine complaint against history, the Marxist an avowed apotheosis of it" (ibid.).

A full-blown historicism, however, conflicts with the presupposition of eventual or inevitable perfectibility. In *The Ethical Dimensions of Marxist Thought* West defines historicism as the notion that there are no extrahistorical metaphysical foundations on which we might ground our ethical practices (1991:67). In this respect, the historicist position renders problematic any metaphysical claims regarding, for example, the eventual triumph of the working class, the teleological necessity of capitalist crisis and collapse, or the ontological inevitability of socialist revolution. Marxism promotes neither a particularly optimistic nor pessimistic opinion about humanity's fate. Marxism may be said to be both optimistic and pessimistic regarding the human condition—optimistic in that it regards human beings as capable of creating more life-enhancing circumstances and pessimistic in that it offers no metaphysical guarantees that humanity will create such circumstances. Capitalism does not derive from humanity's innate avaricious tendencies any more than socialism will emerge from humanity's altruistic tendencies. Corporate executive officers do not exploit workers because they, like all human beings, are naturally greedy. Rather, they exploit others because the obligations and constraints imposed on them as a result of their positions within the division of labor and property (e.g., their responsibility to stockholders and the competitive nature of the market) powerfully compel, even if they do not totally dictate, that they behave as representatives of capital (e.g., by cutting workers' wages, relocating plants to production sites where labor is cheaper, or violating health and safety regulations). In other words, nothing about capitalist social relations is simply natural. Indeed, a central task of critical theory is precisely to denaturalize capitalism by demonstrating its historical particularity and elaborating the human decisions and actions that produce and reproduce the capitalist mode of life.

History with a capital *H* does nothing. It never has. This profoundly anti-Hegelian position denies that human beings are governed by laws that remain forever beyond their theoretical grasp and practical mastery and places the responsibility for the organization of human relations and development squarely on the shoulders of human beings. There is not the slightest reason to assume that everything will end up all right, that human perfectibility is inevitable. Although communism may be, as Marx once wittily remarked, the answer to the "riddle of history," there are no metaphysical grounds for assuming that the riddle will be solved (indeed, there is ample evidence to support the claim that it will not be solved in this manner). How things turn out depends on nothing other than how we individually and collectively turn them, and whether we make things turn in the direction of a more humane future in no small measure depends on resisting beliefs that prevent human beings from working to realize that future.

Although West is entirely correct to argue that Marxism and Christianity posit "irreconcilable" concepts of human nature, history, and change, his account of what makes them irreconcilable is only partially correct (1982:99). Moreover, the differences between Marxist and Christian theories have decisive consequences for social practice. Our theories of human nature significantly shape how we understand what can and cannot be done to improve human life. Marxism presupposes the radical Enlightenment notion that all human beings can rationally and deliberately shape their world to meet their needs. Human beings transform themselves, their nature, by transforming their material circumstances. Marx writes: "The human essence is no abstraction inherent in each single individual. In its reality it is the ensemble of the social relations" that are themselves the product of human labor as human beings take up and transform their natural and social conditions of existence (in Tucker 1978:145). Human nature may be conceptualized as a *result-in-process* of the relationships that human beings establish in and through labor between social and natural laws, processes, and relations and simultaneously as a principal or even the primary *condition of possibility* for the creation of new "natures." From a Marxist perspective, the work of creating a society in which citizens actively participate in the democratic planning of development cannot be grounded on, and certainly not guaranteed by, the existence of abstract essences (e.g., an innate moral inclination or God-given disposition to act "rationally" on the basis of a "good will" to "do the right thing"). Rather, the creation of new "essences," essences that derive from the relations that human beings establish with one another and nature, are forged from the "essences" produced through their current relations (e.g., capitalism creates the objective *and* subjective prerequisites for the creation of a communist society inasmuch as it organizes human beings, quite often through force, into international relations of cooperation). Human nature, history, and society are dimensions of and inescapably dependent on nature even while human nature, history, and society are theoretically distinguishable from nonhuman nature. Human beings take up and transform natural materials and in so doing fabricate a *second nature* that remains rooted in and conditioned by natural laws, relations, and processes and yet immanently transcends the limits given in and imposed by *first nature* (nowhere is this process more evident than in the revolutionary field of genetic research and engineering).[7] Humanity is not absolutely determined by prevailing material and spiritual conditions but rather is capable of cognitively discerning the nature of these conditions and deliberately transforming them. Indeed, the concept of freedom presupposes that we possess the capacity to alter our naturally given and socially created circumstances, in short, to choose to pursue one course of action over others. Ruling-class ideologies often elide the difference between what is given and what is created by human beings by reducing social relations to natural determinations. In *The Poverty of Philosophy* (1963 [1847]) Marx elaborates on the methodological limitations and political implications of bourgeois political economy:

> [Bourgeois] economists have a singular method of procedure. There are only two kinds of institutions for them, artificial and natural. The institutions of feudalism are artificial institutions, those of the bourgeoisie are natural institutions. In this way they resemble the theologians, who likewise establish two kinds of religion. Every religion which is not theirs is an invention of men, while their own is an emanation from God. When economists say that present-day-relations—the relations of bourgeois production—are natural, they imply that these are the relations in which wealth is created and productive forces developed in conformity with the laws of nature. These relations therefore are themselves natural laws independent of the influence of time. They are eternal laws which must always govern society. Thus there has been history, but there is no longer any. (120–21)

To paraphrase Marx, nature does not produce enormous wealth for a few and brutal impoverishment for the many. Rather, these conditions result from human actions undertaken within a definite system of social relations (e.g., the so-called natural rate of unemployment is deliberately manufactured to prevent workers from raising their wages through collective action). At the same time, however, humanity creates its mode of life through its relationship to nature. Thus, while first and second nature may be theoretically distinguished, the latter's transcendence of the former is always relative, for human beings never transcend their dependence on nature. The emergence of ecological theologies reveals an attempt to come to terms with our dependence on nature as continuing environmental degradation threatens our existence as a species.[8]

Human nature is not simply equivalent with or reducible to human practice, as in the idea that we are what we do. Rather, human beings produce their own nature or way of life by transforming their natural and social circumstances. Human beings are first and last natural beings who possess the creative capacity to alter existing circumstances of self-development—a condition from which follows Marx's concern for property relations as mediating not only diverse institutions and ideas but also the development of this capacity. At its heart, the struggle to expand the realm of self-determination and freedom, that is, to secure humanity's conditions of material reproduction and to expand its capacities to engage in creative work, is a struggle to transform existing "natures" through the practical transformation of natural and social conditions of production, reproduction, and free creation. Efforts to expand the realm of self-determination and free creation are fueled by an awareness that the present mode of human life, as well as the present state of human nature, is neither ontologically necessary nor theologically inevitable. Rather, such struggles are fueled by the recognition that our present mode of life may be created differently, that we may organize our relations with one another and nature so that every person enjoys the opportunity to develop his or her individual capacities in a manner that empowers all other persons to do the same.

Human nature is not some eternal, transhistorical "essence," whether the terms in which this essence is conceived are natural (as in the mechanical reductionism of E. O. Wilson's sociobiology) or ontological (as in the Christian notion of a soul stained by an essential and consequently untransformable "sinfulness"). On the contrary, human nature emerges from the interaction between human beings and nature as it is mediated by humanity's mode of social organization. Individual self-creation is fundamentally and inescapably natural and social. No individual creates him- or herself except through his or her relations with nature and other human beings. Although some philosophers, activists, and political leaders who identify themselves as Marxists have explicitly asserted or implicitly assumed human perfectibility within history to be inevitable, in fact Marxism presupposes the opposite: namely, that nothing is inevitable, necessary, or guaranteed in advance of what human beings do. The theory of economic determinism, the notion that capitalism will inevitably collapse as a result of its own contradictory laws of motion is, wrote Gramsci, a pernicious "substitute for the Predestination or Providence of confessional religions" (1971:336).[9] It is pernicious because it fosters the conservative view that history is governed by laws, forces, or spirits that have little, if anything, to do with individual or collective decisions and actions. To generate revolutionary agency requires adopting the opposite view that "if it was made, it can be made otherwise."[10] Or, following David F. Noble's comments in his prologue to *Global Productions: Labor and the Making of the "Information Society,"* we might say that today the work of generating revolutionary agency requires that workers pierce the veil of digitally generated lies and grasp that "beneath their electronic enhancements and omnipotent corporate personas, the gods [CEOs] are actually mortals themselves, however deformed by greed and power," and that those "who make, operate, and repair the things that make the gods gods—the electronic components, the computer assemblies, the telecommunication links, the data entry"—outnumber their all-too-mortal masters "millions-to-one" and possess the power to end their servitude and create a masterless, though not spiritless, future (1998:x).

The Tragic Nature of (This) Life

For West, however, the goal of preventing myopic Prometheanism makes it pragmatically necessary to posit a theological anthropology in which human nature is marked by dignity and depravity:

> For Christians, the dimension of impotency of all historical projects is not an excuse which justifies the existing status quo, but rather a check on utopian aspirations which often debilitate and demoralize those persons involved in negating and transforming the status quo. Ultimate triumph indeed *depends on the almighty power of a transcendent God* who proleptically *acts* in history but who also *withholds* the final, promised negation and transformation of history until an *unknown* future. In the interim, imperfect human negations and transformations must persist. (1982:96 [emphasis added])

In "Pragmatism and the Sense of the Tragic," West argues that, in addition to the Christian ideas of humanity's imperfectibility, a "deep sense of evil and the tragic must infuse any meaning and value of democracy" (1993d:114).[11] Democracy, he adds, "requires not only the civic virtues of participation, tolerance, openness, mutual respect and mobility, but also dramatic struggles with the two major culprits—disease and death—that defeat and cut off the joys of democratic citizenship. Such citizenship must not be so preoccupied—or obsessed—with possibility that it conceals or represses the ultimate facts of the human predicament" (114). In other words, a tragic sense of the human condition is vitally important to the collective work of humanizing our relationships with one another and with nature.[12]

In "Black Strivings in a Twilight Civilization," an essay published in *The Future of the Race,* a work coauthored with Henry Louis Gates Jr., West offers a critical assessment of the work of W. E. B. Du Bois. In the opening pages West indicates that his "fundamental problem with Du Bois is his inadequate grasp of the tragicomic sense of life—a refusal candidly to confront the sheer absurdity of the human condition" (1996:57). Elaborating on this point, West explains that his "major intellectual disappointment with the great Du Bois lies in the fact that there are hardly any traces in his work of any serious grappling with the profound thinkers and spiritual wrestlers of the modern West," individuals such as Leo Tolstoy, Fyodor Dostoyevsky, Anton Chekhov, Franz Kafka, or Karl Kraus, who were "major figures obsessed with the problem of evil in their time" (75–76). Du Bois's Enlightenment-inspired commitment to the power of reason and science and his unwillingness to wade into the deep cross-currents of black culture left him almost completely disabled when it came to dealing with evil and absurdity in his own life, particularly the death of his eighteen-month-old son. The "tragic plight and absurd predicament of Africans here and abroad requires a more profound interpretation of the human condition," an interpretation that would lead to "more democratic concepts of knowledge and leadership which highlight human fallibility and mutual accountability; notions of individuality and contested authority which stress dynamic traditions; and ideals of self-realization within participatory communities" (64).

Yet is this really the case? Will confronting the "sheer absurdity of the human condition," cultivating "a deep sense of evil and the tragic," and struggling with "disease and death" foster the development of "more democratic concepts of knowledge and leadership," keep citizens from repressing "the ultimate facts of the human predicament," and enable "struggles for justice" (1996:57; 1993d:114, 107)? Is the struggle for liberation more productively advanced when viewed as a theological-existential struggle with the "tragic," "evil," and "absurd" nature of the human condition? In a critique of Cornel West, Lorenzo C. Simpson argues that "not only is a sense of the tragic and of evil as deep as West commends not requisite for meliorative action, it is, to the contrary, precisely what makes such action seem *futile* unless we resort to devices to mitigate that sense" (1993:42). Indeed, this sense of the tragic is so profound that West, like all those informed by similar theological notions, is compelled to believe in the existence of an "almighty power" that can sustain a sense of hope and rescue human beings from their plight (1982:96). When all is said and done regarding human beings' need to liberate themselves, it is God who finally effects their liberation/salvation.

Thus, although West contends that progressives must come to terms with the absurd, tragic, and evil nature of human existence, these categories essentialize or, to use Marx's concept, fetishize and thereby mystify the *social* roots of what he names "evil," "absurd" and "tragic." Such theological, literary, and existentialist categories encourage the acceptance of the existing order of things at least as much as they discourage it, even though, as West points out, this order has resulted in the murders of over 200 million human beings in the twentieth century (1996:57). The attempt to confront honestly and straightforwardly the "ultimate facts of the human predicament" is thwarted by their metaphysical mystification as expressions of the purportedly tragic or even tragicomic nature of the human condition and hence as conditions about which we can do little other than come to terms and make do. Honestly confronting the nature of our situation and responding progressively to it requires, above all else, recognizing that our current situation is not the most recent historical expression of the human predicament but rather a consequence of our particular mode of social organization. It is not that "life sucks, and then you die," as T-shirts worn by Americans in the 1980s boldly declared. Rather, it is more accurately that "life under capitalism sucks, and then you die." The difference between these two interpretations makes all the difference in the world. The first leads to a pessimistic acceptance of the status quo, whereas the second may foster a desire to work to create a world in which such declarations no longer appeal. It is not the gods whom workers must defeat but rather the mortals who pose as gods. The struggles for self-determination and freedom are fueled by a recognition that the immediate facts of life are not manifestations of a general human predicament but rather indicators of our specific historical situation.

Such a recognition is revolutionary precisely because it cuts through reifying representations and grasps that oppression, degradation, and exploitation are not the results of sin, evil, or the tragic nature of life but rather the specific effects and causes of what John McMurtry (1996) calls the "cancer stage of capitalism." Although the conditions of our lives run the spectrum regarding the extent to which we can improve them, metaphysical categories such as sin, evil, absurdity, and tragedy often do more to confuse than clarify what we can and cannot change. The death of Du Bois's son was tragic, but its real tragedy lies in the fact that death and disease are rarely simply "natural" phenomena. The fact that average infant mortality rates are substantially higher among black Americans than among white Americans, for example, suggests that death and disease are in some measure socially determined "ultimate facts." They are always *relatively* ultimate facts—that is, mediated by specific modes of social organization. Although the death of Du Bois's son may not have been directly caused by racism and class oppression, the fact that Du Bois was taxed so deeply by the work of fighting these social maladies and that access to medical care was in part raciallty determined certainly made providing optimal care more difficult. That the conditions required to enjoy good health (e.g., clean water, medicine, shelter, and sanitation) are distributed so unevenly around the world, such that today "one-quarter of the world's people are starving and one-third of all children are malnourished" (McMurtry 1996:11), results from humanly created conditions and specifically from decisions made by individuals who are compelled by their positions as property owners within the capitalist division of labor to invest capital to make capital. Starvation and malnutrition are tragic not because they reveal the absurd nature of the human condition but because, along with poverty, inadequate health care, poor sanitation, and high infant mortality rates, they need not exist.

Arguing that disease and death constitute ultimate facts of the human predicament raises the problem of death and disease out of the realm of history and into the realm of metaphysics. And as Simpson writes, a metaphysical problem can be solved only through a metaphysical intervention. Alternatively, to conceive of death and disease not as ultimate facts but as conditions whose meaning and reality vary according to humanly created circumstances places human beings in a proactive position in relation to these circumstances. Not all societies have conceived and related to death and disease as do individuals under capitalist society. For example, Rosemary Ruether, drawing from Vine Deloria's *God Is Red* (1973), points out that the "Indian is fearless toward death because the Indian lives on, not as an isolated individual but in the collective soul of the tribe" (1983:251). Such a person "accepts personal finitude and can receive death as the proper culmination of life. Since Indians do not live individualistically, death is not the end but only a point of transformation to another state of life. Earth and people are one" (ibid.). Although Ruether bases her comments on questionable generalizations, her discussion of the meaning and value of death and disease within different societies suggests these "ultimate facts" are not transhistorical givens but rather always historically mediated or even created phenomena that are not the same for all human beings in all places and at all times. Death is not the great equalizer in that its reality, which arrives only *in life,* arrives far from equally. All human beings perish, but it is the matter of when, why, and how our death arrives that makes the difference to us. Indeed, it is precisely the difference these matters make that fuels efforts to end suffering made needless by the power that, through its own acts, humanity has won over its destiny. We do not struggle against painful circumstances to abolish death (although scientific research is radically transforming the status of death as an absolute limit to human development as it moves toward cloning human organs and body parts and toward discovering the biological mechanisms that induce the processes associated with aging). Rather, we struggle to reduce, for example, the infant mortality rate by changing the socioeconomic structures that unequally distribute its tragic, because ontologically unnecessary, occurrence. Moreover, it is reasonable to assume that our experience of being-unto-death would be qualitatively different from what most people experience today if we lived in a society based on democratic planning of development. Growing old and dying under capitalism quite often means growing old and dying under conditions of severe material deprivation and spiritual alienation. The "Pascalian wager of Marxism," says Fredric Jameson, is that growing old and dying within a genuine human community, with a sense of connection to society as a whole and to history, would be less painful than doing so under capitalism and perhaps might even be experienced as a fulfillment of one's life (1981:261).

The meaning of death has more to do with our experience of life and especially our sense of being connected to other human beings, society, history, and nature than it does with death in itself. Although the transformation of existing social relations will not eliminate death, there are good reasons to believe that individuals living personally satisfying and socially meaningful lives would experience death quite differently than many currently do under conditions of alienation. By positing death and disease as absolutes, however, West establishes the necessity to believe in, for example, "a transcendent God who proleptically acts in history but who also withholds the final, promised negation and transformation of history until an unknown future" (1982:96). To the extent that individuals believe the causes of suffering and even suffering itself to be inevitable (holding, e.g., that God ordains suffering as a necessary component of learning important lessons), they will be inclined to appeal to superhuman powers to liberate them from the cruelty of this order, to seek, in short, extrahuman powers to save them from humanly created circumstances. Assuming that human beings are fundamentally incapable of saving themselves, that the root of human suffering is sinfulness and that sinfulness can be cleansed only by God's mercy, makes Christianity incompatible or, as West suggests, irreconcilable with the notion of human being as *ontoformative.*

Given humanity's ontoformative powers, we have no stake in establishing a priori limitations on the possibilities for individual and collective development. In this regard Marxism shares much with pragmatism's optimistic conception of human nature and reality as unfinished works in process. Yet West's theological premises set such limitations on the extent to and manner in which human beings create themselves. Moreover, West's theological and philosophical premises conflict with each other. Whereas his theological narrative claims that human history is an already written book in which human beings will eventually be saved by an all-powerful God, his pragmatist outlook holds that our future is open-ended and that human beings are solely responsible for their own "salvation."

West leaves this theoretical contradiction mostly unexplored even as he occasionally gestures toward resolving it by suggesting that his religious commitments have more to do with their personal and political *utility* than with faith in the absolute reality of a transcendent, omniscient, omnipotent God.

The "self-understanding and self-identity that flow from this tradition's insights into the crises and traumas of life are," says West, "indispensable *for me* to remain sane. [The Christian tradition] holds at bay the sheer absurdity so evident in life, without erasing or eliding the tragedy of life" (1989:233). As to whether God exists and the Gospel is true, West says, "I reply in the affirmative, bank my all on it, yet am willing to entertain the possibility in low moments that I may be deluded" (ibid.). In addition to adducing his existential reasons for believing in God and the Gospel, West notes that "the culture of the wretched of the earth is deeply religious [and to] be in solidarity with them requires not only an acknowledgement of what they are up against but also an appreciation of how they cope with their situation. This appreciation does not require that one be religious; but if one is religious, one has wider access to their life-worlds" (ibid.). In short, it is pragmatically and politically advantageous to be religious.

Theological Reflections and Social Contradictions

West affirms the historicist axiom that, like all human creations, the production of theological discourse is determined by historically specific cultural, social, political, and economic conditions. In other words, West affirms the premise that human beings create religious ideas, institutions, and practices and that their religious creations are "conditioned by a definite development of their productive forces and of the intercourse corresponding to these" (Marx and Engels 1970:47). On the basis of these premises, liberation theologians analyze and explicate the ways in which religion and theology support the division of labor, power, and property, including, for example, as West writes in *Prophesy Deliverance,* "the ways in which the racist interpretations of the gospel . . . encourage and support the capitalist system of production, its grossly unequal distribution of wealth, and its closely connected political arrangements" (1982:113).

At the same time, liberation theologians maintain the metaphysical assumption that their own claims are based on the transcendental authority of God. Thus, while it may be fated to be human, cultural and historical, "in respect of the meaning intended by its discourse, theology, all theology, is necessarily transcendent," working to "look inside liberation, and search out its transcendent, supernatural, salvific dimension," seeking that which is not merely human and historical but also divine and eternal (Boff 1987:41; Boff and Boff 1984:95). In accordance with the fundamental premises of the irreligious criticism of religion, liberation theologians assume that theological discourse is material and historical, the product of particular human beings living under and responding to specific social conditions, *and* simultaneously grounded on the authority of a transhistorical, immaterial God. Yet they must exclude their own claims (e.g., that God sides with the oppressed) from a materialist critique because their truth value depends on the assumption that, as Martin Luther King Jr. indicates, "there is a God in the universe who is the ground and essence of all reality . . . , [a] Being of infinite love and boundless power . . . [who] is the creator, sustainer, and conserver of values," and that "man cannot save himself, for man is not the measure of all things and humanity is not God. Bound by the chains of his own sin and finiteness, man needs a Saviour" (1981:98).

Again, liberation theology deploys this dualistic conception of reality, at once both materialist and idealist, natural and supernatural, in its conception of human nature as well. On the one hand, human nature is not fixed and unchanging for all time but rather results from the ensemble of social relations. As West suggests in *The Ethical Dimensions of Marxist Thought*, human nature is subject to deliberate alteration (1991:66–67). Changing existing circumstances changes existing "natures," or as Clodovis and Leonardo Boff contend, "conversion may be reunderstood as social transformation" (1984:38). On the other hand, human nature is understood as something that is constituted once and for all. The "power of the risen Christ [is] present in all humanity," and love "is not a product of man but man a product of love" (Bonino 1974:117). This leads liberation theologians to the paradoxical conclusion that, on the one hand, human nature is constituted through humanity's transformation of natural and social conditions of existence and that, on the other, humans are called *not* "to 'invent' or 'create' a reality which does not exist, but to be what they are, to come to be themselves children of the ultimate, shared and communicated love" (106). Human beings are the creators of their own mode of living, yet their efforts to create a just society are ultimately manifestations of a plan that is determined by "the will of God . . . , [who is] Lord of history. God acts through history, and through its laws," and is "the subject, the agent, of everything" (Boff and Boff 1984:90, 100). As West writes in the last paragraphs of *Prophesy Deliverance:* "Revolutionary Christian perspective and praxis . . . [are] informed by the social theory and political praxis of progressive Marxism which proposes to approximate as close as is *humanly* possible the precious values of individuality and democracy," that is, "as soon as *God's will* be done" (1982:146 [emphasis added]).

Like other liberation theologians, West on the one hand adheres to a Christian view of human nature as depraved (sinful) and dignified (worthy of God's love) and of history as an already written book (the story of humanity's fall and ultimate salvation), yet on the other hand he affirms a pragmatic view of human nature and history as open-ended and transformable. This contradiction may be interpreted not only as expressing what appear to be opposing philosophical formulations regarding the human condition but also as representing the difference between a society in which the majority of citizens enjoy little control over their own productive activities or the products of these activities and a society in which citizens are able to coordinate their productive activities democratically to satisfy their material needs and further their spiritual development. Prophetic pragmatism, like other theologies of liberation, uses theological categories to represent the conflict between private control over labor and its fruits and the potential to create a society based on democratic control. By arguing that human beings must assume responsibility for their own liberation (an argument that assumes that humanity is capable of liberating itself) and yet also maintaining that humanity's fate rests in the hands of God (an argument that assumes that humanity cannot liberate itself from conditions of its own making), prophetic pragmatism, like other theologies of liberation, presents a problem that has profoundly secular implications: either our development is subject to forces beyond our control (e.g., God, our own natures, or the free market), or we possess the capacity to understand and master these forces.

Resolving this philosophical-sociological problem requires transforming the mode of production that generates this theoretical contradiction as a practical secular problem. This is of course precisely what prophetic pragmatism and liberation theology seek to do. Indeed, this fact leads me to posit the following, admittedly optimistic, hypothesis: what the Protestant Reformation was to feudalism, liberation theology is to capitalism, namely, its theological death sentence. Nevertheless, to the extent that liberation theology calls us to create a nonexploitative mode of social life—a classless society, according to Gutiérrez—it calls us to create a society in which the need for liberation theology would not exist. We might say, paraphrasing Marx, that the essence of liberation theology can be realized only by negating the world that produces the need for a theology of liberation, and the world that produces this theology can be negated only by realizing the essence of liberation theology. Once realized, liberation theology loses its raison d'être (Tucker 1978:59). To realize the essence of liberation theology, then, liberation theologians ought not seek "to possess the theological battlefield wrested from their foes," that is, to reproduce the fundamental assumptions that inform Christian theology (e.g., that sin is the root of humanity's suffering or that humans need a savior); rather, they should work to support agents and organizations that possess the potential to abolish the earthly mode of existence that produces the need to be spiritually liberated from this world (Long 1986:195).

Such a project not only depends on transforming theological problems, explanations, and solutions into political problems, explanations, and solutions. It also requires resisting the metaphysical temptation, the otherworldly seduction, to translate political problems into theological categories and to argue, for example, both the productive claim that sin ought to be conceived in structural terms and the unproductive claim that "structural sin" is a product of "human sinfulness." Liberation theologians who emphasize that human beings make their own history and must assume responsibility for the history they make do not and cannot abandon the idea that "the evil of the world is rooted within man himself" and can be uprooted only by God (Marable 1983:214).[13] Although liberation theology places God on the "right" side (that is, on the left) and is critical of those who do otherwise, liberation theologians are reluctant to criticize, let alone abandon, the metaphysical premises informing their theory and practice. Nevertheless, it is precisely these premises that reflect and reify the relations of alienation characteristic of capitalist production. To the extent that liberation theology maintains a conception of human nature, the universe, and history as governed by forces that remain beyond theoretical cognition and practical control, such that liberation is, in the last instance, the result of God's will being done here on Earth as it is in Heaven, liberation theology sacralizes the linchpin of ruling-class ideology. Whereas bourgeois political economists invert the relationship between commodity producers and the commodities they produce, liberation theologians invert the relationship between religion producers and the religion they produce. In this way, human beings, "the creators [of the gods, the state, capital, the division of society into propertyless workers and owners of money], bow down before their creations" (Marx and Engels 1970:37); in so doing, they act as if they must adjust their existence to these realities rather than adjust these realities to their existence. In this way, liberation theology thus helps to reproduce the social relations of alienation it aims to abolish.

The reproduction of the notion that our destiny is controlled by God reinforces a world in which those who own and control productive property are daily represented as being akin to God, operating everywhere at once, dictating conditions of life for many, and yet responsible only to the few. That my fate is controlled by "God" makes perfect sense in a world in which my fate is controlled by social, political, and economic forces seemingly beyond my control. Indeed, "the gods are everywhere, instantaneously. They know everything. Their companies are transnational but they are transcendent" (Noble 1998:ix). It thus often seems as if no individual or class of individuals exploits mortals to live as gods. When "pop" philosophers, theologians, and psychologists offer explanations for why "bad things happen to good people," they frequently fail to examine the bad things that the gods/owners do. In this way they help to reinforce a psychology that is increasingly willing to accept the free market as a god, a force in relationship to which we must adjust ourselves rather than a force we must adjust to us (Cox 1999:18).[14]

But these "gods" are not gods, even if they currently possess the power to determine living conditions for the rest of us. They are dependent on those whom they claim to sustain through their "provision of jobs," "superior work habits," "creative genius," and "generous charity." Moreover, while human beings around the world see through claims regarding the sanctity of private property, competition, and the market and resist corporate exploitation of their land, labor, and lives, it remains difficult to resist the temptation to translate political into religious problems. Indeed, it may not be possible to do so under present conditions. Perhaps Marx was right when he argued that religion cannot be superseded within a context in which human beings do not exercise effective control over the conditions of their own material and spiritual production, in other words, one in which they suffer alienation. Marx writes: "The religious reflections of the real world can, in any case, vanish only when the practical relations of everyday life between man and man, and between man and nature, generally present themselves to him in a transparent and rational form" (1977:173). Only by changing our mode of material production is it possible to create a genuinely new mode of spiritual expression. As long as our material relations with one another and with nature remain beyond our comprehension and control, theology not only will find fertile soil but will in all likelihood flourish (witness, for example, the rise of religious fundamentalism in response to capitalism's transformation of previously noncapitalized societies and spheres of production and consumption).[15]

West rightly points out that in a world in which love, care, service, and sacrifice are negated by the unrelenting and unforgiving competition for profits, Christianity "provides us with a way to demand that service and sacrifice, love and care sit at the center of what it is to be human" (West and hooks 1991:53). In a world in which human beings are dehumanized and degraded, oppressed and exploited, Christianity, like Judaism and Islam, "reaffirms that we are human to the degree to which we love and care and serve" (ibid.). Liberation theology calls on Christians to demonstrate their faith by engaging in actions that transform humanly made causes of suffering. In this way theologies of liberation sow the seeds of their own destruction since, as suggested previously, to create a society in which "the free development of each is the condition for the free development of all" (in Tucker 1978:191) would be to create a society from which human beings would no longer feel the need to be saved. The practical reality of human beings consciously and collectively forging their destiny in a spirit of universal brother- and sisterhood would dissolve the basis of this need.

Lest we grow nostalgic regarding the possible demise of Christianity, we should recall that it did not exist as a distinct religious tradition all that long ago; that it has undergone nothing but continuous transformations, dividing into denominations that bear little resemblance to one another; and that it will likely cease to exist—if it has not already done so—as a mode of spiritual life with the passing of the alienating circumstances that generously fuel the desire, if not the need, to believe in a power capable of saving human beings from these circumstances. In any event, there is no more reason to assume we have reached the end of spiritual history than there is to assume we have, as the sponsors of capitalism contend, reached the end of social history.[16]

Interestingly, theologies of liberation are transforming the conservative, otherworldly orientation of ecclesiastical institutions, theological discourses, and religious practices and challenging the international mode of material production that fosters an otherworldly yearning. Theology and the Church are, like society itself, divided into factions that favor those that are indifferent toward, and those that reject, the world as it is. The liberationist perspective rejects the reconciliatory project of forging peace without transforming the existing system of social relations and ultimately without ending the division of human beings into appropriators and producers, exploiters and exploited, ruling and ruled classes. Rather, the liberationist position affirms the need to replace the existing system to create a classless society in which real peace is possible. Liberation theology subordinates the goal of personal salvation through faith alone to the goal of social emancipation through works. Liberation theology insists that the purpose of ecclesiastical institutions, theological discourses, and religious practices is not to interpret the world but to change it.

The significance of churches', temples', and mosques' supportive engagement with individuals and organizations seeking to better their living conditions cannot be overestimated. The extent to which religious leaders and institutions lend their support will greatly determine whether efforts to gain control over work, schools, neighborhoods, and the environment and to expand support for education, health care, child care, workplace safety, social security, a living wage, and environmental protection prove successful and whether these struggles rise to the level of a political struggle to abolish private ownership of productive property and to subordinate societal planning to democratic modes of authority. But the theologians, priests, ministers, imams, rabbis, and educators must themselves be educated about the social sources of human suffering and ways to end it. In this respect West's efforts as a critical organic catalyst striving with religious leaders and theologians to develop a combative spirituality, in solidarity with labor, social, and environmental movements, provides a model to theologians committed to the struggle for human liberation. West reminds church leaders of their ethical obligation to carry on the legacy of the prophetic tradition and the prophetic mission of Jesus. In this way religious leaders and institutions may provide even more than solace and comfort to the alienated, degraded, and exploited. They may offer support to those seeking to build a society from which no one will feel the need or desire to be saved.[17]

2. Race, Class, Power

> Furthermore, it follows that every class which is struggling for mastery, even when its domination, as is the case with the proletariat, postulates the abolition of the old form of society in its entirety and of domination itself, must first conquer for itself political power.
>
> —Karl Marx, *Capital,* vol. 1

> Power must be analyzed as something that circulates, or rather as something which only functions in the form of a chain. It is never localized here or there, never in anybody's hands, never appropriated as a commodity or piece of wealth.
>
> —Michel Foucault, "Two Lectures"

Understanding what must be done to improve the human condition entails understanding the conditions that constitute the social and natural bases of productive labor and creative work. We must grasp what is before we can "say anything significant about what can be," for the "possibility of liberation is found only in the depths of the actuality of oppression" (West 1982:112). To this end West has made and continues to make significant contributions to the task of grasping what is and discerning what must be done to expand democratic authority over social production and planning. In addition to providing detailed descriptions and passionate denunciations of the dreadful conditions that characterize everyday labor and life for hundreds of millions of people around the world, West has made valuable contributions to our *theoretical* understanding of the forces that generate these conditions. Among the most important of West's theoretical contributions is an essay entitled "Race and Social Theory: Towards a Genealogical Materialist Analysis," in which he articulates "a new conception of African-American oppression that tries to bring together the best of recent Marxist theory and the invaluable insights of neo-Freudians (Ranke, Becker, Kovel) about changing forms of immortality quests and perceptions of dirt and death in the modern West, along with the formulations of the poststructuralists (Derrida, de Man, Foucault, Said) on the role of difference, otherness and marginality in discursive operations and extradiscursive formations" (1993d:265).[1] West calls his method for explaining the formation of racial identities, relations, and inequalities "a genealogical materialist analysis: that is, an analysis which replaces Marxist conceptions of history with Nietzschean notions of genealogy, yet preserves the materiality and multifaceted structured social practices" (ibid.). As I will show, however, some of these multifaceted structured social practices—namely, property relations—are given less explanatory weight in the analysis of racism than are discursive, institutional, and subjective factors.

West initially outlines his genealogical materialist methodology in *Prophesy Deliverance.* Drawing from the work of Michel Foucault, West delineates the discursive strands from which the ideology of white supremacy has been woven.[2] West's genealogy of modern racism is meant not to supplant historical materialist analyses but rather to complement them by providing a more complete account of the complex social forces that constitute racism. There are, says West, "powers immanent in non-discursive and discursive structures" (1982:49). The latter structures are not superficial "expressions" or passive "reflections" of the former; rather, they possess their own "materiality," operate according to their own relatively autonomous laws of development, and shape the development of nondiscursive structures. West begins his analysis of the discursive variable in the constitution of modern racism by examining the roles that the scientific revolution, Cartesian philosophy, and the revival of classical Greek aesthetic ideals played in the formation of modern discourse that, says West, "'secretes' the idea of white supremacy" (48).

The scientific revolution, initiated by such European thinkers as Copernicus, Kepler, Galileo, Newton, Descartes, Leibniz, and Bacon, constituted a radical critique and revolutionary rejection of theological metaphysics (even as many of these figures tempered, modified, and in some cases concealed their work to avoid the less than merciful wrath of Catholic magistrates). Scientific method demanded that divine revelation be replaced by empirical evidence and logical argumentation as the bases for determining the adequacy of competing truth claims. Moreover, scientific observation and experimentation were linked theoretically and practically to a conception of the scientist as an objective observer and to a theory of knowledge as representing a preexisting, nonrepresentational reality. These premises led many thinkers to conclude that the "fruits of scientific research do not merely provide more useful ways for human beings to *cope* with reality; such research also yields a true *copy* of reality," a position West criticizes throughout his work as philosophically naive and politically myopic (1982:51; 1989; 1991). During what are today known as the Early Renaissance and High Renaissance, ocular metaphors (e.g., the "eye of the mind" and "mind as mirror of nature") and classical Greek norms of beauty were grafted onto the emerging discourse and practice of what later became known as modern science. "The creative fusion of scientific investigation, Cartesian philosophy, Greek ocular metaphors, and classical aesthetic and cultural ideals constitutes the essential elements of modern discourse in the West. In short, modern discourse rests upon a conception of truth and knowledge governed by an ideal value-free subject engaged in observing, comparing, ordering, and measuring in order to arrive at evidence sufficient to make valid inferences, confirm speculative hypotheses, deduce error-proof conclusions, and verify true representations of reality" (West 1982:53 [emphasis omitted]). As important, modern science developed at the same time as the emerging European bourgeoisie began to explore, colonize, and enslave the rest of the world, and it was mobilized by European scientists, theologians, and philosophers as a method for classifying and evaluating, among other "discoveries," non-European human beings according to a schema in which European notions of intelligence, knowledge, beauty, philosophy, morality, law, and civilization were employed as the ideal standards by which to measure all "others." Although Linnaeus argued in his *Natural System* (1735) that human types ought not be hierarchically ordered in terms of their respective moral, intellectual, and spiritual value, his descriptions nevertheless disclose the unexamined values that inform his "objective" observations.

> European. White, Sanguine, Brawny. Hair abundantly flowing. Eyes blue. Gentle, acute, inventive. Covered with close vestments. Governed by customs.
>
> African. Black, Phlegmatic, Relaxed. Hair black, frizzled. Skin silky. Nose flat. Lips tumid. Women's bosom a matter of modesty. Breasts give milk abundantly. Crafty, indolent. Negligent. Anoints himself with grease. Governed by caprice. (cited in West 1982:56)

Linnaeus's failure to distinguish objects belonging to the natural sciences from those appropriate to the social sciences signifies not only his time (he wrote during the initial development of modern scientific theory and practice) but also the degree to which his observations were anything but value neutral. Like many Enlightenment philosophers, Linnaeus failed to differentiate sufficiently between what is given by nature, that is, what exists independently of human societies, and what is created by human beings in and through their interaction with nature and one another. Consequently, skin color and forms of governance, hair type and clothing, and body proportions and moral dispositions form an organic totality and in so doing create the basis for the most perilous sort of ideological reductionism. Erasing the difference between humanly created and naturally given conditions of life makes it possible to advance defenses of the existing social relations by explaining these relations as manifestations of natural laws about which little, if anything, can be done. The reduction of humanly created conditions, conditions created through individual and collective labor, to purportedly natural conditions is a key ideological operation deployed to enforce the "noble lie" regarding an ontological hierarchy of distinct racial "types" (see Aptheker 1987; Lerner 1992; Mills 1997, 1998).

It was in the fields of phrenology and physiognomy that the idea of racial types and the vertical ordering of these types—according to a "great racist chain of being"—assumed its clearest and most grotesque formulation. Fascist mythmakers, for example, used the Dutch anatomist Pieter Camper's theory of the "facial angle" to differentiate "Aryan" from "non-Aryan" types.[3] Camper measured facial types according to classical Greek ideals of beauty, proportion, and moderation, standards against which everyone other than the Europeans who articulated these standards were found to be deficient. Camper, Johann Kaspar Lavater, and Franz Joseph Gall were instrumental in promoting what West, borrowing from Foucault, calls the "normative gaze." The normative gaze presumes the observer's ideological innocence and a relationship of epistemological immediacy between the knowing subject and the object known. As West indicates, many abolitionists were transfixed by this gaze, assuming a natural division of human beings into biologically distinct races even as they struggled to abolish slavery. By the end of the eighteenth century, he says, the ideology of racism was no longer subject to serious theoretical dispute.[4] The scientific truths posited by European intellectuals had been naturalized to such an extent as to appear self-evident. Not only did these intellectuals elaborate racist theories; in many cases they believed their theories to rest on scientific inquiry, evidence, and reason (West 1982:61).

West draws two general conclusions from his genealogy of modern racism: first, the advent of modern science played a "crucial role . . . in highlighting the physical appearances of people in relation to what it is to be human, beautiful, cultured, and intelligent" and hence in promoting the notion of white supremacy, a notion purportedly "grounded" in racially categorical biological differences (West 1982:64 [emphasis omitted]); second, "there was no iron necessity" compelling theorists to articulate the metaphors, notions, categories, and norms that constituted the discursive actuality of racist ideology. They might just as well have been articulated differently or perhaps not at all. To trace the genealogy of modern racism is not to explain the totality of the conditions of its emergence, West adds. Rather, it is to identify the roles that science, philosophy, and aesthetics played in the construction of racism.

> This variable is significant because it not only precludes reductionistic treatments of modern racism; it also highlights the cultural and aesthetic impact of the idea of white supremacy on black people. This inquiry accents the fact

> that the everyday life of black people is shaped not only simply by the exploitative (oligopolistic) capitalist system of production but also by cultural attitudes and sensibilities, including alienating ideals of beauty. The idea of white supremacy is a major bowel unleashed by the structure of modern discourse, a significant secretion generated from the creative fusion of scientific investigation, Cartesian philosophy, and classical aesthetic and cultural norms. Needless to say, the odor of this bowel and the fumes of this secretion continue to pollute the air of our postmodern times. (Ibid.)

West's description of this variable provides vital knowledge about the forces that perpetuate racial identities, inequalities, and relations and indicates the importance of researching those conditions. An adequate understanding of the category of race must grasp not only the ways in which racial divisions are reproduced through socioeconomic processes, particularly that of capital accumulation (note that such studies are, especially in the U.S. academic context, relatively rare), but also how racism is ideologically and institutionally reproduced (see, e.g., Marable 1981; Alexander 1987; Callinicos 1993; Malik 1996). Although racial inequalities cannot be fully eliminated without transforming the property relations that produce a society marked by average social, political, and economic inequalities between persons identified as belonging to different "races," establishing democratic control over productive property will not in itself eliminate racial inequalities because, as West notes, racism is economic, political, *and* cultural. Subordinating productive property to democratic authority would merely make it possible to utilize these vast resources to combat the division of human beings into different races (e.g., through state-coordinated programs designed to ensure equal educational opportunities, universal access to quality health care, good housing, employment, and safe natural environments for all individuals).

The Theoretical Sublation of Racism

West's genealogical materialist approach to racism has increasingly led him away from the strongly Marxist-informed analysis he advanced in *Prophesy Deliverance.* Before 1989, in his pre-*Evasion* works, West argued that the fundamental cause of powerlessness for black as well as white citizens derives from lack of control over productive property, that is, from class position, not racial identity. Although he maintains some aspects of this argument in his later works, West's materialist genealogy privileges discursive formations and institutional arrangements (e.g., culture, morality, the law, and other superstructural elements) over property relations as the fundamental causes of persistent average inequalities for black and white citizens (Unger and West 1998:15, 16, 34, 74). In *The Future of American Progressivism* Unger and West write that "the United States has a relatively well-defined class structure," that "the class system has remained as stable in American reality as it has been clouded in American consciousness," and that the United States "has seen increasing inequality of wealth and income, driving the life chances of individuals apart" (15, 16 [emphasis omitted]). The agenda they advance to address this situation, however, seeks not to transform capitalist property relations and the goal of capitalist production but rather to reform the law, education, and tax code; create joint ventures between private capital and public institutions; and increase spending on job-training and employment services to narrow the income gap and foster greater upward mobility. West has in large measure moved away from his argument, advanced in *Prophesy Deliverance* and *Prophetic Fragments,* that we must build an international movement against capitalist globalization of nature and society. Thus as West's thought has developed, his "hesitant rejection" of the Marxist view that economic considerations are paramount in the explanation of racism's role and function has become a sophisticated evasion or an outright rejection of class struggle and the necessity to socialize productive property.

Although West explains that his genealogical materialist analysis is not meant to replace Marxism as the explanation for the formation of modern racism, he nevertheless contends that racism is a "logical consequence of the quest for truth and knowledge in the modern West" and that the notion of white supremacy is "unleashed by the structure of modern discourse" (West 1982:65). Moreover, this claim appears to suggest that creating a postracist society would entail terminating this quest. Although West maintains that racism is both a discursive *and* extradiscursive reality, his genealogical materialist method represents and contributes to the development of a post-Marxist propensity to begin within the heavenly realm of ideas and rarely, if ever, return to Earth to examine the relationship between these ideas and property relations. Without examining this relationship, it is difficult to determine how discourses protect the interests of the ruling class. West's approach downplays, even though it does not totally disregard, the necessity to explicate the relationships between racist discourses and the processes of capital accumulation. By downplaying this relationship, the genealogical materialist method supports superstructural and in some cases manifestly *idealist* explanations for the existence and persistence of racism. Such explanations emphasize the independence of institutions and discourses from the division of labor and the processes of capital accumulation to such an extent that the struggle against racist practices and inequalities is reduced to, for example, constructing more affirming representations.[5] The problem, then, is not so much that West abandons a concern for the role that class relations play in determining societal development; he most certainly does not, and this remains a strength throughout virtually all his works. Instead, it is that as far as racism is concerned, he ascribes to institutions, discourses, and subjectivity a causal force equal to or, in works such as *Race Matters, The War against Parents,* and *The Future of American Progressivism,* greater than that of private ownership of productive property and transnational processes of capital accumulation.

In "Race and Social Theory" West explains that "a genealogical materialist conception of social practices should be more materialist than that of the Marxist tradition, to the extent that the privileged material mode of production is not necessarily located in the economic sphere" (1993d:266). By arguing that "decisive material modes of production at a given moment may be located in the cultural, political, or even psychic spheres," West usefully reminds us of the need to resist the methodological inclination to explain all social phenomena as being the product of a single factor. Not all that exists warrants the adjective "capitalist," as if everything that exists embodies the essence of capitalism or functions only as a condition for the reproduction of the labor-capital relation. West opens the space for investigating society as a complex of interrelated spheres of practice that must be studied afresh to grasp their historically specific constellation.

Nonetheless, for many post-Marxist and anti-Marxist leftists and in West's post-Marxist works, the argument that cultural and psychic spheres may at any time assume dominance in relationship to economic and political spheres and operate as decisive *material* modes of production has frequently become an argument that the former spheres virtually always exercise greater influence on societal development than do the latter spheres. Discourse, culture, and subjectivity dominate or simply eclipse the categories of class, class struggle, and state power. Moreover, the argument that discourse, culture, and subjectivity are as material as class, class struggle, and state power has even become an argument that the former create the latter. From this perspective, social problems, including racial divisions, are thought to be constituted primarily or even singularly by discourse, culture, and subjectivity, and on occasion by legal, political, and educational institutions, and consequently to be resolvable through the transformation of these realities. The limitation of this perspective, a perspective central to social constructionism, is that it tends not to link the analysis of law, discourse, and culture to a critique of a capitalist political economy. In this way, "the relation between the social divisions created by an economic and social system and the strength of racial feeling is obscured" (Hadjor 1995:22; see also T. Allen 1994; Roedigger 1994). Individuals may be led to believe that racism "can be challenged by building a Black counterculture, by encouraging a sort of alternative version of a subjectively constructed identity"; nevertheless, although "promoting many different cultures in this way may well strike a blow against the *notion* that one group is superior . . . , it can also end up excusing and reinforcing racial divisions in a language that is far more acceptable today than the old ideologies of White supremacy" (Hadjor 1995:22–23 [emphasis added]), a point I consider in greater detail chapter 3. Although legal reforms may benefit a small proportion of racially identified individuals in their efforts to gain access to educational, political, and economic institutions, they do not alter the division of labor and society into warring classes. Such reforms would at best distribute persons ascribed to distinct racial groups equally across employment categories and class positions. Thus, although social construction theorists have contributed significantly to our knowledge of the cultural, legal, and political factors that contribute to the formation and perpetuation of racial identities, relations, and inequalities, by leaving the linkages between these factors and the processes of capital accumulation largely unexamined, the political horizon of their solutions remains limited.

West's rejection ("hesitant," perhaps, but still a rejection) of the claim that material production fundamentally determines all other aspects of social life leads him to formulate "methodological moments" for analyzing racist ideologies and practices:

> (1) A *genealogical* inquiry into the discursive and extra-discursive conditions for the possibility of racist practices, that is, a radically historical investigation into the emergence, development and sustenance of white-supremacist logics operative in various epochs in the modern Western (Eastern or African) civilizations. (2) A *microinstitutional* (or localized) analysis of the mechanisms that promote and contest these logics in the everyday lives of people, including the ways in which self-images and self-identities are shaped, and the impact of alien, degrading cultural styles, aesthetic ideals, psychosexual sensibilities and linguistic gestures upon peoples of color. (3) A *macrostructural* approach which accents modes of overdetermined class exploitation, state repression and bureaucratic domination, including resistance against these modes, in the lives of people of color. (1993d:268)

West's refined post-Marxist macrostructural moment, in which one examines class exploitation, state repression, and bureaucratic domination, has increasingly become little more than a moment. With each new work by West, these categories attract increasingly less attention in the task of discerning the spiritual and material conditions of freedom and determination and the changes that must be made if human beings are to assume greater mastery over their own conditions of material production and creative work. In his post-*Evasion* works West proposes that labor, business, and government ought to work together to achieve common ends, for example, to save America from decline, a position that discloses a non-class-based analysis of politics. With the publication of *The War against Parents* (Hewlett and West 1998) and *The Future of American Progressivism* (Unger and West 1998), West no longer clearly and consistently connects socioeconomic inequalities to the structural operations of the capitalist mode of production. Rather, he views socioeconomic inequalities as being what results when those who own and control the means of production and who appropriate the fruits of other people's labor appropriate too much: "Despite an official effort to blame the wage squeeze on foreigners, declining levels for the average American worker and frightening levels of insecurity have little to do with Korean workers or global competitive pressures; rather, they are the result of rampaging managerial greed, newly endorsed and facilitated by government" (Hewlett and West 1998:61).

The extraordinary greed of American managers and CEOs has undoubtedly contributed to the dramatic growth of income and wealth disparities over the past twenty-five years. American managers and CEOs take a far bigger slice of the globally produced pie than do managers and CEOs in most other rich capitalist nations and defend their gluttonous behavior on the grounds that they "risk so much" (of value created by others) and "work so hard" (compared to workers laboring in fields, factories, and mine shafts around the world?) to "run their business" (expand and intensify the processes of surplus-value extraction). Today, the United States is "the most [economically] unequal country in the advanced industrial world. The top one percent of the American population now controls 39 percent of national wealth, compared to 26 percent in France, 16 percent in Sweden, and 18 percent in Great Britain" (Hewlett and West 1998:83). There is no question that American workers would enjoy higher standards of living if managers and CEOs embraced the Christian love ethic and as a consequence shared wealth. Nonetheless, such changes would not alter the organization of productive property, labor, and nature for the purpose of profit making.

There is no question that U.S. CEO compensation is obscene, but the deeper social obscenity, the heart of capitalism's antisociality, lies in the fact that private ownership of the means of production denies hundreds of millions of human beings around the world control over the resources required to satisfy basic needs and to ensure the universal development of rich individuality. If one argues, as West and Hewlett do in *The War against Parents,* that the fundamental cause of social, political, and economic problems is "pure, unadulterated greed," then the solution becomes one of lessening greed and, as they suggest, having the appropriators distribute the pie more fairly to those who make and serve the pie. In other words, their argument assumes that societal problems are rooted in the subjective dispositions of those who own, control, and appropriate the fruits of the means of production rather than in the institutionally sanctioned, buttressed, and protected structures of production and appropriation. A CEO, whether greedy or generous, is still a CEO, which is to say, a capitalist—that is, a person whose function is determined less by his or her individual disposition than by his or her position as an investor or owner of means of production and, as such, whose aim is to ensure the valorization of value, the self-augmentation of capital, through the "greedy" or "generous" (whatever works) exploitation of labor. Indeed, without abolishing the division of society into classes of individuals whose economic and political interests conflict, there is little reason to assume that even the most kindly of capitalists will remain charitable toward their less fortunate brethren if they believe, rightly or wrongly, that their personal existence is threatened. What is needed is not a new social compact between the working and owning classes but rather the institutionalization of a mode of production and distribution in which no individual or class of individuals is capable of making publicly unaccountable decisions, a mode in which, as West wrote in *Prophesy Deliverance,* the associated citizens "participate substantively in the decision-making processes in the major institutions that regulate their lives" (1982:112).

In his desire to develop a method that is "more materialist than that of the Marxist tradition" by viewing discourse, representation, culture, and subjectivity as material, West has articulated a post-Marxist genealogical materialist analysis that has led not only to a concrete and significant analysis of the genealogical, microinstitutional, and macrostructural aspects of racial oppression but also to a position that makes the conditions identified by a genealogical analysis primary in the constitution of international social, economic, and ecological problems. Thus, for example, as I will examine in chapter 4, West argues in *Race Matters* that "the major enemy of black survival in America has been and is neither oppression nor exploitation but rather the nihilistic threat" (1993a:15). Once this theoretical step has been taken, once everything becomes material and one begins to speak of the constitution of social problems as being a consequence of discourse, representation, culture, or subjectivity, the space is cleared to argue that racism is, as West says in *Prophesy Deliverance,* a product of "the underside of modern discourse—a particular logical consequence of the quest for truth and knowledge in the modern West"—or, as Hewlett and West argue in *The War against Parents,* that class inequalities are the result of "greed" (West 1982:48; Hewlett and West 1998:83).

The division of human beings on the basis of skin color did not initially derive from scientific laboratories, philosophical associations, or aristocratic clubs. Members of the slave-holding class developed racist ideologies and legally codified racial divisions to justify and perpetuate the enslavement of Africans and divide workers who had proven themselves capable of acting in solidarity against their exploiters (see Aptheker 1992; Jones 1998).[6] The racialization of socioeconomic inequalities, notes Marable, "was always [and remains] fundamentally a product of class domination" (1995:217). The association of slavery with "blackness," now so firmly cemented in historical memory that it seems as if the two must have always been linked, did not exist from the beginning. Rather, the ruling economic class institutionalized the racialization of slavery through legislative decisions and criminal punishments to ensure its domination over black, red, and white labor. Prior to the institutional racialization of socioeconomic divisions among the laboring class, workers across the color spectrum lived, labored, and parented children together, and most significant from the point of view of the exploiting class, they acted in solidarity with one another, killing their masters, burning their masters' houses and fields, and running away. The ruling class carefully crafted a complex of laws in the seventeenth and eighteenth centuries proscribing sexual relations and marriage between "Europeans," "Indians," and "Africans" and codifying unequal punishments for each (see Aptheker 1992; Goldfield 1997:36–49; Jones 1998:76–77).

Even after the link between slavery and skin color was established, that is, after the racial ontology of slavery in the United States was juridically, politically, and economically formalized, it was less a case of racial divisions being reproduced via the perpetuation of racist ideologies than of the perpetuation of such ideologies being made possible, as it is today, by residential and employment segregation. It is also true, however, that racist ideologies facilitate the reproduction of exploitation. As West's genealogical materialist analysis indicates, science, philosophy, and religion have all contributed to the rationalization of socioeconomic inequalities by justifying their existence and directing attention away from their economic sources. At the same time, average inequalities between black and white citizens cannot be eliminated by transforming racist discourses, practices, or prejudices alone. Inasmuch as capitalist development generates inequalities, their elimination, whether between or within racial categories, cannot be achieved without also eliminating class divisions and production for the sole purpose of profit making, as West argues in *Prophesy Deliverance*.[7] At the same time, antiracist campaigns are not secondary or superfluous to class struggle. Indeed, efforts to overcome racial, ethnic, national, gender, and sexual forms of discrimination are key to building an effective movement for democratic globalization.

Marxism, Racism, and Science

By arguing that racism is a consequence of the modern West's quest for truth and knowledge, West makes the scientific quest for truth and knowledge complicit with racism. Putting aside for now questions concerning the substitution of cultural for economic categories and the problematic status of the concept the "modern West" (e.g., where and what exactly is the modern West, and how might it be transformed?), it is worth noting that scientists almost universally claim that "race has no scientific validity, as a meaningful biological or genetic concept" (Marable 1991:188).[8]

West's argument regarding racism's connection to the Western quest for truth and knowledge is problematic both because it reduces the meaning and consequences of this quest to the support that particular individuals and theories have given to racism and because it makes science the private property of a quasi-metaphysical entity called "the West." West does not critique capital's use of science and technology to increase the rate of surplus-value extraction, that is, the exploitation of labor, but rather critiques scientific method as such. In this respect, his critique shares more with Luddite than Marxist critiques of capitalist society, for it directs attention away from the class powers that control the processes and products of scientific production and toward the processes and products themselves. His argument buttresses those who believe that economic and ecological problems derive from science itself rather than from the social relations that make it possible for a small minority to determine the needs scientific production will satisfy and that compel this minority to make their decisions according to what might best increase the rate of surplus-value extraction (see, e.g., Lauritsen 1993; Clorfene-Casten 1996; Marsa 1997; Lappe, Bailey, and Lauritsen 1998).

West focuses his critique of modern science on Marxist science. According to West, Marxism's optimistic outlook regarding humanity's capacity to assume control over its own conditions of production reveals an "uncritical valorization of scientific method—more specifically, dialectical method" (1982:99). Marxism's uncritical valorization of scientific method

> not only reflects the origins of Marxism in the heyday of European modernity when the authority of science flourished; it also reveals the captivity of Marxism to the modern ideology of science initiated by the Enlightenment. The fundamental tenet of this ideology is the desirable creation of a scientific monopoly over a subject matter, a master discourse on particular phenomena. Marxism prides itself as warranting its own scientific monopoly over discerning and explaining power and wealth in modern societies; it prides itself as the master discourse on capitalist societies. . . . the Marxist clamor for scientific standing discloses the will to power which rests at the center of European modernity: the will to cognition and control, manipulation and mastery. (99–100)

West's claim is partially accurate yet misleading. His claim is accurate to the extent that Marx drew from and developed advances in the fields of sociology, economics, and philosophy made prior to and during the Enlightenment. Moreover, West is correct when he claims that Marxism is continuous with efforts to develop humanity's capacities for cognition and control, manipulation and mastery. To say only this much and to say it in this way, however, confuses more than it clarifies. The development of Marxism as a distinct, albeit (as Marx himself repeatedly stressed) barely outlined, approach to the study of society was in part premised on advances made in German philosophy, French social science, and English political economy;

the material conditions of possibility for these advances were in turn premised on the colossal transformations that characterized the emergence, development, and consolidation of capitalism as the dominant mode of socioeconomic organization in Europe and eventually around the world. Claiming that Marxism's valorization of science indicates a "will to power" central to European modernity excludes consideration of the antagonistic social forces that constitute the reality designated by the concepts of European modernity and the Enlightenment. It was not the *European* will to power but the European *bourgeoisie's* will to expand its control over land and labor that revolutionized conditions of existence in and beyond Europe. These efforts conflicted with the progressive Enlightenment ideal of universal human rights. The concept of European modernity remains insufficiently differentiated to the extent that it does not account for the bourgeoisie's subjugation of people at home prior to its expansion abroad. By arguing that Marxism is a manifestation of the "will to power . . . at the center of European modernity," West elides the role Marxist theory and practice played in the struggle against exploitation and colonization, including its critique of capital's use of science and technology as means for extending exploitation and colonization.[9] Indeed, it would be difficult to explain why European powers have sought to expel, imprison, and execute Marxists, most notably Marx himself, if Marxism was, as West argues, only another expression of the European will to power.

Moreover, Enlightenment thinkers did not all share the same views on society, history, progress, human nature, race, and rights. Many espoused inconsistent and often contradictory views. Whereas Rousseau maintained that intellectual, imaginative, and moral capacities are distributed in equal proportions among all human beings, Jefferson held these capacities are distributed unequally among biologically distinct human groups or races. Whereas Rousseau argued that observable differences among human groups were due to social-historical factors and were superficial compared to what human beings share in common, Jefferson held that observable differences among human groups, especially between Europeans and Africans, were due in large measure to biological differences. The shift from Rousseau's to Jefferson's perspective on human nature, race, and rights coincides with the bourgeoisie's position of power. Initially the rising middle classes fought the feudal nobility and Catholic clergy under the banner of universal rights and equality of persons. Having assumed state power, however, the slaveholding, merchant, and factory-owning elite sought to rationalize colonialism, slavery, and class domination to protect itself against movements calling for democratic control of economics. Thus, while Jefferson wrote in the Declaration of Independence that "all men are created equal," in his *Notes on Virginia* he maintained that some men, most notably the Africans he owned as slaves, were inferior to other men, most notably the class of slaveholders to which he belonged. The principal point I wish to emphasize here is that Enlightenment thinkers assumed different and opposing positions on everything from capitalism and slavery to socialism and equality. The European will to power is, in other words, more accurately described in terms of competing wills seeking to maintain and challenge different systems for organizing the production and distribution of power.

The methodological limitations and conservative nature of West's argument derives in part from his use of concepts drawn from Nietzsche's metaphysics. Nietzsche's concept of the will to power is conservative inasmuch as it suggests, in the vein of Spenser's social Darwinism, that the capitalist mode of production is only another manifestation of a universal metaphysical law: not life under capitalism but "life itself is *essentially* appropriation, injury, overpowering of the strange and weaker, suppression, severity, imposition of one's own forms, incorporation and, at the least and mildest, exploitation," said Nietzsche in a characteristic aphorism from his later speculations on—or rather "revelations" regarding—the will to power (1977: 229–30).[10] Contrary to claims made by socialists, democrats, and levelers, said Nietzsche, "'Exploitation' does not pertain to a corrupt or imperfect or primitive society: it pertains to the *essence* of the living thing as a fundamental organic function, it is a consequence of the intrinsic will to power which is precisely the will of life" (230). Interestingly, this speculative reduction of the historical particularities of capitalism finds a curious parallel in Hegel's reduction of objectification under capitalism to the transhistorical alienation of Spirit, even as Hegel was Nietzsche's sworn enemy.

The problem of science and technology is not, as Heidegger argued, so much a spiritual problem, a problem that may be solved through spiritual means (e.g., by thinking the Being of beings), but rather, at least initially, a problem rooted in the question of who decides the social ends realized through and interests served by science and technology (Heidegger 1969). Science and technology in themselves are not the problem (even though some technologies—e.g., nuclear ones—should not be developed at all). Rather, the problem lies in the fact that science and technology are controlled by private investors competing with one another to make profits. Science and technology are therefore developed with little or no regard for the social and natural consequences of their development not because private investors suffer a lack of morals, though some no doubt do, but because global competition penalizes those who do consider these consequences. Questions concerning development's impact on the environment, health care, housing, literacy, and employment are not figured into cost-benefit analyses and decisions. As long as money can be made, the Earth's forests will be cut down and burned out of existence. As long as money can be made, ozone will be depleted and the

Earth's temperature will rise. As long as money can be made, the diversity of animal life will be relegated to picture books and genetic banks. All these things and worse are occurring and will continue to occur unless factors other than profits figure into the mathematics of development.[11]

Scientific knowledge and technologies are not value neutral. Clearly, technologies of repression are necessary only in a society based on the domination of one group or class over another. However, a politically productive critique of science and technology must be linked to a critique of the social interests that science and technology protect and promote. Interpreting science and technology as manifestations of "the will to power," "European modernity," "the West," or "the Enlightenment" does not provide a basis for understanding what must be done to ensure that they are used to enrich human beings. Indeed, it is not even clear what it would mean to abolish the will to power, European modernity, the West, or the Enlightenment. What is clearer, however, is that the will to power, specifically the will to political power, must be developed among U.S. workers if science and technology are to become the shared property of all persons and used to enrich humanity's collective life.

Capitalist development establishes conditions that make democratic determination of material production and free creation not only possible but also increasingly necessary in addressing the global problems that challenge humanity today. The subordination of social planning and production to democratic, rather than privatized, modes of authority is vital to creating the structural basis for ensuring that the material and spiritual needs of all human beings are satisfied. Regrettably, scientific and technological producers, production, and products are, as previously indicated, increasingly organized to meet the goal of capital accumulation. In *Biotechnology: The University Industrial Complex,* Martin Kenney writes: "Behavior that is normal in industry or the professions—secrecy, evasiveness, and invidious competition based on pecuniary motives—threatens to disrupt the social relationships based on non-commercial motives that are expected in and have characterized the university" (1986:131; see Soley 1995). Thus, even as the mode of scientific and technological production is socialized, creating an international scientific community, the fruits of science are increasingly subject(ed) to private appropriation and subordinated to the antisocial teleology of private profit making. Valuable scientific knowledge and technologies that could be made available to every human being are increasingly controlled by multinational corporations and made accessible only to those who can pay the price.[12] Cures for physical, mental, and emotional diseases will be found not by ridding humanity of science and technology but rather by freeing both from the antisocial fetters of private property. Arguing that science *in itself* is the poison is little better than arguing that science in itself is the cure. Both positions accept a reified understanding of science as the cornerstone on which rests liberation or damnation. Although West does not argue that we should jettison science and technology, his claim that science, technology, and modern racism represent expressions of the European will to power supports those who mistakenly believe that our salvation lies in resisting "the will to cognition and control, manipulation and mastery" (West 1992:100). To do so, however, means to deprive human beings of powers that derive from their own blood, sweat, and tears, powers that, if organized democratically, offer the potential for dramatically expanding our abilities to meet humanity's biological requirements on a global scale and to support the work of free creation.

The problem facing humanity is not whether the power to conceptualize and control reality should exist. Rather, the problem is a matter of *who* commands and *whose* needs will be satisfied by science and technology. In fact, West's project presupposes as much. Although he critiques the Western drive toward scientific mastery, his own project seeks to theorize what must be done to expand humanity's capacity to master and control its own material and spiritual conditions. Exercising freedom as the capacity to achieve consciously determined goals depends on having the ability to choose one's goals and having access to the resources required to achieve the goals chosen. Individuals may decide to eat organically grown food, yet as long as the resources required to grow such food are used to grow chemically enhanced food products, the ability to realize this choice will be seriously limited (as it is throughout the world today). The value of power cannot be assessed abstractly; rather, power must be evaluated by assessing the extent to which its utilization minimizes the time required to satisfy humanity's biological needs, maximizes the time and resources available for all human beings to engage in creative work, and accomplishes these goals in a manner that generously replenishes the natural basis of human life. Although science and technology have never before been as subordinated to the reproduction of exploitative relations as they are now, those seeking to improve our social and natural conditions of life cannot afford to reject science and technology.

Marxism, Science, and Elitism

West largely accepts the postmodernist critique of the claim that science has an epistemological advantage over other means for theoretically grasping the nature of "reality." Following Nietzsche's "Truth and Lie in the Extra-Moral Sense," postmodernists from Agger to Zizek have argued that science is a metaphorical construct, mobilized less to understand how things work (a project that many postmodernists argue mistakenly assumes that something called "reality" exists prior to and independent of its discursive representation) than to advance the interests and ends of this or that social group. According to this view, Marx was an ethical philosopher who was motivated less by a desire to investigate, analyze, and determine how capitalism works than by a desire to provide "scientific" "evidence" to buttress his a priori commitment to justice, liberty, and fraternity. In *The Ethical Dimensions of Marxist Thought* West writes that for Marx, "'objective truth' should not be associated with representations *copying* the world, but rather with *coping* in the world, that 'objective truth' should not be associated with representations *agreeing with* objects in the world, but rather *with people transforming* circumstances and conditions in the world" (1991:65). West elaborates on this point: the "scientific or objective status of theories is not linked to philosophic notions of verification, or of correct correspondence relations (e.g. idea/object, words/things, propositions/states of affairs)" but rather rests "on the sensitivity expressed [by theoreticians] towards pressing problems, the solutions offered for urgent dilemmas, and openings made into new areas of self-criticism" (98).

Nonetheless, West's interpretation of what he describes as Marx's "metaphilosophical" move from philosophical to theoretical formulations undermines the possibility of critiquing the conditions that give rise to a suspicion regarding science and technology. Rather than critique this suspicion as a partially accurate comprehension of the everyday consequences of science and technology for most working people (e.g., they are deployed by capital to replace workers and increase the rate of exploitation), West makes this suspicion the basis for his critique of science and technology as such and, by extension, of the elitism of those who, like Marxists, claim to know more than others about, for example, the operation of capitalism, technology, science, and racism. But some do know more than others about some things, and this fact is less about elitism than it is about uneven access to knowledge and the means of knowledge production. Assuming otherwise undermines the practice of critique, since criticism depends on the epistemological premise that some understand reality not merely differently but actually better than others do. Moreover, although many postmodernists assert the contrary with unbridled confidence, it does not follow that knowing more than others about some things necessarily leads individuals to assume they are morally superior. Marxists and Marxist organizations have used scientific rhetoric to legitimate their authority as the "revolutionary" leaders. Such individuals should be exposed for using scientific rhetoric to advance their own sectarian interests in the same manner that religious leaders should be exposed for using religious rhetoric to support their kingdoms here on earth. Nonetheless, such critiques are not advanced in the least by positing a historically abstract link between elitism and science, as if science *is* elitist. The danger here is not merely one of surrendering to the anti-intellectualism that derives in part from the fact that many people have little understanding of or involvement in the production of scientific knowledge, although this would be damaging enough, but also one of misidentifying the cause of elitism as a matter of claiming scientific status. It is not the "rhetoric of science which surreptitiously manipulate[s] and control[s]" the working class and the poor, any more than it is the rhetoric of science that gives "prestige and status to those [Marxists] who have the method" (West 1982:100); in any case, history does not offer much evidence to support the claim that Marxists have gained much prestige or status by claiming the authority of science for their theories. It is not the *rhetoric* of science but rather capital's development and deployment of science and technology for its own purposes that justifies the well-founded suspicion that they are not all for the good, or rather not good for all. At the same time, it is precisely a scientific understanding of capitalism's modes of operation that makes it possible to move from being passively suspicious of science and technology, as so many working people are, to being actively engaged in the struggle to subordinate science and technology to democratic authority and create the political basis for placing both in the service of universal human emancipation.

Marx and Foucault on Power

The complications resulting from West's synthesis of Foucault's genealogical materialism with Marxism's historical materialism derive in part from the fact that Foucault and Marx theorize opposing conceptions of power. Foucault remarks that perhaps "Marx and Freud cannot satisfy our desire for understanding this enigmatic thing which we call power, which is at once both visible and invisible, present and hidden, ubiquitous" (1977:213). "We know with reasonable certainty who exploits others, who receives the profits, and which people are involved, and we know how these funds are reinvested," but "it is often difficult to say who holds power in a precise sense" (ibid.).

I share Marx's view that power ultimately derives from the degree of control that an individual or class of individuals exercises over the means of production, that is, over property and specifically over productive property. It is the dominant economic class that largely controls the political, financial, legal, educational, and media institutions that determine the form and content of policy debates and which policies will be implemented by those who are ruled. Thus, although the state may assume the form of democracy, state apparatuses are largely controlled by the dominant class or, as is most often the case, the strongest factions of this class. The state represents this class's or class-faction's problems as if they were those of society as a whole (e.g., a president claims that a trade policy or military action is necessary and good for "America" when in fact it is undertaken to advance specific class interests; the North American Free Trade Agreement [NAFTA] and the "humanitarian" intervention in Yugoslavia are recent cases in point). Although the state, with its sundry ideological and repressive apparatuses, remains a site of political conflict, in general it functions, just as Marx noted, as an instrument for managing the common concerns of the capitalist class. Today, in the era of transnational capitalism, the "state not only must facilitate conditions of unfettered cross-national movement of commodity capital; it must also guarantee unrestricted conditions for international investment" (Yaghmaian 1998–99:251). Among all states worldwide, the U.S. state plays a pivotal role in protecting and propping up the international system of capital accumulation. In all likelihood capitalism would not last long without the U.S. state's ideological, political, financial, and military support, support funded primarily through taxes collected from U.S. workers (Greider 1997:192).

Corporations outsource production and market their commodities around the world, but they nevertheless turn to representatives from their "home" nations to negotiate agreements (e.g., NAFTA and GATT [General Agreement on Tariffs and Trade]) that support their efforts to expand control over labor and resources beyond their own borders. Cyril Siewert, head of the Colgate-Palmolive Company, admits that their home nation "doesn't have an automatic call on our [corporation's] resources [and that] there is no mindset that puts this country first" (in Parenti 1995:31). Yet Siewert and his fellow CEOs are quick to plunder their country's public treasury when it comes to protecting their financial interests. U.S. workers cover the costs associated with U.S. military interventions that protect U.S. corporate investments, create new investment opportunities, and preserve high rates of capital accumulation. They also fund corporate access to foreign labor markets, lose their jobs, see their own wages devalued, and even lose their lives as a result. Indeed, it is this difference—*the difference of class*—that explains why the state is willing to spend more to bomb Yugoslavia than is gained in revenues as a result.[13] Although the state is becoming less responsible to the needs of the people it claims to represent (a fact that may explain why most citizens in nations such as the United States do not vote), it has nevertheless remained crucial to keeping the world safe for "freedom and democracy," that is, capital investment. This above all else explains why the Pentagon budget remains a sacred cow even in the post–cold war era and even as politicians make balancing the budget—that is, eliminating programs that benefit the working class and poor—a centerpiece of their party platforms and legislative agendas. By controlling the state, the capitalist class is able not only to maintain and expand control over land, labor, and resources but also to socialize the costs of production through tax write-offs, guaranteed rates of return, and taxes on citizens to cover the costs of building transportation and communication systems, as well as research and development. The fact that many corporations operate above the laws of any particular nation has in no sense lessened the significance of the struggle to control the state. Indeed, without state support, especially the U.S. military's support in the form of direct interventions and indirect military aid, democratic movements around the world would enjoy much greater success. While the sunny day of the post–World War II economic boom is setting for many workers, the U.S. state remains key to preserving global capitalism.

Foucault rejects the Marxist concept of power, based as it is on one class's possessing power over another, insisting instead that "power in its exercise goes much further, passes through much finer channels, and is much more ambiguous since each individual has at his disposal a certain power" and is simultaneously "had" by power (1980:72).

> [Power] is not that which makes the difference between those who exclusively possess and retain it, and those who do not have it and submit to it. Power must be analyzed as something which circulates, or rather as something which only functions in the form of a chain. It is never localized here or there, never in anybody's hands, never appropriated as a commodity or piece of wealth. [Rather] power is employed and exercised through a net-like organization. And not only do individuals circulate between its threads; they are always in the position of simultaneously undergoing and exercising this power. They are not only its inert or consenting targets; they are always also the elements of its articulation. In other words, individuals are the vehicles of power, not its point of application. (Ibid.)

Foucault challenges the Marxist theory that power derives from control over productive property. By displacing the Marxist concept of power, Foucault displaces the need for workers to take control of state apparatuses and democratize control over social resources and institutions. Foucauldian and Marxist theories of power yield decidedly different understandings of what must be done to emancipate humanity from oppressive circumstances. Whereas a Marxist analysis illuminates what working people must do to gain and use power as a means for building a democratic society, a Foucauldian analysis suggests that individuals should displace the dominant discursive regime by resisting localized sites of its specific operations. Inasmuch as Foucault theorizes power as some thing or force that enables and disables every individual, regardless of racial, sexual, ethnic, national, religious, or class position, he advances a political position from what might at best be called "some vague libertarian standpoint" (Eagleton 1996:31). Given the anarchist implications of his rejection of utilizing power to build a workers' democracy, it is perhaps not surprising that, when Foucault was asked to identify precisely the subjects who oppose each other, he offered an answer that would surely have made Hobbes grin: "It's all against all. There aren't immediately given subjects of the struggle, one the proletariat, the other the bourgeoisie. Who fights against whom? We all fight each other" (208). Foucault then added that "there is always within each of us something that fights something else" (ibid.), leaving his befuddled disciples to ponder what these somethings might be.

The victims of racism, sexism, and exploitation would not get very far in their struggle to rid the world of these social ills on the basis of Foucault's concept of power. By making power virtually coextensive with all of reality ("power is co-extensive with the social body"; it is "a machinery that no one owns"), Foucualt's theory of power loses its capacity to explain who uses power against whom and for what (1980:142, 156). If power is "never localized here or there, never in anybody's hands, never appropriated as a commodity or piece of wealth," if no one owns the machinery of power, power-producing machines (e.g., fighter planes, electrical generators, food-harvesting tractors), if everyone is done by and does power, then it becomes difficult, if not impossible, to say that an individual or class of individuals, say, the ruling economic class, is exploiting another individual or class of individuals, say, workers whose labor produces the machinery of power. Foucault's concept of power shares more in common with pantheological formulations of divinity than it does with sociological formulations of power that understand power as deriving from an individual's or group of individuals' possession of some natural resource (e.g., an oil field, forest, or uranium deposit) or machine (e.g., a tractor, refinery, missile) and the authority and ability to use them to realize determinant goals.

Although we sometimes, but not always, "fight each other," it is also true that the labor, suffragist, and civil right movements would never have gotten off the ground without the solidarity that comes from unified actions. Foucault's concept of power does not illuminate the ways in which the competition for jobs, resources, and commodities that characterizes civil society encourages individuals to fight one another. Only by explicating these relationships can we begin to appreciate that our tendencies to fight one another, for example, as Muslims and Jews, Protestants and Catholics, or Albanians and Serbians, derive not from some mysterious force "within each of us" or a primordial "fear of the other" but rather from humanly created, entirely knowable circumstances that pit human beings against one another and in so doing ensure that the existing mode of power production remains unchanged.

Although in *Prophesy Deliverance* West advanced a primarily Marxist explanation of racism and articulated a primarily Marxist conception of what we must do to end it, he also initiated a project that characterizes most of his work: namely, eclectically amalgamating diverse methods and concepts. In *Prophesy Deliverance* West contended that we need "a clear-cut social theory" to clarify our situation and to change it (1982:112); in *The American Evasion of Philosophy,* published seven years later, he says that "the crucial task is to pursue social and heterogeneous genealogies, that is, detailed accounts of the emergence, development, sustenance, and decline of vocabularies, discourses, and (non-discursive) practices in the natural and human sciences against the background of dynamic changes in specific (and often coexisting) modes of production, political conflicts, cultural configurations, and personal turmoil" (1989:208). Prophetic pragmatism, says West, incorporates "the genealogical mode of inquiry initiated by the later phase of Foucault's work," as well as the "continental traveling theories such as Marxism, structuralism, post-structuralism" (223, 239). In "The New Cultural Politics of Difference," published four years after *The American Evasion of Philosophy*, he adds to this list "Heideggerian *destruction* of the Western metaphysical tradition, Derridean *deconstruction* of the Western philosophical tradition, Rortian *demythologization* of the Western intellectual tradition, and Marxist, Foucaultian, feminist, antiracist or antihomophobic *demystification* of Western cultural and artistic conventions" (1993d:21). Although it is difficult to imagine how one might apply these theories to a particular problem in a meaningful fashion, such eclecticism is nevertheless commonplace among academic intellectuals. Many theorists, including West, have attempted to reconcile Marxist and non-Marxist categories, an attempt that more often than not has led to the subordination of Marxism to nonrevolutionary perspectives or, in some cases, to the rejection of Marxism altogether in favor of, for example, semiotics, deconstruction, psychoanalysis, genealogical materialism, or postcolonial discourses. This development, which has been philosophically facilitated by poststructuralist discourses, involves not only what Barbara Epstein calls a "turn away from class as a key category of left politics" but also a turn toward a politics that seeks to create a gentler capitalism (1996:129). The strength of West's prophetic pragmatism lies precisely in the fact that, unlike many self-identified left intellectuals today, he does not completely abandon the category of class. At the same time, however, West's eclecticism has diluted the clarity of the Marxist-informed, anticapitalist, democratic socialist arguments he advanced in *Prophesy Deliverance* and *Prophetic Fragments* and weakened the contribution that prophetic pragmatism can make to the theoretical and practical task of waging a successful campaign against "common capitalist foes" (1988a:77). Indeed, as I will show in later chapters, with each new work West has moved away from the Marxist critique of capitalism he advanced in *Prophesy Deliverance* and with it from the necessity to build a global society based on "democratic control over the institutions in the productive and political processes" (1982:112).

3. Racism and the Struggle for Working-Class Democracy

> I believe that there will be a clash between those who want freedom, justice and equality for everyone and those who want to continue the system of exploitation. I believe that there will be that kind of clash, but I don't think that it will be based upon the color of the skin . . .
>
> —Malcolm X,
> "Nature of the Coming World Showdown" (1965)

> Class war, not race war.
>
> —Anonymous, painted on a wall in Richmond, Va., 1999

ONE HUNDRED YEARS AGO Henry Sylvester-Williams organized and convened the first Pan-African Conference. Held in London, the conference brought together representatives from African nations and the African diaspora in order to form a unified international position to combat the "aggression of white colonizers and, at the same time, to make an appeal to the missionary and abolitionist traditions of the British people to protect the Africans from the depredations of the Empire builders" (Du Bois 1969:20). The African American sociologist W. E. B. Du Bois attended the conference, was made honorary chair of the Resolutions Committee, and gave a memorable address in which he argued that "the problem of the twentieth century is the problem of the color-line, the question as to how far differences of race . . . will hereafter be made the basis of denying to over half the world the right of sharing to their utmost ability the opportunities and privileges of modern civilization" (ibid.). Today, almost a century after Du Bois gave his now famous and frequently cited address, racism continues to flourish within and contribute to a mode of life that prevents the vast majority of human beings from enjoying "the opportunities and privileges of modern civilization." As we begin the twenty-first century, racism remains an imposing obstacle on the path to building a humane global society.

Cornel West has contributed significantly to the work of explaining why racism remains a recalcitrant problem. His work, perhaps more than that of any other contemporary figure, has deeply enriched the development of North American religious and secular liberationist criticism.[1] In *Prophesy Deliverance* West began where Malcolm X and Martin Luther King Jr. had arrived at the ends of their lives, arguing that, if we are to advance the struggle for justice, we must examine the productive processes that generate income and wealth inequalities between and within the categories of individuals socially designated as "white" and "black." Without analyzing and clarifying the role that private control and appropriation of collectively manufactured wealth plays in the reproduction of social, political, and economic inequalities, liberationists are unable to give their definitions of liberation any substantial material content. Unfortunately, most North American liberation theologians do not consider how efforts to eliminate racial inequalities and racial prejudice are seriously compromised by the fact that, as West noted in 1982, "one-half of 1 percent own 22 percent of the wealth, 1 percent own 33 percent of the wealth, the lower 61 percent own only 7 percent of the wealth, and the bottom 45 percent own only 2 percent of the wealth" (1982:113)—statistics that describe wealth distribution before Reagan initiated his upward distribution program. Liberationists have not explored and explicated the causal connections among racial prejudice, socioeconomic inequalities, and the structural relations that generate these inequalities. Without challenging these relations, their antiracist efforts can at best result in an equal distribution of differently racially identified persons across the employment and income spectrum and between the exploiting and exploited classes. Such efforts would not alter the unequal distribution of income, wealth, and power or the mechanisms behind those unequal distributions.

To create a society based on genuine equality of opportunity for all persons consequently requires examining the connections between racism and capitalist production and accumulation. Power derives from control over productive property and the institutions that regulate individual and collective development. Marxist criticism is key to the analysis of race, according to West, for it reveals that "racist practices intensify the degree of powerlessness among black people," yet that powerlessness fundamentally derives from the fact that, like most nonblacks, most black citizens do not control any of "the major institutions that regulate their lives" (1982:114, 115). In short, most citizens are excluded from participating in the planning of societal development. In this regard, said West, "class position contributes more than racial status to the basic form of powerlessness in America. . . . Only class divisions can explain the gross disparity between rich and poor, the immense benefits accruing to the former and the depravity of the latter" (115, 116).

This does not mean that the category of class should replace the category of race in the analysis of the conditions that constitute black life in the United States. Although it may be the case, as Ice-T indicates, that "South Central [Los Angeles] is not a black community, it's a poor community[; you] live there 'cause you're broke, not because you're black'" (in hooks 1995:165), you are on average three times more likely to live in poverty if you are black than if you are white. An adequate analysis of racialized inequalities requires examining how racial prejudice and class exploitation shape each other's development. Based on these assumptions, West initially argued that revolutionary theorists should investigate and explicate the role that racist ideas and actions "play in buttressing the current mode of production" in order to foster the development of an international *working-class* movement against "common capitalist foes" (1982:114; 1988a:77). Moreover, they should seek not merely to reform capitalism but to reconstruct the entire system of property relations on the basis of "collective control of the major institutions of society" (1982:114). Anything less than socialized control would leave the ideal of democracy unrealized.

> Capitalism is an *anti-democratic* mode of socioeconomic organization in that it requires the removal of control of production from those engaged in production. At present, capitalism is inseparable from imperialism in that the latter is an extension of capitalism across national boundaries. Imperialism is a system of capital accumulation for profit maximization based on a developed country's acquisition of control over the land and means of production in less developed countries. . . . Capitalist civilization remains racist and sexist at its core and based upon class exploitation and imperialist oppression. (122, 125)

West's definition of capitalism needs the following points of clarification. Capitalism is antidemocratic because it denies producers control over production and reduces the object of production to the goal of producing capital rather than enriching humanity. Corporations have in recent years introduced a multitude of management strategies that involve workers more fully in tasks associated with production, including being involved in decisions about ways to operate the machinery of production most efficiently and on occasion more humanely, even as their involvement remains subordinate to the goal of capital accumulation (see Moody and McGinn 1992; Moody 1997; Brouwer 1998; and Brecher 1998). The "team concept" has become one among a variety of management strategies to contain worker unrest and solidify worker allegiance to the bottom line of profit making. Formal control over productive processes does not equal democratic control over production, for workers remain excluded from determining such things as what needs will be satisfied and how will they be satisfied. In short, such "democratic" control does not alter the basic aim of production under capitalism. In addition, it is imprecise to describe imperialism in terms simply of one country's acquisition of control over another, less developed one; rather, imperialism is a system in which a wealthier country's *ruling class*, especially the most powerful factions within this class, controls the land, labor, and resources of poorer countries, often in collaboration with the latters' "indigenous" bourgeoisie and petit-bourgeoisie. This qualification avoids a nation-based analysis of social, political, economic, and ecological problems. The fundamental antagonism is not between nations but rather between capital and labor. Echoing Marx, William Greider notes that the "global economy divides every society into new camps of conflicting economic interests [and] mocks the assumption of shared political values that supposedly unite people in the nation-state" (1997:18). Revolutionary democratic politics are, as West wrote in 1986, necessarily internationalist (1988a:74–78).

Of course, to create such an internationalist revolutionary movement, workers must first overcome racial, ethnic, and nationalist prejudice and act as a class. Although such prejudice has proved to be a major obstacle to developing working-class solidarity, in 1982, as Reagan was ascending on the profane wings of the religious right, West optimistically proclaimed that "the future looks different," supporting his claim by arguing that the "expansion of interracial unionization in the South, the radicalization of integrated unions in blue- and white-collar occupations, and the concerted push for federalized policy concerning national problems of unemployment and health care may provide the framework for a new era, an era in which the black and white poor and working classes unite against corporate domination of the economy and government" (1982:90).

Unfortunately these projects did not get off the ground to the extent or in the manner West envisioned. No one could have fully anticipated the retrogressive political effects that an all-out business-class assault on labor would have on struggles for progressive social change. Capital waged its war against labor on ideological, political, and economic fronts. Economically, corporations intensified their disaggregation and dispersion of productive operations around the world. Advances in communication, transportation, and financial technologies made it possible for corporations to institute more flexible mechanisms of capital accumulation (see Yaghmaian 1998–99; Burbach and Robinson 1999). Corporations seek out and invest in production where labor and associated costs of production are lowest. Corporations have as a consequence been able to drive down wages and working conditions worldwide, even while average worker productivity has increased steadily.

As capital has become more mobile and pursued an aggressive policy of downsizing labor by replacing full-time with part-time and contingent workers and by outsourcing production to regions and nations where components of production, especially labor, are cheaper, Democrats and Republicans alike have been madly dismantling New Deal legislation, programs, and institutions. Between 1977 and 1994, while average hourly wages among private-sector employees fell more than 13 percent, Democrats and Republicans gutted social programs that might have softened their landing. In the name of creating a "smaller government," "deregulating the economy," and "liberating individual initiative," Democrats and Republicans, spending as if there were no tomorrow, lavished funds on programs beneficial to the wealthiest corporations, families, and individuals and passed legislation that liberated corporate operations from the "restraints" of prolabor regulations. Thus, after twenty years of "trickle-down" (i.e., neoliberal) economic policies, the "degree of inequality in the United States is now so extreme that we have returned to the ignominious levels of the 1920s" (Brouwer 1998:14). Mishel, Bernstein, and Schmitt add that the "distribution of wealth is even more concentrated at the top than is the distribution of income, and wealth inequality has grown worse in the 1990s. Between 1989 and 1997 (projected), the share of wealth held by the top 1% of households grew from 37.4% of the national total to 39.1%" (1999:8). The much-celebrated "stock market boom of the 1980s and 1990s has had little or no impact on the vast majority of Americans for the simple reason that most working families do not own much stock. . . . Projections through 1997 suggest that 85.5% of the benefits of the increase in the stock market between 1989 and 1997 went to the richest 10% of households" (9).

During this same period, while masses of wealth were redistributed from working people to the richest dividend-collecting families, corporate-sponsored scholars, politicians, media pundits, and television and radio talk-show hosts successfully encouraged workers to adopt a social Darwinian ethic of every individual for him- or herself. As "labor" and "union" were ideologically transformed into four-letter words, workers embraced individualistic and identity-based solutions to problems associated with their depreciating circumstances. They sought psychological therapy; participated in self-help programs; joined religious cults and ethnically, religiously, racially, and sexually based organizations and movements; and supported corporate-sponsored state and federal legislation on the mistaken assumption that lifting government restrictions on their exploiters would somehow improve their circumstances. They were systematically depoliticized and are only now beginning to recover their collective bearings and fighting back.

Meanwhile, as workers retreated in response to the ruling class's successful economic, political, and ideological assaults, many on the left retreated from Marxism, class struggle, and socialist politics (see Wood 1986). Rather than advance the kind of revolutionary project that West articulated in *Prophesy Deliverance,* many sought to reform capitalist property relations. They no longer asked the question West argued is necessary to foster the struggle for genuine democracy, namely, why the social pie "never gets recut more equally or how it gets baked in the first place" (1982:116). Many contended that Marxism does not address the heterogeneous nature of oppression, and in place of Marxism's "totalizing tendencies," they elaborated critical theories that examined, for example, sexism, heterosexism, and racism in abstraction from capitalist political economy. Theorists who pursued post-Marxist paths often lost sight of the global socioeconomic forces that were creating local problems. They did precisely what West argued ought not be done: they became "silent about class divisions . . . and how they undergird discrimination against regions, impose ceilings on upward social mobility, and foster racism, sexism, and ageism" (1982:116). Thus, during the 1980s and 1990s, when identity-based politics proliferated, conditions of labor, leisure, and life for the majority of all working people and nonworking poor declined.[2] In the last years of the twentieth century, it became increasingly evident that identity-based projects disconnected from questions concerning economic power are virtually powerless to achieve their local goals. What remains to be done is not to abandon the specific claims advanced by women, gays and lesbians, blacks, Latinos/as, indigenous peoples, environmentalists, and others about the need to improve such things as health care, education, employment, housing, literary, retirement, and the environment. Rather, what must be done is to connect these claims to the struggle for economic power. West began this work in *Prophesy Deliverance* by establishing a general explanation of the connection between race and class and by showing how the struggle against racism must be connected to the struggle against capital. It remains necessary, however, to analyze the specific formation of race and class relations within the context of transnational capitalism. Only in this way can we comprehend what must be done to abolish the forces that reproduce the insidious partition of human beings into separate "races."

The Racial Mode of Production in the Era of Transnational Capitalism

The symbolic character and material content of the racial mode of production have not remained the same since Du Bois delivered his momentous address one hundred years ago or even since King expressed his memorable dream almost forty years ago. The transnationalization of capitalist production and the creation of a transnational capitalist class have significantly transformed the relationship between economic exploitation and racial oppression. In short, the skin color of the exploiting class, as well as its professional-managerial allies, is no longer as exclusively white as it was at the time of the first Pan-African Conference in 1900.[3] This is not to say that the color composition of the exploiters was ever monochromatic or that black and white individuals are now distributed in equal proportions among the exploiting and exploited classes. Rather, it is to say that relative to the first period of colonialism, the present period is characterized by the existence of both a multiracial, -ethnic, and -national class of owners and investors whose aim is to make profits and politicians, bureaucrats, educators, religious leaders, and military officers whose function, in the pay of capital, is to ensure the reproduction of conditions propitious to profit making. This new capitalist class and its professional-managerial allies not only serve up their own workers and resources to foreign investors at bargain-rate prices, a function that allows them "to line their pockets with the foreign aid sent by the U.S. [and other powerful capitalist] governments" (Parenti 1995:16).[4] They are increasingly principal beneficiaries of exploitation and competitors with First World capitalists, a fact that is radically dissolving the social adequacy of the concepts of First and Third Worlds (as well as the associated binary categories core/periphery, developed/underdeveloped).[5] Although transnational capitalism has not eliminated nation-states as regulatory agencies for capitalist development, it has developed supranational regulatory institutions such as the World Bank, International Monetary Fund, and World Trade Organization. The transnational capitalist form of political and economic domination differs from the monopoly capitalist form in that the exclusive geographical association of the exploiters with only the core or developed nations and the exploited with only the periphery or underdeveloped nations is breaking down.[6] Although there are on average very wealthy and very poor nations, there has been a notable increase in poverty within wealthier nations (in a process sometimes referred to as "thirdworldization") and the development of a rich elite within poorer nations. The development of transnational capitalism involves, then, not only the transnationalization of productive operations and finance capital but also the emergence of a transnational bourgeoisie that, as Burbach and Robinson indicate, "has become in the 1990s the hegemonic class fraction globally" (1999:34). Members of the exploiting class are becoming as racially, ethnically, and nationally diverse as are the members of the exploited class—a fact that should forever lay to rest the metaphysical assumption of a necessary connection between personal identity and political perspective (Greider 1997:390).[7]

Similar changes have occurred in the United States. Since the passage of civil rights legislation, a significant number of African Americans have entered the ranks of the professional-managerial and wealthy business classes. As Stephen Steinberg notes in *Turning Back: The Retreat from Racial Justice in American Thought and Policy:* "Never before have so many blacks been represented at the higher echelons of the occupational world—in the professions and in corporate management. Never before have so many blacks found employment in core industries, in both white and blue-collar sectors" (1995:195). Indeed, never before have so many blacks exercised so much economic, political, and cultural power and authority.[8] In 1965 neither black nor white citizens would have predicted that a black man would have a good chance to win the presidency of the United States before the end of the century, and yet by the mid-1990s many Americans across the color spectrum felt that Colin Powell was the best candidate for the job. Although the post–civil rights class of black professionals, managers, entrepreneurs, executives, and investors remain financially insecure relative to their white counterparts (Farley 1997:253), they have nevertheless assumed an increasingly important role in the reproduction of capitalist relations of exploitation as both supporters and beneficiaries of these relations. Like the wealthy and their allies in poorer capitalist nations, members of this class have become deeply involved in supporting capitalist policies. In 1983 Marable projected that members of this class might well invest a substantial portion of their time, energy, and money to a "political drive to discipline the entire Black [and nonblack] working class" (1983:167). As already briefly described, the 1980s saw the advance of just such a business-class offensive. Unlike previous assaults against labor, however, in this offensive a multiracial cadre of conservative pundits, politicians, and business leaders led the charge. In fact, the post–civil rights black middle class and capitalist class not only helped to co-opt and contain the revolutionary potential of 1960s and 1970s liberationist movements; they have also aided in the expansion of transnational capitalist culture, politics, and economics.

Although there are important strategic and tactical differences regarding public policy specifics within the conservative camp, in general black conservatives oppose unionism as being antithetical to individual freedom, affirmative action as being detrimental to meritocracy, and tax-funded services for the poor, including health clinics, child-care centers, Head Start, and welfare, as being disincentives for the development of the Protestant work ethic. Most conservatives in general support strict limits on, if not the outright abolition of, welfare for the poor and working poor; a "get-tough" criminal justice philosophy, including increased spending on police, security, and prisons; continuing cold war levels of military spending; deregulation of the economy; and the "free market" as the best mechanism for improving the life of all Americans.[9] Not only have black and Hispanic conservatives "gone out of their way to distance themselves from the Black poor, branded the 'underclass.' They have proved willing to echo the ruling elite's messages about individual responsibility, crime, and enterprise, as a sign that they are qualified to be considered as decent Americans, on the 'right' side of the divide in American society" (Hadjor 1995:173). Like their comprador comrades, this conservative "rainbow coalition" provides crucial ideological and political support to American capital in particular and global capitalism as a system.

Although a historically unprecedented number of black citizens are now members of the professional-managerial and owning-investing classes, life for a large percentage of blacks is as bad as it was prior to passage of civil rights legislation, and in some respects worse. From the growth of neo-Nazi groups committed to upholding the rights of the so-called white race, the spread of hate literature, and everyday acts of racial prejudice to the mobilization of racially coded sound bites by politicians seeking the allegiance of economically falling white workers (especially males) and the continuing reality of discrimination in banking, employment, housing, and recreation, all these realities demonstrate that blacks remain subject to racist prejudice and practice across class divisions.[10] Some scholars have even argued that over the past thirty years race relations have deteriorated to such an extent that the United States could find itself embroiled in a full-scale race war if the growing class inequalities that exacerbate racial conflict are not addressed.[11] The resurgence of racist ideologies and actions is alarming. There is no adequate means for measuring the everyday existential damage caused by racism. Equally damaging, however, if not more so, is the fact that the gap between average conditions of life, labor, and leisure for whites and those for blacks remains wide—in terms of many basic quality-of-life indices, as wide as it was when apartheid was the law of the land (see Chideya 1995:215; Farley 1997; Massey and Denton 1993; Conley 1999).[12]

The Economics of (Racial) Inequality

The extent to which average inequalities between black and white citizens persist because of the legacy of slavery and segregation, present-day racial discrimination, or the economic processes of capitalist production is the subject of extensive scholarly debate. The following are less debated points, however: first, access to everything from housing, health care, and good education to leisure time, safe environments, and recreational opportunities depends on possession of money, and second, blacks, as well as Hispanics and Native Americans, on average have less money than do whites. Although the number of blacks making over $50,000 per year has increased over the past thirty years, a fact that conservative white and black politicians and pundits cite to support their case that the "free market" provides every individual willing to work the opportunity to improve his or her lot in life, in 1997 fully 26.5 percent of blacks lived, worked, and died in poverty, while the corresponding figure for whites was 11 percent (Mishel, Bernstein, Schmitt 1999:280). Indeed, the number of children of all races living in poverty increased steadily over the past twenty years, a period mainstream economists describe as one of the best in history, but poverty rates for children under eighteen are especially high among minorities: in 1997, 37.2 percent of black children lived in poverty, as did 36.8 percent of Hispanic children, but only 16.1 percent of white children did so (9).

These figures reflect blacks' disproportionate presence at the lowest rungs of the economic hierarchy. In 1997 "only 16 percent of employed African Americans held professional or managerial jobs, compared to 31 percent of employed whites. By contrast, black workers were overrepresented in the service sector, with its low wages: 26 percent of employed African Americans worked in service industries in 1997, while only 15 percent of their white counterparts held jobs in this sector" (Conley 1999:11). Not surprisingly, in 1997 the median hourly wage for whites was $18.20, whereas for blacks it was $12.92 (Mishel, Bernstein, and Schmitt 1999:171). To make matters worse, most of the job growth over the past twenty-five years has occurred in the service sector, where most jobs pay low wages and offer no health insurance or retirement benefits. As Jeremy Brecher and Tim Costello note, this sector is "crowded with those who face discrimination in U.S. society: people of color, women, immigrants, the young, and the elderly. Two thirds of all part-timers and 60 percent of all temporary workers are women" (1998:23) Meanwhile, blacks remain more than twice as likely as whites to be unemployed. Indeed, for the majority of black workers, "there was a general downward shift out of better-paying and middle-wage employment into low-wage employment from 1979 to 1989, with modest growth of very high earners" (Mishel, Bernstein, Schmitt 1999:138). Although black women fared better on average than did most black men between 1979 and 1990, by 1997 a significant proportion of blacks (33.2 percent of black men and 42.6 percent of black women, constituting 38.2 percent of all black workers) held jobs paying wages below the poverty level (139). In short, the job crisis "is the single most important factor behind the familiar tangle of problems that beset black communities" (Steinberg 1995:199).[13] A "young black man has, statistically, a greater likelihood of being jailed or arrested than he has of obtaining a job that can adequately support himself, a partner, and family" (Marable 1997a:46).[14] As is painfully obvious to working people (though largely ignored by politicians who chant about family values yet do nothing to support most working-class families), without good jobs, health care, and leisure time, it is difficult to keep families strong.

In addition to being overrepresented in the lower rungs of the occupational world, blacks on average have far less wealth in the form of property, stocks, and savings than do whites on average. In "1995, average wealth in black households was $43,000, just 16.8% of the average for white households ($255,300). . . . average financial wealth in black households was about $23,300, compared to $198,400 in white households. . . . the homeownership rate for blacks was 46.8%, about two-thirds the rate for white households (69.4%)" (Mishel, Bernstein, and Schmitt 1999:266). Whereas in 1865 blacks owned 0.5 percent of the total wealth in the United States, 135 years later, they owned just 1 percent yet comprised almost 13 percent of the population (Conley 1999:25). These numbers not only expose the insecure position of the black middle class; they also go a long way toward explaining the inequalities that exist in other aspects of black life, for under capitalism wealth inequalities tend to reproduce themselves from generation to generation. Given that, as Dalton Conley argues in *Being Black, Living in the Red,* "wealth, not occupation or education, is the realm in which the greatest degree of racial inequality lies in contemporary America" (1999:152), we should not expect any significant closure of the racial gap any time soon, if ever, without state intervention to distribute wealth more equitably.

The economic realities just described mean that many societal goods (e.g., housing, health care, and good education) remain out of reach for a large portion of black citizens in the United States. Past and present social, political, and economic factors make it difficult for blacks to earn sufficient money and accumulate sufficient wealth to gain access to these goods. Certainly, as Douglas Massey and Nancy Denton (1993) argue, racial discrimination plays no small part in determining access to jobs, credit, bank loans, housing, legal representation, and so on. Skin-color prejudice perpetuates occupational, residential, and recreational segregation and fosters average socioeconomic inequalities between black and white citizens. Conley explains how continuing prejudice affects housing values and segregation. In general, housing in predominantly black neighborhoods is worth less, appreciates more slowly, and depreciates more often than comparable housing in predominantly white neighborhoods: "White housing is worth more precisely because it is not black housing" (1999:38). "White flight" occurs when white residents move out of a neighborhood as black residents begin to move in. Whites move out, says Conley, because they "fear that their property values will drop. Why might they drop? Values fall because white flight creates a vacuum in the market—in other words, the anticipation of a market drop in housing prices becomes a self-fulfilling prophecy. This pernicious circle sustains racist residential ideology and directly links it to economics in the housing market" (39).[15] Moreover, residential segregation affects all aspects of life. Inasmuch as blacks are more highly concentrated in poorer neighborhoods than are whites, more blacks are more likely to suffer unsafe environmental conditions, higher crime rates, and inferior schools—all of which, in turn, weaken opportunities for blacks to improve their overall life circumstances.

Racial discrimination continues to play a role in determining living conditions for black citizens, but as Steinberg asserts, the "essence of racial oppression is not the distorted and malicious stereotypes that whites have of blacks" but rather "a racial division of labor, a system of occupational segregation that relegates most blacks to work in the least desirable job sectors or that excludes them from [some] job markets altogether" (1995:179, 180). The racial division of labor is more fundamentally responsible for average income and wealth inequalities between black and white citizens than is racial prejudice. Moreover, the racial division of labor is reproduced with *and* without the aid of white racism. The exploitation of labor, the investment goal of profit maximization, and global capitalist competition are the principal forces responsible for the regeneration of racialized occupational segregation and the resulting average income and wealth inequalities *between* and *within* groups of persons designated "white" and "black." Civil rights legislation redistributed not a single penny's worth of wealth, and since life conditions, opportunities, and outcomes are in large measure predicated on wealth possession, it should come as no surprise that thirty-five years after this legislation little has changed for most blacks. Again, life has if anything become more difficult for virtually all workers. Indeed, if race were the principal factor determining powerlessness in the United States in the post–civil rights era, it would be difficult to explain the slight gains blacks made during a period of declining wages for most workers: between 1979 and 1997 the overall percentage of blacks living in poverty decreased from 31.0 percent to 26.5 percent, while the percentage of whites living in poverty increased from 9.0 to 11.0 percent; between 1989 and 1997 black median family income grew 1.1 percent, whereas it rose 0.1 percent among white families and fell 0.9 percent among Hispanic families (Mishel, Bernstein, and Schmitt 1999:280–81, 44–45).[16] These gains notwithstanding, poverty rates for blacks are two to three times higher than they are for whites. Nor should these trends obscure the previously mentioned fact that whites on average have higher incomes and possess significantly greater wealth assets (e.g., stocks, homes, and other properties) than do black citizens (266–67). Moreover, they do not demonstrate clear or direct causal connections or the absence of racial prejudice and practice. Although average black poverty rates have declined and white poverty rates increased over the last twenty years, this does not mean that blacks are not subject to discrimination (although the work of William Julius Wilson and Dalton Conley suggests that class position—that is, wealth—may play a greater role than racial discrimination in the determination of black life).

My primary point is not to downplay the importance of racist prejudice and practice. Rather, it is to emphasize the fact that capitalist development has never led to a relatively equal distribution of opportunity, income, wealth, and other social goods. Indeed, the capitalist mode of socioeconomic organization cannot achieve this end, since it involves the systematic transfer of value from those who produce society's wealth to those who own the means of producing wealth (it is not merely that African slaves were poor when European masters were rich but that the latter grew rich through their exploitation of the former). Thus, even if civil rights legislation had completely eliminated racial discrimination (and it has not), there would be no more reason to expect that life would necessarily improve for all blacks than there is to expect that life will necessarily improve for all whites under capitalism; indeed, as was already noted, income and wealth have declined for most workers across the color spectrum since the end of Jim Crow. Because black Americans were systematically underdeveloped under slavery and segregation, they were poorer, less healthy, and acquired fewer skills, both at school and in the workplace, than did whites (in 1959 55.1 percent of all blacks fell below the poverty line, while only 22.4 percent of all whites did so). It is thus not surprising that blacks have not achieved parity with whites since the abolition of *legalized* segregation. What is remarkable is that so many blacks have accomplished so much with so little in such a short time, doing so within the context of continuing discrimination and increasing economic inequality. Historical evidence and structural analysis, however, suggest that capitalist development is unlikely to result in equality between black and white or, for that matter, male and female workers, and capitalist development of course cannot result in class equality. If current economic and political trends continue, living conditions for most black workers, as well as for most white workers, will probably continue to worsen. Antiracist and multicultural appreciation programs will never equalize the overall distribution of societal goods even though they may improve everyday interactions between black and white citizens. Such programs can make a difference only if they are linked to democratizing property relations. Liberal scholars, activists, church leaders, and politicians who do not connect the struggle against racism to the struggle against the productive processes that produce socioeconomic inequalities are fighting a difficult, if not impossible, battle, for as long as inequalities exist, prejudice will always find fertile soil in which to flourish.

Racial prejudice will not die easily. As manifest in the dense and seemingly indestructible texture of multifarious customs, ethical codes, sexual mores, residential and religious segregation, patterns of bank lending, linguistic systems, and cultural representations, racism constitutes a distinct, if not unique, tradition in the United States of America. Racism is, to shatter the cheerful signifying chain, more American than "baseball, apple pie, and Chevrolet." At the same time, however, the abolition of capitalist property relations and the democratic reorganization of development according to the principle of universal enrichment are necessary conditions for the creation of a postracist society because a postracist society cannot easily, if ever, be constructed on the basis of socioeconomic inequalities. In many respects Derek Bell (1992) is absolutely correct when he argues that racism is a permanent feature of *this* society. Although democratic control of societal planning would not in itself end racism, it would create the political basis for building a society in which all persons could enjoy access to the "opportunities and privileges of modern civilization," as Du Bois hoped, and as a consequence relate to one another on equal footing as human beings. Capitalist development guarantees this dream will be forever deferred.

As we begin the twenty-first century, one hundred years after Du Bois delivered his address and three decades after Martin Luther King Jr. expressed his dream, many of the radical goals of the Second Reconstruction remain unrealized. Although many blacks have entered the ranks of the upper working and capitalist classes, for a greater number life remains much as it was prior to the end of legal segregation, and for some life has become even more impoverished. The following statement made by Malcolm X remains as true today as when he voiced it more than thirty-five years ago: most blacks "were—and still are—having a nightmare" (1964:281).[17] Ending this nightmare, however, requires transforming the capitalist property relations that make a beloved community impossible to achieve. The economic roots of racial inequality also mean, as West argues in *Prophesy Deliverance* and *Prophetic Fragments,* that "class politics must be the prism through which black politics are elaborated" (1988a:137).

Multiculturalism, Inequality, and Exploitation

That there are now more blacks in the upper working and capitalist classes than ever before and, simultaneously, more blacks among the working and nonworking poor constitutes what Henry Louis Gates Jr. (1998) calls the "central paradox" of contemporary black life in the United States. The solution to this paradox is to be found, as the previous section indicates, in the fact that capitalism presupposes and produces class divisions and that with the abolition of legal segregation, existing class divisions among blacks were able to develop and express themselves more fully (e.g., through black flight to "white" suburbs). Ruling-class ideology supports the reproduction of class domination by concealing the relations of exploitation that produce them. As long as socioeconomic inequalities corresponded highly with racial divisions, with class divisions within black communities remaining underdeveloped and largely invisible to whites, they could be ideologically justified as reflecting the "naturally" unequal capacities of distinct racial "types." The abolition of segregation, the integration of blacks and nonblacks in virtually every area of society, and the growth of class divisions within black America have dissolved the material basis of such "biological" explanations. They prove largely inadequate to explain—and justify—these post–civil rights realities. Of course, this does not mean that pseudobiological concepts of race no longer inhabit capitalist culture (the Ku Klux Klan and miscellaneous academic scholars, e.g., still employ such concepts). Nevertheless, there has emerged a new discourse that, like biological racism, can account for these realities in ways that reinforce the social relations that generate socioeconomic inequalities.

This multicultural discourse emphasizes cultural rather than biological differences between "ethnic" traditions, communities, and individuals as a means for explaining societal divisions. The concept of ethnicity provides a way to explain both inter- and intraracial class divisions in a manner that buttresses the relations of exploitation behind these divisions. According to this more enlightened discourse, humans are not divided into biologically distinct races. Rather, they are born into and shaped by distinct cultures that differently appreciate the principles and practices required to ascend the ladder of opportunity. The shift in ideological emphasis from the biological condition of race to the cultural condition of ethnic identity makes it possible not only to explain class divisions within black America but also to subject every individual to the ideology of the self-manufacturing "self." The concept of ethnic identity loosens the causal link between color and class enough that, on the one hand, the ideology of individualism may be applied to everyone and yet, on the other, the essentialist stereotypes associated with biological racism may be easily invoked (many of the traits that biological racism causally ascribed to skin color are now ascribed to culture). In the post–civil rights era, neither the law nor biology stands in the way of upward mobility. You have no one to hold responsible for your circumstances, whether good or bad, but yourself. If Bill Cosby can succeed, then so can you—and Cosby is the first to say so.[18] According to this new ideology, since the proverbial "playing field" was leveled by 1960s civil rights legislation, and since we now recognize that biological claims regarding white superiority/black inferiority are bogus, all individuals, black and white, are now, as the high priest of free-market economics Milton Friedman explains, free to "choose" values conducive to upward mobility as long as they are "willing" to do so. Thus, as bell hooks indicates, although "class divisions among blacks in a racially desegregated society have been the breeding grounds for those who are privileged to internalize contempt and hatred of the black poor and underclass" (1995:166), this postmodern Horatio Alger myth fertilizes this soil by eliding the class relations that unequally divide access to collectively produced wealth, power, and privilege. Multiculturalism has in this regard proven to be a valuable cover for ruling-class efforts to dissolve programs that benefit working-class and nonworking poor citizens across the color spectrum.

Corporate Multiculturalism

Multicultural theory and practice, as an updated expression of liberal pluralist ideology, have proven pivotal to corporate owners seeking to negotiate alliances and market products, as well as to managers responsible for administrating a diverse international workforce. Achieving these objectives requires owners and managers to understand the ways in which individuals from other cultures interpret, evaluate, and respond to the realities of transnational capitalism. In *Managing Cultural Differences,* a book financed and published by the procapitalist, British-based Economist Intelligence Unit of *The Economist* magazine, Lisa Hoecklin states: "As markets, competition and organizations globalize, the business-people, politicians and consumers who comprise these institutions are increasingly having to interact, manage, negotiate and compromise with people from different cultures" (1995:1). The bottom line is that "ignoring or mishandling differences can mean inability to retain and motivate employees, misreading the potential of cross-border alliances, marketing and advertising blunders, and failure to build sustainable sources of competitive advantage" (21). In the world of transnational capitalism, multiculturalism is key to establishing, maintaining, and expanding profitable relationships among transnational corporate investors and owners.

Corporations are not only learning how to negotiate ethnic, racial, and religious differences to form alliances; they are also increasingly mobilizing ethnic, racial, cultural differences to create and satiate consumer desires. From the Gap's washed-out rainbow of young adults selling "Everyone in Yellow" and Aboriginal elders using Visa cards to the United Colors of Benetton and Masai making cellular phone calls, the corporate creation, co-optation, and commodification of cultural diversity has become standard operational policy. Products are sold to specifically targeted consumers and marketed as possessing authentic cultural "essences." The "African-American aspects of Jordan's game are indissolubly linked to the culture of consumption and the commodification of black culture," writes Michael Eric Dyson, adding that "he and his shrewd handlers have successfully produced, packaged, marketed, and distributed his image and commodified his symbolic worth, transforming cultural capital into cash, influence, prestige, status, and wealth" (1993:69–70). Using any means necessary, corporations encourage consumers to, for example, "love blackness" by purchasing products associated with being authentically "black" (e.g., hip-hop fashion and rap music). At the level of exchange, diversity is another name for the free-marketing game, as corporations invent and mobilize diversity to market commodities and produce a desire to consume the commodities that are produced.

Capital not only markets diversity; it also takes advantage of socially generated wage differentials between and within different regions, states, and nations.[19] Globalization simultaneously dissolves, often violently, all fixed and frozen bonds of community, affection, and tradition and integrates, for example, Africans and Europeans, Muslims and Christians, blacks and whites, and men and women into networks of productive and consumptive global relations. In doing so, capital creates the force on which it lives and that potentially represents its nonexistence. To prevent this potential from being realized, corporations symbolically celebrate the diverse cultures of the individuals who constitute their "work teams." Multicultural celebrations of diversity, diversity sensitivity training, and antidiscrimination policies are not only compatible with continuing corporate domination; in addition, they have become key to expanding the processes of capital accumulation. Corporate multiculturalism provides a useful means for managing a diverse workforce, for it offers symbolic recognition, what the philosopher Norman O. Brown called "psychic salary," in place of substantive social, political, and economic power. In the era of transnational capitalism, notes Greider, management teams increasingly look "like a visionary's ideal of multicultural cooperation" (1997:84). Motorola's Malaysian team of "Chinese, Malay, Indian, black, yellow, pale, brown, Christian, Buddhist, Muslim, and Hindu" individuals is typical of transnational corporate management personnel (ibid.). The transnational nature of capitalist relations of production and distribution has in fact created "one of the ripe anomalies of global economic revolution: while conservative ideologues in America fiercely contested the threat of multiculturalism, conservative American corporations were out around the world doing it" (ibid.). The legitimization of cultural diversity as a positive social good is less a progressive political achievement than it is a transnational corporate accomplishment. Indeed, this is why politics organized to support cultural differences—rather than politics organized to combat capitalism's mobilization of difference in support of exploitation—may impede workers from recognizing and acting on shared socioeconomic interests as much as, if not more than, it enables them to do so. "The message embedded in the cult of diversity celebration is that if we all simply get to know each other a little better we will 'all get along,'" and yet, as chair of the African American Studies program at Virginia Commonwealth University Njeri Jackson indicates, "multiculturalism shifts our focus away from the political and economic arenas" and obscures the class dynamics that support and are supported by multiculturalism (1999:3). In the light of these changes, we might paraphrase the last paragraph in the chapter entitled "The Sale and Purchase of Labor-Power" in Marx's *Capital,* vol. 1, to read: "Yes, you *are* different. Your needs are different, and your dreams are different. You *are* culturally different. We understand your reluctance, even resistance, to identify with those who might claim, falsely, they share common interests with you." So declares Mr. Moneybags who, like his postmodern allies, rejects Enlightenment ideals as unjustly imposed Western prejudices. He knows his workers have received a proper multicultural education and will, as a consequence, work more efficiently as persons who have "brought their own hide[s] to market and now [have] nothing else to expect but—a tanning" (Marx 1977:280).

Multiculturalism in economics is expressed in the realm of politics as well. Thus, although Clinton ran his first presidential campaign on the promise to create a government that *looks* like America and although he partly made good on this promise, his commitment to "egalitarianism is," as Adolph Reed indicates, primarily "a token issue," as it is with his corporate sponsors, more a matter of good public relations than any serious effort to distribute power more equally among those who lack power (1997a:18). And though Clinton's administration includes more women and minorities than did any other previous administration, "all of his appointees are centrist insiders, committed to his neo-imperialist foreign policy and his 'bipartisan,' pro-corporate retreat from a program of democratic redistribution" (ibid.). Hiding behind the representational cloak of diversity, Clinton serves the same multinational corporate interests his Republican predecessors served. Indeed, even Republicans now recognize the need to put on a multiracial, multiethnic, multicultural face to win elections, after which they implement their procorporate, neoliberal policies. Even Clinton's clamoring about race is superficial, for he remains unwilling to invest serious money to support this conversation or any policy proposals that may result from interracial dialogue. Clinton ran for and won the White House without enlisting the support of black political and religious leaders. Clinton kept his public contact with blacks to a minimum to procure support from the torn and tattered remains of the white poor and working class. Although Clinton affirms diversity in word, he has supported policies that exacerbate inequalities and, as Reed observes, "pandered to the resurgent racist tendencies he purports to bemoan" (1997d:19).

Multiculturalism provides a sophisticated mechanism for interpreting and simultaneously mystifying the political and economic roots of inequalities. It makes it possible to explain class divisions within racial categories in a manner that diverts attention from the relations of exploitation that create these divisions. Multicultural theory and practice help corporations establish international business relations, market products, manage a diverse workforce, and replace financial rewards with symbolic recognition. Moreover, multiculturalism has become part and parcel of higher education ideology and is key to successful capitalist politics in the post–civil rights era.

The Struggle against Racism and for Working-Class Democracy

None of what I have so far described is meant to suggest that multiculturalism is *inherently* racist or conservative. Multiculturalism is not a fixed object but rather a complex network of ideas and practices that are subject to diverse theoretical interpretations and tactical deployments. Even as deployed by corporations, multiculturalism may foster the development of counter-hegemonic working-class consciousness and organizations to the extent that it enables workers from different cultural backgrounds to appreciate and understand one another and consequently to discover points of shared interest. Corporate promotion of multiculturalism, including cultural appreciation and tolerance programs for workers, may indeed prove to be a case of the capitalist class creating its own grave diggers.

Still, although multiculturalism may prove to be a progressive force in the struggle for working-class democracy, the struggle against racism is most progressively advanced not in the name of black politics or even black freedom but rather as an integral dimension of the struggle for working-class power. To fight against racism in the name of black politics is problematic for the reasons already outlined and, most important, because it presupposes that blacks share common interests even though they are now more than ever divided by class interests that place individuals on opposing sides in the struggle to change the system that produces inequalities, creating a situation in which, as Gates notes, "the mounting intraracial disparities mean that the realities of race no longer affect all blacks in the same way" (1996:36). The category "black" does not signify homogeneous social, political, or economic interests. Conceptual formulations such as "the black community" or "black folk" are inadequate because they perpetuate the sociologically false notion that blacks share similar conditions of labor, leisure, and life. Indeed, economic inequality is greater among blacks than it is among whites as we begin the twenty-first century (Conley 1999:28). And here is the key to my proposal regarding the struggle against racism: although all blacks would gain from the end of racism, not all blacks would gain from the abolition of capitalism. To the extent that capitalism produces average inequalities between workers socially designated as black and white, with skin-color prejudice being fostered by and fueling the reproduction of these inequalities, and to the extent that black members of the capitalist class (as well as, though to a lesser extent, their professional-managerial allies) benefit from the social relations that produce these inequalities, working-class blacks and owning-class blacks cannot be unified in the struggle against these relations. Although they may share skin color, they are divided by antagonistic economic and political interests. Blacks have no more forgotten where they came from when they move to affluent neighborhoods, send their kids to private schools, and join expensive country clubs than have whites when they do the same. They are simply pursuing the American Dream of upward mobility. When it comes to post–civil rights politics, it is less a "black thing" or "white thing" than it is a "money thing" that unifies and divides individuals.

So what is to be done? How should the struggle against racism be advanced in the light of these transnational conditions of ideological, political, and economic freedom and determination? In many respects I have little to offer that is new, and most of what I have to say West said clearly and boldly in *Prophesy Deliverance* and *Prophetic Fragments.* As has been the case in the past, the struggle against racial prejudice is today most progressively advanced as part of the larger working-class struggle against the system that produces socioeconomic inequalities. This struggle involves, among other projects, exposing how racial prejudice and class exploitation reinforce each other, encouraging white workers to wage war against racial discrimination, and building working-class solidarity across racial, ethnic, national, sexual, and gender lines to create organizations capable of fighting against capitalist domination.

Racist ideologies, in both their crude biological and sophisticated multicultural forms, explain why, or at least make it more acceptable that, some human beings clean classrooms, offices, and bathrooms while others write articles, essays, and books about racism. "Biological" racism reduces inequalities to the uneven distribution of abilities among different races. A man is poor because he is deficient in some capacity (and not the other way around). "Cultural" racism weakens, but does not completely sever, the link between privilege, property, and power and phenotypic traits. It provides a way to explain intraclass differentiation within racial categories and yet makes culture nearly as determinative as biology. Whereas the old racism says "lazy," the new, more enlightened racism says "more relaxed." Poor blacks suffer from a "culture of dependency," "culture of violence," or "matriarchal culture." Thus, although biological racism and cultural racism differ in the manner in which they explain inequalities, they both mystify their economic source and encourage workers to labor under the illusion that their problems derive from anything other than class domination.

Racism inclines white workers to identify and collaborate with their white bosses.[20] By acting on the basis of skin color, they work against the development of working-class solidarity. They may consequently defend their relatively better position within the division of labor as resulting from their "superior work ethic" rather than from inequalities stemming from slavery and segregation in the past and discrimination and uneven exploitation in the present. Racism impedes the development of class consciousness and impairs workers' capacities to act in solidarity with one another across color and culture. Racism encourages black and white workers to blame each other for their problems rather than to organize against the class and class system that exploits all workers.

White workers have gained certain benefits from racism, and they continue to do so in the short run. Nonetheless, white workers and the poor suffer higher rates of poverty, infant mortality, illiteracy, homelessness, and drug addiction in states in which workers are racially divided and union solidarity is weak. The scholarly works of Du Bois (1976), Foner (1974), Zinn (1980), Goldfield (1997), and J. Jones (1998) demonstrate that "although the material benefits of racial exclusion may be quite real in certain venues for white workers . . . , for most white workers, especially those with the more typical, limited ability to control the labor market in their occupations and industry, the opposite has been the case" (Goldfield 1997:14). In regions and states where racial inequalities in wages, property, and benefits have been the greatest, white workers have been among the least well paid. On the other hand, where interracial union solidarity has been strongest, both black and white workers have been among the best paid. The reasons for this are fairly straightforward. Racial divisions among workers , as well as ethnic and gender divisions, support the capitalist class's efforts to reduce the costs of labor across the board. Thus, whatever short-term advantages white workers may gain from discrimination are quite often mitigated by the fact that racial divisions generally raise the rate of exploitation and in so doing empower the owners of productive property at the expense of those who labor. White capital—not white labor—gains from the exploitation of racially divided workers. In 1995 the top 20 percent of U.S. households owned almost 84 percent of wealth assets. The next 20 percent owned a little more than 11 percent of the wealth assets, whereas the bottom 60 percent of families divided up the remaining 5 percent of the wealth (Mishel, Bernstein, and Schmitt 1999:263). Thus, although working class whites on average possess greater access to social, cultural, political, and economic resources and opportunities than do most, though certainly not all, working-class blacks, most whites own little or no wealth assets. Moreover, if, as West argues in *Prophesy Deliverance,* powerlessness derives primarily from class position, that is, from controlling productive property and extracting surplus value from the exploitation of labor, then black and white workers can achieve power only through acquiring control of this property and thus over their own productive capacities. Although working-class whites on average have greater access to social, political, and economic resources and opportunities, few will ever become members of the property-owning class. They remain, along with their black brothers and sisters, subject to global capitalist exploitation, the largely unpredictable fluctuations of the international market, and the anarchic rule of the law of value. History clearly indicates that capital has proven itself to be entirely pragmatic when it comes to pursuing profits, replacing white workers with black, American with non-American, and male with female if doing so increases the rate of surplus-value extraction and capital accumulation.

The resurgence of racism in the last few years is an effect of growing class inequality, with workers unable to identify the class roots of their declining wages. The general decline of wages, benefits, and security for white workers over the past thirty years provides a key to understanding their generally positive response to the absurd claims made by Democratic and Republican politicians—for example, that the poor, criminals, blacks, and immigrants are the cause of their difficult situations. Welfare reform initiatives, as well as criminal justice, affirmative action, and immigration legislation, find receptive ears among those who believe that their interests derive from skin color rather than class position.

Although most workers, especially white male workers, have been blinded to their shared class interests by identity-based issues, the owning class and their allies have not succumbed to similar confusions. Over the past thirty years the owning class and its representatives have consciously promoted "racial awareness." Interestingly, "the most important initiatives that have turned race into the number one issue in the United States today have come largely from the top of society downwards" (Hadjor 1995:28). In this regard, Clinton's national conversation on race keeps us from talking about class.

> The net result of this pattern of elite manipulation has been to instill White [and Black] America with a heightened sense of race—effectively giving the green light to every redneck and bigot who wants to abuse Black people in public, to take a baseball bat to a Black youth in Bensonhurst, or to acquit police filmed beating a Black man in Los Angeles. . . . The majority view in White America today holds Black America responsible for major social problems. This view is the pay-off for the hard work that the political elites have done in connecting insecurities to racial issues and diverting attention away from the failures of their economic and political system onto the supposed shortcomings of those at the bottom of society. (29, 59)

The media focus on Christian racist organizations, the anti-Semitic pronouncements of Louis Farrakhan, and sensational incidents of racist discrimination and violence. However, they rarely expose the role that CEOs, legislators, judges, and politicians play in supporting forces that maintain many black and white communities in a state of perpetual underdevelopment. The premeditated exportation of well-paying manufacturing jobs, along with welfare reform, capital gains tax cuts, and criminal justice legislation, may be less obviously damaging than individual acts of racist violence. They are nevertheless more profoundly responsible for impoverishing working-class communities and, in doing so, creating conditions that foster racial discrimination and violence.

Indeed, with the collapse of the Soviet Union, the discourse of a dark, chaotic world threatening imminent destruction from within (the inner cities and welfare mothers) and from without (illegal immigrants and rogue nations) now assumes a function similar to that of the "red threat." Attacks on welfare recipients, the poor, and immigrants provide middle- and lower-working-class white Americans with an appealing, however mistaken, explanation for their worsening conditions of life and, unfortunately, an equally appealing rationale for keeping the military-industrial juggernaut, forces of state repression, and the national security state steaming full-speed ahead, extending surveillance of all citizens and punishing those who, as President Clinton is fond of repeating, "refuse to play by the rules." With the assistance of corporate-sponsored scholars, politicians, and pundits, Democrats and Republicans alike have thus far been able to divert public attention away from the economic sources of their increasingly difficult situations. Although capital's manic pursuit of profits is the primary force responsible for driving down wages for most working-class whites, the most vulnerable social groups, the poor and single mothers—groups disproportionately populated by blacks—have taken the heaviest blame for this decline.

Racism undermines working-class solidarity and the struggle for genuine democracy. Efforts to end racism, as well as ethnocentrism, nationalism, and sexism, are necessary to build solidarity and carry out this struggle. Although all workers and their allies ought to fight racism, white workers bear particular responsibility for abolishing racism both inside and outside working-class organizations because they have tended to perpetuate it. White workers must gain the trust of black workers by fighting all forms of discrimination. They must act on the basis of the Industrial Workers of the World and Knights of Labor idea that "an injury to one is an injury to all" and that "all of the working class is one big union." As Goldfield writes: "For workers to unite and find common cause for struggle, all workers—and especially white male workers—will have to act in solidarity and mutual support, giving central attention to the grievances of the most oppressed groups" (1997:357), namely, blacks, Hispanics, Asians, Native Americans, immigrants, women, and gays and lesbians, as well as the world's factory and agricultural workers. At the same time, however, black and white workers and their allies must, as West argues in *Prophesy Deliverance,* contest petty-bourgeois black nationalist and black capitalist perspectives. These perspectives, popular among academic intellectuals, impede the development of working-class solidarity and revolutionary praxis. The successful 1997 United Postal Service strike provides one of the most significant recent examples of workers across the color spectrum fighting together for common ends. Brecher reports that Gloria Harris, a thirty-nine-year-old single mother, felt that "the strike brought people together in a way that company picnics and bowling leagues never could. 'We now feel more like brothers and sisters than co-workers,' she said, noting the diversity of the strikers, who, until the walkout, had often kept to their own racial or ethnic group. 'We all learned something about color. It comes down to green'" (1998:361). To build a revolutionary socialist movement, it is necessary to work against the grain of capitalist ideologies and grasp the specific class interests fostered by policies implemented by whites and blacks for the purported "good of all Americans" (e.g., welfare reform and crime legislation), determining how this discourse obscures class domination and the economic and political sources of racial discrimination and inequality. It is also necessary to advance a political agenda that speaks to shared interests. In this regard, in line with proposals West made in 1986 in an article entitled "Left Strategies Today," "four major issues—issues visibly associated with the common good and public interest—should play a central role in our efforts to initiate a class counteroffensive to the business assault: jobs, national health care, the unjust distributive effects of prevailing taxation, and the deplorable plight of homeless people and poor women and children" (1988a:142). I would modify West's proposals by adding that today the framework for advancing these issues ought to be international. We ought to continue the work of building alliances with all organizations concerned with fostering democratic globalization through the formation of institutions and constitutions that make the provision of jobs, health care, housing, education, and safe environments fundamental principles of societal development. Such an agenda provides a common ground on which to build the kind of movement that West contended in *Prophesy Deliverance* and *Prophetic Fragments* is central to creating a society in which all human beings will enjoy "the right [and reality] of sharing to their utmost ability the opportunities and privileges of modern civilization" in the context of equality, fraternity, and peace (Du Bois 1969:20).

4. The Pragmatic Concepts of Truth, Reality, and Politics

Dewey's metaphilosophy and his accentuation of the role of critical intelligence are inseparable from his promotion of creative democracy.
—Cornel West, *The American Evasion of Philosophy*

In his writings prior to *The American Evasion of Philosophy* (1989), West articulated a revolutionary socialist political project on the basis of a predominantly Marxist analysis of racial oppression, class exploitation, and capitalist imperialism. In *Prophesy Deliverance* West staked the future of liberation on "an alliance of prophetic Christianity and progressive Marxism," an alliance that he claimed to offer "a last humane hope for humankind" (1982:95). Whereas prophetic Christianity provides a moral vision of the good society, a society guided by libertarian and democratic norms, progressive Marxism grounds this vision and these norms by providing "a clear-cut social theory about what is" (112). We must grasp what is in order to "say anything significant about what can be," for the very "possibility of liberation is found only within the depths of the actuality of oppression. Without an adequate social theory this possibility is precluded" (ibid.).[1] The most adequate social theory for expressing the depths of racism, West argued, is Marxism.

Marxism examines racism in terms of "America's system of production, foreign policy, political arrangement, and cultural practices"; elucidates the social, political, and economic causes of racism; and clarifies what must be done to construct a postracist society (West 1982:113, 115).[2] As I noted in chapter 3, West uses his Marxist analysis to argue that, although "racial status contributes greatly to black oppression . . . , class position contributes more than racial status to the basic form of powerlessness in America" (115), a form that affects both blacks and whites. Most blacks, like most whites, own no productive property and derive no value from the exploitation of labor. Indeed, the vast majority are exploited, not exploiters. As individuals they exercise little or no significant control over their cultural, social, political, economic, and environmental conditions of life, labor, and leisure. Most black and nonblack citizens do not control the means of production or participate in planning societal development. For this reason, said West, any serious definition of liberation must include the notion of a society that lets workers "participate substantively in the decision-making processes in the major institutions that regulate their lives," including the means of production (114, 90). In a genuine democracy, those who produce wealth have the power to decide what is produced, who produces it, how it is produced, and how the goods produced are distributed. Possessing the power to make these decisions constitutes a necessary, if not sufficient, condition for citizens to coordinate their use of the Earth, societal powers, and productive labor in a manner that allows for the satisfaction of basic needs and the all-around development of individual abilities. Building such a society can be accomplished only by workers who, as detailed in the previous chapter, have overcome the racial, ethnic, national, and gender prejudices and practices that would prevent them from acting together "against common capitalist foes" (West 1988a:77). West argued that workers across the color spectrum must follow the tradition of the Knights of Labor and the Industrial Workers of the World by "develop[ing] a revolutionary praxis beyond capitalist civilization" that seeks to realize the "democratic socialist ideals of freedom, equality, and democracy" (21, 108).

In subsequent publications, however, West did not pursue the working-class, internationalist, anticapitalist, anti-imperialist revolutionary socialist theory and politics he elaborated and argued for in his pre-*Evasion* works. Between the publication of *Prophesy Deliverance* and *Race Matters* in 1993, West developed (and has continued to develop) a progressive pragmatist theory and politics. Rather than continue to develop the radical project bequeathed to him by Martin Luther King Jr. and Malcolm X, West has followed a post-Marxist path of theoretical and political development.[3] Following this path involved, above all else, marginalizing and in some cases jettisoning the Marxist theory of class, class struggle, and socialist transformation. Although many academicians made race, class, and gender their conceptual scaffolding, class realities (e.g., exploitation) received the least attention, and sometimes none at all (see Wood 1986; Eagleton 1996). Academicians theorized racism, ethnocentrism, nationalism, sexism, and heterosexism as being fundamentally the consequence of ideological and institutional forces (e.g., racist discourses and the legal system, respectively) but not of capitalist property relations. They thus proposed ending these oppressive phenomena by transforming ideologies and institutions, not by transforming the system of property relations that these superstructural forces regulate and reproduce.[4] So, for example, West contends in *Race Matters* that the "major enemy of black survival in America has been and is neither oppression nor exploitation but rather the nihilistic threat—that is, the loss of hope and absence of meaning" (1993:15). This problem can be "tamed [only] by love and care," that is, by "a politics of conversion," by "a turning of one's soul [and] one's own affirmation of one's own worth—an affirmation fueled by concern for others" (18, 19).[5] Alternatively, in *The War against Parents,* he and Hewlett argue that CEO greed, not private ownership of the means of production and global competition for profits, is the fundamental cause of inequalities (Hewlett and West 1998:61, 87).

Having rejected the Marxist analysis he advanced in *Prophesy Deliverance* and *Prophetic Fragments,* West no longer seeks to replace private with public control of "the major institutions that regulate [workers'] lives"; rather, he now wants to ensure that "the grid of class, gender, and race weigh less heavily upon our life in common" and to increase "the ability of the determined individual to climb the ladder of class distinctions" (West 1982:114; Unger and West 1998:60, 24). Indeed, the contrast between the theory and politics of his pre-*Evasion* works and those of his post-*Evasion* writings could not be more striking. As West writes in *Race Matters*, his post-Marxist politics seeks not to build an international movement against corporate-controlled globalization but to save America from racial division, moral dissolution, and political balkanization and to establish "a freer, more efficient, and stable America" (1993a:7). Rather than argue for developing a counterhegemonic working-class movement to turn back the business-class assault, Hewlett and West urge us to empower heterosexual parents to raise their children well so as to "increase America's store of human capital and help this nation compete with the Germans and Koreans" (1998:93). Rather than propose revolutionizing a system that West previously described as "anti-democratic to the core," he and Unger argue that our overarching goal should be "to democratize the American economy and reenergize American democracy" (1998:93).

Not only has West come to accept private property—"the market" and "free enterprise"—as an inevitable fact of life, but he argues explicitly against what he now calls the "paralyzing" belief,

> recommended by European theories like Marxism, in the existence of a system out there—"capitalism," for example—with its driving laws, its inner logic, and its indivisible unity. Either you change the whole system, or you merely try to soften its harsh effects through "reformism." This simple and sincere progressive fails to cross the threshold of questioning and reimagining American institutions, or crosses it only under pressure of extreme crisis and with the help of the collective anxieties and enthusiasms crisis generates. The believer in the idea of the "system" places the institutional arrangements of the country beyond effective reach of deliberate, piecemeal reconstruction. (Unger and West 1998:29–30)

West is certainly a long way from his earlier claims that Marxism is essential to liberation in that it clarifies in "an extremely clear and convincing way" the causes of racism and what must be done to fight capitalist imperialism and to build a genuinely humane, free, and democratic society. A progressivism that incorporates "the truth about political possibility," as West indicates his now does, rejects "the simple contrast between governmental activism and free enterprise, not because it wants to have a little of each, but because it insists upon having more of both" (Unger and West 1998:57, 3). Unlike those who believe in a capitalist system "out there," prophetic pragmatists, as members of a large progressive coalition, do not assume "primacy for one causal factor," such as property relations, and are not committed to "any preordained historical agent, such as the working class" (West 1989: 235). Rather, they take the high road and "condemn oppression anywhere and everywhere," promote "an all-embracing democratic and libertarian moral vision," and "invite all people of goodwill both here and abroad to fight for an Emersonian culture of creative democracy" in order, ultimately, to "alleviate the plight of the wretched of the earth" (235, 232, 235). Whereas the aim of West's African American revolutionary Christianity was to build a socioeconomic system based on "collective control of major institutions," the aim of his prophetic pragmatism is to "revitalize our republic" and "democratize the market economy" (West 1982:114; Hewlett and West 1998:258; Unger and West 1998:49). The goal is no longer to develop "a revolutionary praxis beyond capitalist civilization" but rather to improve conditions of labor, leisure, and life within the limits of capitalist property relations. Interestingly, following West's earlier Marxist analyses, which he now views as being based on a "paralyzing" belief in a reified system, nothing could be more utopian.

How does this transition relate to West's epistemology and ontology? Is it possible that West's prophetic pragmatist theories of knowledge, reality, and politics support one another? In the remainder of this chapter I explore these questions and attempt to explicate how West's philosophical perspectives are related to his political theories. I pursue the following hypothesis: West's earlier socialist politics presuppose a realist epistemology and materialist ontology, whereas his transition to the left-liberal reformist politics he presently supports was aided by his adoption and development of what he designates as an antifoundationalist epistemology and an antirealist ontology. I do not argue that West's philosophical perspectives and political positions necessarily support each other. In fact, his left-liberal reform politics presuppose many of the same philosophical assumptions that supported his revolutionary socialist politics. Rather, I argue that his philosophical critiques of foundationalism and realism indirectly support his transition from a revolutionary to reformist political theory by weakening the metaphysical foundation on which his former politics were so resolutely advanced. West's philosophical critiques make it possible for him, first, to place Marxism alongside other theories as merely one method among others or, as he says in an interview with David Lionel Smith, "just one story among others" (1999b:588) and, second, to abandon the revolutionary politics that follow from Marxist analyses of capitalist social relations (see Unger and West 1998:29–30).[6] Having made these moves, West is free to interpret and propose solutions to social problems in abstraction from the realities of class struggle. In the remainder of this chapter I (1) describe how West's development of an antifoundationalist epistemology and antirealist ontology complicates the practice of ideological criticism, (2) explicate his post-Marxist theory of society, and (3) critique his initial application of this theory to race matters.

The Theory and Practice of Ideological Criticism

In *Prophesy Deliverance* West argued that Marxist social theory is "the most powerful and penetrating social criticism in modern times" and that it "is first and foremost a critique of inadequate theories of capitalist society and subsequently a critique of capitalist society" (1982:111, 110). Religious and secular liberationists ought to use Marxism to demystify "the systematic misunderstandings of capitalist society . . . [and] put forward the correct understanding of this society in order to change it" (110). A correct understanding of capitalist society is fundamental to developing counterhegemonic working-class consciousness, organizations, and movements. Only in this way may revolutionary theory become a material force in the struggle for liberation.

Although West does not explicitly say so, this conception of criticism presupposes some kind of realist epistemology and materialist ontology to the extent that it assumes, as I believe it must, that reality and claims about it are distinct from each other and that it is possible to distinguish the relative truth values of claims made about reality through the process of empirical research, theoretical analysis, and practical engagement. West's claim that some theoretical perspectives (e.g., Marxism) grasp nontheoretical conditions of existence more truthfully than others (e.g., liberalism) presupposes these premises. Although a variety of ideological, institutional, and historical factors make it difficult for most citizens in the United States to consider the significance of class divisions, "one is forced," West contended, "to posit them in the light of the overwhelming *evidence* for their existence" (1982:116 [emphasis added]). Contrary to what most Americans think, feel, imagine, or believe, class exploitation best explains why the rich are rich, the working class is sinking, and the poor are poor (ibid.). In short, there is what we think is the case and what really is the case. Ideological criticism both exposes the difference between our thoughts and reality and suggests means by which we can improve our individual and collective conditions of life.

West's epistemological and ontological positions are relatively clear, even though they are not explicitly stated in his earliest writings. In *The American Evasion of Philosophy* and subsequent works, however, West elaborates an antirealist, antifoundationalist perspective that at the least complicates and may even undermine the practice of ideological criticism. West offers mixed, often contradictory, epistemological and ontological formulations. In *The American Evasion of Philosophy* he writes that the following theses are basic to pragmatism:

> (1) antirealism in ontology, so that the correspondence theory of truth is called into question and one no longer can appeal to Reality as a court of appeal to adjudicate between conflicting theories of the world; (2) antifoundationalism in epistemology, so that one cannot in fact invoke noninferential, intrinsically credible elements in experience to justify claims about experience; and (3) detranscendentalizing of the subject, the elimination of mind itself as a sphere of inquiry. . . . these three theses (mainly Dewey's) are underpinned by the basic claim that social practices—contingent, power-laden, structured social practices—lie at the very center of knowledge. (In Ross 1988:269)

In fact, it is this "basic claim" that prevents pragmatism from succumbing to the cynical relativism and political quietism that characterize much of postmodernist theory and practice. Given the preceding philosophical theses, however, the interpretation of the epistemological status and critical significance of Marxist theory that West offers in *The Ethical Dimensions of Marxist Thought* differs from the interpretation he offered in *Prophesy Deliverance.* Again, in the latter work West argued that Marxism provides not just one among many productive critical theories but the best theory for advancing the goal of human liberation. He added, however, that although Marxism "provides the most powerful and penetrating social criticism in modern times," it is problematic to the extent that it claims to be "the master discourse on capitalist society" and in so doing reveals its complicity with "the will to power which rests at the center of European modernity: the will to cognition and control, manipulation and mastery" (1982:111, 100). For Marxism to remain politically useful, it must be understood as providing one among many productive critical theories rather than being the "master discourse on capitalist society."

In the works following *Prophesy Deliverance* West has articulated increasingly elaborate justifications for placing Marxism alongside, rather than above, other critical theories. Pragmatism, says West in *The American Evasion of Philosophy,* holds that there cannot be "privileged representations because [its antifoundationalism] views knowledge as relations to propositions rather than as privileged relations to the objects certain propositions are [or are not] about"(1989:201). Scientific claims, including those advanced by Marxists, must be understood as providing "one kind of description (or set of descriptions) of the world among other kinds of equally acceptable descriptions, e.g., those of art" (98). Although theoretical truth claims cannot be judged on the basis of their correspondence to nontheoretical conditions of existence, pragmatism nevertheless maintains that they may be evaluated in terms of their capacity to generate desired consequences.

Not only is West's interpretation of Marxism informed by pragmatism; in addition, he contends that Marx's "turn toward history resembles the antifoundationalist arguments of the American pragmatists" (1991:xxi). Like James and Dewey, Marx also believed that "philosophic claims must no longer be scrutinized in terms of their objectivity, validity or necessity, but rather described and explained in terms of their function and role in relation to groups, communities, societies, and history" (49). For a radical historicist such as Marx, the criteria for adjudicating between competing claims are not epistemological but rather sociological, not philosophical but political. Critical of traditional philosophical conceptions of truth, Marx held that "'objective truth' should not be associated with *copying* the world, but rather with *coping* in the world, that 'objective truth' should not be associated with representations *agreeing with* objects in the world, but rather *with people transforming* circumstances and conditions in the world" (1991:65). Alternatively, as West writes in "Pragmatism and the Tragic," "when you talk about the truth, you are talking about the consensus forged by human beings who agree upon certain common ends and aims" (1993b:50). In other words, truth is an essentially practical rather than philosophical matter.

According to West's reading, Marx was a romantic philosopher whose work was less concerned with penetrating bourgeois ideology to reveal the anatomy of capitalist society than with providing empirical "evidence" and "scientific" explanations to support his a priori commitment to aid in the larger task of building a humane, just, and democratic society. The "Marx who became obsessed with the scientificity and the scientific status of his work," says West, "brought in a certain kind of orthodoxy and dogmatism to his work" (1993c:139).[7] West admits that Marx believed "the theories of bourgeois economists are, in some important sense, wrong" and that his own theory is, in some important sense, right (1991:95). But "right" in relationship to what? If we cannot "compare theories with anything that is not a product of another theory" (1989:197), a proposition West follows Rorty in asserting, if there is no determinate reality described by theories of the world, then it is not clear how one determines whether one theory is more right/true/correct than another. How does Marx justify the superiority of his theory of capitalism over others? For that matter, how does West justify his claim in *Prophesy Deliverance* Marxism is "the most powerful and penetrating social criticism in modern times" and more recently in *The Future of Ameri-*

can Progressivism that Marxism holds to a "paralyzing" "European" belief (West 1982:111; Unger and West 1998:29)?

Although evidence suggests that Marx understood his work as superior to that of the classical political economists because it grasped more accurately the social nature of the relations of production peculiar to capitalism, especially the nature of value, West defends the superiority of Marxism in *The Ethical Dimensions of Marxist Thought* on the grounds that "his theory provides the most thought-provoking and ultimately devastating self-criticism of the discipline" and not, apparently, of capitalist society (1991:97). Marx's "augmenting or enlarging of the conversation among political economists, coupled with an augmenting or enlarging of the awareness of concrete problems or impending crises, signifies that this theory is 'scientific,' 'objective,' and not mere ideology"—in short, that it is true (98). Here the criteria on which the explanatory truth value of a theory is determined are *intra*discursive.[8]

Viewed from the perspective that West presents here, many claims made by Marx would constitute merely rhetorical strategies deployed to give his research the appearance of "scientificity." The following claims would fall in this category: "the ideal is nothing but the material world reflected in the mind of man, and translated into forms of thought"; "[in] the succession of economic categories, as in any other historical, social science, it must not be forgotten that their subject—here, modern bourgeois society—is always what is given, in the head as well as in reality, and that these categories therefore express the forms of being, the characteristics of existence"; and "economic categories are nothing but the theoretical expressions, the abstractions of social relations of production" (Marx 1977:102; Tucker 1978:242; Marx 1963:109).[9] Although Marx appears to assume that his theory's truth value derives from its capacity to express theoretically the forms of being, the characteristics of existence, in *The Ethical Dimensions of Marxist Thought* West writes that a theory's status as scientific rather than ideological derives from its capacity to augment or enlarge "the conversation among political economists [and] the awareness of concrete problems or impending crises" (1991:98). To this definition he adds that "the status of the theories depends upon the *sensitivity* expressed toward pressing problems, the solutions offered for urgent dilemmas, and openings made into new areas of self-criticism" (ibid. [emphasis added]).[10] From this perspective, the generation of scientific knowledge is not a matter of investigating, analyzing, and explaining the natural and socially created characteristics of existence but rather a matter of enlarging or augmenting, for example, discourse among specialists and awareness of specific issues and events, as well as the "sensitivity" that a theory or theorist expresses with regard to "pressing problems," "urgent dilemmas," and "new areas of self-criticism." But who and what determine when a problem is pressing or a dilemma is urgent? How might an insensitive and uncritical theory or theorist become more sensitive and self-critical?

Although West does not answer these questions, he does offer a clue in *The American Evasion of Philosophy* when he points out that American pragmatists have failed to be sensitive or provide solutions to pressing problems and urgent dilemmas confronting the majority of women living and laboring in a sexist and racist capitalist society, adding "that the issue is how American women will reshape and revise pragmatism" (1989:181). Why must women assume primary responsibility for making pragmatism more responsive to women's problems and dilemmas? West explains this issue as a matter of "how their *appeal to their own experiences* can enrich and promote an Emersonian culture of creative democracy," assuming a culture formed around a figure West identifies as a "mild-racist" is a culture women would seek to enrich and promote (ibid. [emphasis added]).[11] Redressing pragmatism's feminist "lack" is less a matter of analyzing patriarchal discourses, institutions, and practices to illuminate the causes of women's oppression, a project both men and women might undertake, than one of letting women's *experience as women* reshape and revise pragmatism. Yet the notion that experience provides an adequate epistemological basis to understand the nature of reality is challenged by West's entirely correct argument that experience is mediated by social forces and does not in itself provide a sufficient basis for determining the nature of subjective and objective realities.

In addition, the fact that a theory augments and enlarges a conversation and awareness also fails to provide an adequate basis for determining whether that theory is scientific or ideological or precisely whose "pressing problems" and "urgent dilemmas" that theory practically represents. It does not provide a strong philosophical foundation from which to advance ideological criticism. Matters are not made clearer by the following passage from *The American Evasion of Philosophy:*

> [Dewey] promotes a critical intelligence that defers to no authority other than the enrichment of human experience and the alleviation of the human plight. Dewey's conception of truth reflects an Emersonian refusal to posit any authority other than human efforts and creation. Therefore he rejects Reality as the ultimate court of appeal in adjudicating between conflicting theories—and subsequently any correspondence theory of truth or realist ontology. . . . The crucial question according to Dewey is whether ideas are reliable, worthy of acting upon given the ways in which we accept them. (1989:98–99)

Thus any theory is to be judged only by its ability to enrich human experience and to alleviate suffering. Not only are these criteria imprecise, however; they frequently conflict, for the former is subjective and the latter is objective—that is, if we assume, as West does throughout his work, that suffering is both a mental and physical matter. Although it might be argued that President Reagan's "truth" regarding the "communist threat" in Central America enriched experience, it would be difficult to argue that it alleviated suffering.[12] Reagan's truth appears to be subjectively true and objectively false. To the extent that pragmatism rejects reality as the arbiter of a theory's value, it is not clear how we might discern whether Reagan was telling the truth or lying. In fact, as Jack Nelson-Pallmeyer indicates, the "U.S. government officials who labeled Nicaragua a 'totalitarian dungeon' and the contras 'freedom fighters' knew that these were rhetorical abuses that trampled upon the truth. Rhetoric is not designed to serve the truth. It is calculated to serve political objectives. The contras were created by the U.S. government to inflict terror on civilians in service to U.S. political objectives" (1989:6).[13] Thus, at the same time that postmodern radicals were arguing that reality is a discursive construct, the elite were mobilizing carefully crafted discourses to protect the nondiscursive reality of their rule.[14]

Although all theories about reality are socially circumscribed, they are not therefore all equally adequate with regard to representing theoretical and nontheoretical conditions of existence—a point West accepts in practice even while he rejects it philosophically. This of course does not mean that human beings may acquire an exact, complete, total, and absolute "replica," "portrait," "representation," "reproduction," or "copy" of reality. Inasmuch as thinking and being, subjectivity and objectivity, are qualitatively distinct, as long as being is not reducible to thinking, thinking cannot be identical to being. This also means that metaphors such as "correspondence" are problematic to the extent they suggest a one-to-one relationship between the object thought and the object in itself. Nevertheless, as has been suggested, the nonidentity of thinking and being, subjectivity and objectivity, does not render the project of discerning the actuality of the latter impossible.

Marx's conception of human nature as practical or sensuous subjectivity, or more accurately, objective subjectivity, proves helpful in this regard in that it locates the problem of the relationship between thinking and being, subjectivity and objectivity, discourse and reality, within the nexus of humanity's ongoing efforts to understand and transform its conditions of existence. The problem of the relationship between thinking and being is not a static problem; rather, it derives from the dynamic relationships established by humans with nature and one another.[15] Human beings practically change the objective world and in so doing objectify their subjectivity. Copying and coping, to use West's terms, constitute interrelated aspects of a single process. That knowledge of the world and the world itself are never identical suggests a more reserved, historically modest conception of truth as that which is *relatively* more productive with regard to grasping the actuality of conditions (some humanly produced) that determine our possibilities for self-determination and relatively more productive with regard to empowering individuals and organizations to "cope" with or even transform these conditions. Still, just because "we do not have the absolute truth or the uniquely true, all-embracing perspective does not mean that some perspectives do not yield more truth, give a more adequate account, than others" (Nielsen 1989:166).[16] Determining which theory yields more truth can be accomplished only if there is an extratheoretical reality in relation to which theories may be tested. Only if capitalism is more than what Marx and others say it is can we discern whether Marx's claims tell us more about the reality of capitalism than, for example, Friedman's do. To accept the notion that we can describe what people believe, think, and feel but never assess the adequacy of those beliefs, thoughts, and feelings would be, to say the least, to seriously limit the practice of ideological criticism and the aim of revolutionary pedagogy.

In his discussion of class consciousness in England, Marx indicated that the bourgeois press encouraged English workers to blame Irish workers for their impoverished circumstances.

> The ordinary English [read: American] worker hates the Irish [read: Mexican, Japanese, Korean, etc.] worker as a competitor who lowers his standard of life. In relation to the Irish worker he regards himself as a member of the *ruling* nation [always using the classless pronoun "we" to refer to "his" nation's interests] and consequently he becomes a tool [i.e., a subject] of the English aristocrats and capitalists *against Ireland,* thus strengthening their domination *over himself.* He cherishes religious, social, and national prejudices against the Irish worker. His attitude towards him is much the same as that of the "poor whites" to the "niggers" in the former slave states of the U.S.A. The Irishman pays him back with interest in his own money. He sees in the English worker at once the accomplice and the stupid tool of the *English domination in Ireland.* This antagonism is artificially kept alive and intensified by the press, the pulpit, the comic papers, in short, by all the means at the disposal of the ruling classes. This *antagonism is the secret of the impotence of the English working class,* despite its organization. It is the secret by which the capitalist class maintains its power. And that class is fully aware of it. (In Selsam, Goldway, and Martel 1970:136)

Ideological criticism depends on disclosing the difference between what people think is the case and what is the case and on identifying how different ways of thinking support or challenge the existing socioeconomic order. In this regard, what makes an idea or system of ideas ideological is not that it constricts a conversation or decreases awareness of problems and crises. Nor is it, as West suggests in *The Ethical Dimensions of Marxist Thought,* that it offers a distorted, partial, or false view of the world, though many ideologies do (1991:95). Rather, what makes an idea or system of ideas ideological is that it fosters actions that, as indicated, support or challenge existing practices, institutions, and property relations and in so doing serve and protect the interests of a particular class or combination of classes. An idea or theory does not assume its ideological character as a result of being produced by individual members of one class or another. Members of the ruling class can and do generate ideas that conflict with their own class interests (e.g., Jefferson claimed that all men are endowed with certain inalienable rights even as he also denied certain categories of men and women these same rights). In a like manner, members of the ruled class can and do generate ideas that support their continuing subordination (e.g., white labor's support of racism). Although ideology is always about power, it is not always about false consciousness. Marxism reveals the anatomy of capitalist society *and* serves the political interests of the working class. By providing solutions to ruling-class economic and political problems, neoliberal theory serves ruling-class interests. In addition, individuals may and often do adhere to perspectives that do not represent their interests. In a class-divided society, to paraphrase Marx, the dominant ideas are almost always the ideas of the dominant class. The ruled often believe in the dominant ideas just as much as do those who dominate economically, politically, and ideologically. This explains why public opinion polls, surveys, and questionnaires, such as those Hewlett and West use in *The War against Parents,* are problematic, for they may do little more than record ruling-class-manufactured ideologies. Brian Lloyd writes: "Marx directed the search for the effects of class interests away from felt, individual or social psychological motives and toward a recurring pattern of *theoretical* 'problems and solutions.' A Marxist conception of ideology does not prescribe an abrupt reduction of ideas to material interest or social position but the thorough and meticulous attention to ideas *as ideas* that one finds in *The German Ideology* and *Theories of Surplus Value*" (Lloyd 1997:12).

It would be a mistake to reduce prophetic pragmatism to West's own socioeconomic position and class interests, a move that several individuals who have read drafts of this book have suggested provides the best explanation for West's political development. West's ideas exceed West. They represent and contribute to the development of the progressive pragmatist reform tradition. The main point I want to stress, however, is the interdependent relationship between discerning the truth about reality and ideology critique. The postmodern rejection of science and more generally the Enlightenment is as problematic as the Luddite rejection of machinery: it confuses effects for causes, reduces social relations to natural properties, and leaves the roots of suffering untouched. Although science, as a mode of knowledge production, has been used to exploit human beings, it has also been used to liberate them. Feminist critiques of Aristotle's theory of gender, which provided the basis for many, if not most, Christian "truths" regarding women, were premised not only on the recognition that Aristotle's theory buttressed patriarchy but also on the biological discovery that females are not, as Aristotle wrongly held, "passive incubators" for the "active male seed." Again, as the opening paragraphs of this section outline, ideological criticism assumes that reality and claims about it are distinct and that it is possible to distinguish the relative truth value of claims made about reality through the process of empirical research, theoretical analysis, and practical engagement.

Thus Marx claims superiority for his theory of capitalist society because it grasps what otherwise remains comprehended only partially (e.g., the circuit of exchange) and often in a reified—that is, naturalized—manner by "bourgeois" economists. These economists reduce the social forms of capitalist production to the natural properties of the material objects (e.g., land, wool, or labor) impressed and organized by these forms. Not only do they fail to identify the social relations peculiar to the capitalist mode of production, but when they do analyze these relations, they tend to reduce their peculiarity (i.e., a historical one) to metaphysical premises regarding the supposed innate disposition of human beings (e.g., that they are greedy).[17] Indeed, this move allows bourgeois economists to claim that capitalism is the most "natural" social system for it reflects and derives from humanity's inherent characteristics and tendencies. Marx denaturalized capitalism by arguing that it was "not the 'natural' propensities of concrete individuals which determined the socially-prevalent patterns of behaviour (much less which determined the movement of the system as a whole), but rather the constraints placed upon such individuals by the structural 'sites' of economic activity they occupied" (Rosenthal 1998a:42). *Pace* West, it is not so much that Marx sought to "pierce the veil of appearance, to disclose, unearth, and reveal what has hitherto been concealed" (West 1991:95)—that is, unless we understand *appearance* as referring to that which takes place during the public processes of exchange and *essence* as referring to that which takes place elsewhere in the private operations of consumption—as it is that he sought to comprehend the historical particularities of capitalist relations of production or, in short, to identify what makes capitalism capitalist.[18]

The practice of ideological criticism assumes we can discern the difference between what people believe to be the case and what is the case. Marx criticizes bourgeois theorists, just as West suggests, because they inadequately comprehend the nature of capitalist realities. Interestingly, West necessarily assumes the possibility that we can discern the difference when he argues, for example, in *Prophesy Deliverance,* that Marxism is "the most powerful and penetrating social criticism in modern times" and, more recently in *The Future of American Progressivism,* that Marxism is a paralyzing European theory that unprofitably clings to a belief in "the existence of a system out there—'capitalism,' for example" (West 1982:114; Unger and West 1998:29).

The Politics of Antirealism

In *The Ethical Dimensions of Marxist Thought* West defines ideology in terms that, given his critique of epistemologically based philosophies, are surprisingly epistemological. A discourse or theory is ideological, he says, when it comprises "ideas which distort reality, impede a clear understanding of reality, and conceal the biases and prejudices of its proponents" (1991:95). Although this definition appears to assume a reality to be distorted, West nevertheless argues that the

> move toward antirealism in ontology leaves no room for a correspondence theory of truth (of any philosophical significance) in that it undermines the very distinctions upon which such a theory rests: the distinctions between ideas and objects, words and things, languages and the world, propositions and states of affairs, theories and facts, schemas and contents. The result is not a form of idealism because the claim of anti-realism is not that ideas create objects, words create things, language creates the world, and so forth. Nor is the result a form of Kantianism because the antirealist claim is not that ideas constitute objects, words constitute things, and the language constitutes the world, and so on. Rather, the result is a form of pragmatism because the claim is that evolving descriptions and ever-changing versions of objects, things, and the world issue forth from various communities as responses to certain problems, as attempts to overcome specific situations, and as means to satisfy particular needs and interests. To put it crudely, ideas, words, and language are not mirrors that copy the "real" or "objective" world but rather tools with which we cope with "our" world. (201)[19]

If the move toward antirealism leaves no room for the distinctions on which a specifically realist ontology rests—for example, between ideas and objects, words and things, languages and the world, propositions and states of affairs, theories and facts, or schemas and contents—then the notion of a world that exists independently of and yet is knowable through our ideas, words, languages, propositions, theories, and schemas is made problematic. Determining whether certain ideas impede the understanding of reality or conceal biases and prejudices necessarily presupposes the categorical distinction between ideas and reality and the idea that reality is not reducible to the ways in which it becomes experientially intelligible to us (West 1991:95). Without maintaining these distinctions, one risks collapsing being into thinking or thinking into being. Kant understood this problem better than any other modern philosopher, which is precisely why he maintained the distinction between, on the one hand, his transcendental idealism, the notion that our perceptions are made possible by the forms of intuition and categories of understanding, and, on the other, an empirical realism holding that we would not have any perceptions apart from a world independent of our experience of it. Said Kant: "Without sensibility no object would be given to us, without understanding no object would be thought. . . . The understanding can intuit nothing, the sense can think nothing. Only through their union can knowledge arise. But that is no reason for confounding the contribution of either with that of the other; rather is it a strong reason for carefully separating and distinguishing the one for the other" (in Colletti 1973:202–3). If ideas do not create objects, words do not create things, and languages do not create the world, as Kant and West also maintain, then objects, things, and the world must exist distinct from and independent of ideas, words, and languages. West's antirealism contains within itself the realist or more accurately materialist (rather than, as in Hegel, idealist) assumption of an independently existing and knowable reality. Furthermore, to claim, as West does, that ideology refers to ideas that "distort reality" or hinder an "understanding of reality" is to assume, first, that some aspects of reality exist independently of our ideas about them; second, that we can acquire a better or worse understanding of these aspects; and third, that we can and do compare ideas with conditions of life that are not products of other theories (e.g., social inequalities result from exploitative social relations, not from theories of these relations).

If it were not possible to apprehend the nature of a world beyond our descriptions of it, albeit always mediated by determinate social conditions, it would be impossible to determine either that description's epistemological adequacy (e.g., whether it represents a truer theory of reality) or its ethical value (e.g., whether it best enables the transformation of the world). To the extent that the struggle for emancipation is discursive and, as West argues, extradiscursive, emancipation will be possible only if we can mobilize explanatory theories that elucidate "the structures of cognitive and non-cognitive oppression, and the possibility of their transformation by women and men" (Bhaskar 1989:114). Conflicts over truth claims always involve a comparison, whether explicitly or implicitly stated, of competing theories with a world that exceeds, exists independently of, and yet also contains theories about the world. The emphasis on the consequences generated by different "versions of the world" merely defers, while remaining completely dependent on, comparisons between our beliefs and the world they describe. Indeed, this is precisely what enables West to argue, as he does in *Prophesy Deliverance,* that "one is forced to posit [class divisions] in light of the overwhelming evidence for their existence," even while he sometimes rejects this point philosophically, as he does when he claims that "appeals to 'the world' as a final court of appeal to determine what is true can only be viciously circular" (1982:116).

In fact, West cannot maintain a consistent antifoundationalist, antirealist perspective.[20] Even the most strident antirealists make claims about reality, even if they do so in negative terms. The greatest difficulty with West's philosophical arguments is not immanent to the domain of philosophy; rather, it is to be found in the political positions his philosophical arguments support. Indeed, West himself stresses the links among pragmatism's concepts of truth, reality, and politics when he notes that Dewey's refusal to privilege any particular version of the world, that is, his privileging of ontological pluralism, constitutes a deeply democratic philosophical gesture:

> The pragmatic conception of truth can be viewed as a kind of Americanization of the idea of truth that renders it "various and flexible," "rich and endless" in resources, and it is hoped "friendly" in its conclusions. More pointedly, pragmatism conceives of truth as a species of the good; the procedures that produce warranted assertions are themselves value-laden and exemplary of human beings working in solidarity for the common good. In this way, Dewey's metaphilosophy and his accentuation of the role of critical intelligence are inseparable from his promotion of creative democracy. (1989:100)

Yet West not only adopts Dewey's concept of "truth as a species of the good"; he also adopts Dewey's opposition to "confrontational politics and agitational social struggle" and his belief that "the political left based on class struggle [can] never win, so cultural politics [becomes the] major terrain for contestation out of pessimism about the American left" (1989:102, 1993b:94). In this way, West's articulations of a pragmatist concept of truth and reality are bound to his politics, just as Dewey's were. West's philosophical position enabled him to move from claiming that Marxism is the "most powerful and penetrating social criticism in modern times" to the claim "that despite its blindnesses and inadequacies—especially in regard to racism, patriarchy, homophobia, and ecological abuse—Marxist thought is an indispensable tradition for freedom fighters who focus on the fundamental issues of jobs, food, shelter, literacy, health and child care for all" (a position that opened a clearing for the radical eclecticism of his post-*Evasion* works), and more recently to the claim that Marxism is a "paralyzing" theory (West 1982:114, 1991:xiv; Unger and West 1998:29). Making these moves allowed West to adopt Dewey's nonconflict model of society and social change. No longer committed to the goal of forging a counterhegemonic working-class movement, in his post-*Evasion* writings West set about articulating non-class-based progressive political agendas.

West notes that Dewey once remarked that "the chief characteristic of the pragmatic notion of reality is precisely that no theory of Reality in general, *überhaupt,* is possible or needed," adding that for Dewey, "the very notion of assigning an exclusive reality to the objects posited by any *one* version of the world is dogmatic" (1989:94, 188). Yet Dewey's philosophical position did not prevent him from affirming the superiority of one version of social reality any more than West's philosophical position has prevented him from doing the same.

Why Can't We All Just Get Along?

In *The American Evasion of Philosophy* (1989) and *The Ethical Dimensions of Marxist Thought* (1991) West "pragmatizes" Marx's historical materialist concept of history.[21] Says Marx,

> In the social production of their existence men inevitably enter into definite relations, which are independent of their will, namely relations of production appropriate to a given stage in the development of their material productive forces. The totality of these relations of production constitutes the economic structure of society, the real foundation, on which rise a legal and political superstructure and to which correspond definite forms of social consciousness. The mode of production of material life conditions the general process of social, political and intellectual life. (1970:20–21)

West reworks Marx's materialist theory, which "holds that a certain kind of social practice (i.e., those directly linked to material production for sustenance) serves as the ground for history (i.e., as the dominant factor in historical explanation and description)," by arguing that "these (as well as other) dynamic social practices are revisable human conventions" (1991:87). West theoretically conceptualizes relatively perdurable structures—structures that he elsewhere admits are difficult to transform because "the powers that be are serious about their entrenched interests" (1993b:62)—as flexible, plastic, dynamic, "revisable human conventions" (1991:87). In short, West conceptualizes capitalist society in what Marx understood to be its "superstructural" dimensions. The "pragmatization" of Marxism's social ontology amounts to "standing Marx on his head" by subordinating what is from Marx's perspective causally fundamental, namely, the economic structure of society, to that which is secondary, namely, the ideological and institutional forces that legitimate, regulate, and perpetuate social relations of production, distribution, and consumption. Although anyone taking the long view of history may think of these relations as akin to social conventions, doing so promotes a theory of society that inadequately represents their greater perdurability and productive primacy relative to legislative, legal, social, and cultural institutions and ideologies. Moreover, West's position supports a theory of politics that at best underestimates the degree to which the propertied and powerful resist the transformation of these relations and at worst supports class-coalition politics that appeal to the moral sensibilities of those in power to work to create a better society for the powerless—precisely the sort of politics West opposed in his earlier works.

West initially applies his post-Marxist theory to social problems in *Race Matters.* West wrote the essays in this book in the aftermath of the riots that occurred in Los Angeles and other U.S. cities following the April 1992 acquittal of four Los Angeles police officers accused of assaulting Rodney King. West's analysis warrants careful examination because, as Kofi Buenor Hadjor indicates, the debate among liberals, conservatives, and radicals regarding what occurred in Los Angeles represents "an ideological contest to decide not just the causes of a particular episode of unrest, but the bigger image which American society holds of itself" (1997:15). To the extent that West's position represents a dominant view among those who identify their work as leftist, examining his position not only tells us something about "the [general] direction in which the political and intellectual wind is blowing in the USA today" (28); it also indicates the direction being taken by the political tradition that West represents.

In "Introduction: Race Matters,"[22] West begins by stating that what took place in Los Angeles was "neither a race riot, nor a class rebellion. Rather this monumental upheaval was a multiracial, trans-class, and largely male display of justified social rage. . . . The Los Angeles upheaval was an expression of utter fragmentation by a powerless citizenry that includes not just the poor but all of us" (1993a:1, 6). What happened in Los Angeles was a product of "the lethal linkage of economic decline, cultural decay, and political lethargy in American life. Race was the visible catalyst, not the underlying cause" (1). To grasp the deeper causes of what took place, West suggests that we must go beyond the narrow margins of mainstream discourse and the "worn-out vocabulary" of conservative and liberal analysts and politicians: the "liberal notion that more government programs can solve racial problems is simplistic—precisely because it focuses *solely* on the economic dimension. And the conservative idea that what is needed is a change in the moral behavior of the poor black urban dwellers . . . highlights immoral actions while ignoring public responsibility for the immoral circumstances that haunt our fellow citizens" (2). Although liberals and conservatives differ with regard to the emphases they place on either structural and behavioral explanatory factors, they share the view that blacks are a "problem people" who must change themselves or be changed by outside forces if racism is to end. In so doing, they fail to analyze what "this way of viewing black people reveals about us as a nation" and consequently fail "to see that the presence and predicaments of black people are neither additions to nor defections from American life, but rather *constitutive elements of that life*" (3).

To move beyond liberal and conservative interpretative frameworks of race and racism, including their shared view of blacks as an "other" who must learn to "fit into" the existing social order, we must begin not "with the problems of black people but with the flaws of American society—flaws rooted in historic inequalities and longstanding cultural stereotypes" (West 1993a:3). In other words, we must consider the very thing that pragmatism's forward-looking orientation leaves pragmatists reluctant to consider: the antecedent *historical* conditions that led to existing social structures of determination and freedom. We must consider, against Emerson's antihistorical dictum, the racist past that stands at our backs and founds the uneven ground on which black and white citizens presently stand. Such a consideration would allow us to appreciate the fact that although black nationalist and Afrocentrist politics may be deeply flawed, as West contends they are, they nevertheless derive from "a fundamental truth: white America has been historically weak-willed in ensuring racial justice and has continued to resist fully accepting the humanity of blacks" (3).

To "establish a new framework" for understanding the causes of the problems associated with racism and for responding to them, we must start by acknowledging "the basic humanness and Americanness of each of us," appreciating our "interracial interdependence," and affirming that "if we go down, we go down together," because the "paradox of race in America," says West, "is that our common destiny is more pronounced and imperiled precisely when our divisions are deeper" (1993a:4). The reality of our increasingly interracial interdependence, an interdependence generated above all by movements for social equality and justice and the integrative force of capitalist productive and consumptive relations, is precisely why we ignore racial divisions at our own peril and why it is crucial to "focus our attention on the public square—the common good that undergirds our national and global destinies" (6). Unfortunately, economic greed, political opportunism, and consumer-driven selfishness have discredited the notion of the common good. To make matters worse, social fragmentation, moral degeneration, and political balkanization are exacerbated by pervasive "appeals to special interests rather than to public interests" (ibid.).

West says that to heal the nation from these ills, we must, among other things, "invigorate the common good with a mixture of government, business, and labor that does not follow any existing blueprint" (1993a:7). The "one essential step" to invigorate the common good and save the United States from the centrifugal forces that threaten to tear it apart is "some form of large-scale public intervention to ensure access to basic social goods—housing, food, health care, education, child care and jobs" (ibid.). At the same time, West cautions, efforts to formulate and forge what amounts to a neo–New Deal social contract between business, labor, and government should not lead us to make "a fetish of the public square. We need to resist such dogmatic swings" (ibid.).[23] In addition to forging a new compact between business, labor, and government, we must also nourish leaders "who can situate themselves within a larger historical narrative of this country and world," who are able to invoke the "ideals of freedom, democracy, and equality" and inspire "all of us, especially the landless, propertyless, and luckless," to work together with business and government to create "a freer, more efficient, and stable America—only that leadership deserves cultivation and support" (ibid.). Drawing from the novelist James Baldwin's prophetic meditation on the future of race relations, *The Fire Next Time* (1962), West concludes: "Either we learn a new language of empathy and compassion or the fire this time will consume us all" (8).

In "Nihilism in Black America," the second essay in *Race Matters,* West further develops his critique of liberal and conservative approaches to the multifarious problems associated with racial identities, relations, and inequalities. Whereas liberals "highlight the *structural* constraints on the life chances of black people," conservatives "stress the *behavioral* impediments on black upward mobility" (West 1993a:11). To provide an adequate theory of racism, writes West, we must go beyond the limitations of liberal and conservative perspectives. To do so we first must "acknowledge that structures and behaviors are inseparable, that institutions and values go hand in hand. How people act and live are shaped—though in no way dictated or determined—by the larger circumstances in which they find themselves. These circumstances can be changed, their limits attenuated, by positive actions to elevate living conditions" (12). "Second, we should reject the idea that structures are primarily economic and political creatures—an idea that sees culture as an ephemeral set of behavioral attitudes and values. Culture is as much a structure as the economy or politics" (ibid.). Finally, going beyond the limitations of liberal and conservative approaches requires us to "delve into the depths where neither liberals nor conservatives dare to tread, namely, into the murky waters of despair and dread that now flood the streets of black America" (ibid.). The fundamental problem with both approaches to race, West contends, is that they conceal "the most basic issue now facing black America: *the nihilistic threat to its very existence,*" that is, "*the lived experience of coping with a life of horrifying meaninglessness, hopelessness* and (most important) *lovelessness*" (12, 14).

"Nihilism is not new in black America," says West (1993a:15). What is new, however, is the dissolution of those religious and secular institutions that once functioned as "powerful buffers to ward off the nihilistic threat, to equip black folk with cultural armor to beat back the demons of hopelessness, meaninglessness, and lovelessness" (ibid.). How did these buffers break down? They were dismantled, West indicates, in large part by "corporate market institutions," a "complex set of interlocking enterprises that have a disproportionate amount of capital, power, and exercise a disproportionate influence on how our society is run and how our culture is shaped" (16). "Needless to say," he adds, "the primary motivation of these institutions is to make profits, and their basic strategy is to convince the public to consume" by the "provision, expansion, and intensification of *pleasure*" (16, 17). The obsessions with pleasure and the reduction of other human beings to means to achieve one's own sensual pleasure and to establish one's own position of power undercut the other-directed values and behaviors, motivated by care, concern, and love for others, that have in the past protected blacks and others from the nihilistic threat and could continue to do so. What is to be done about this threat, and who is to do it?

> If one begins with the threat of concrete nihilism, then one must talk about some kind of *politics of conversion*. New models of collective black leadership must promote a version of this politics. Like alcoholism and drug addiction, nihilism is a disease of the soul. It can never be completely cured, and there is always the possibility of a relapse. But there is always a chance for conversion—a chance for people to believe that there is hope for the future and a meaning to struggle. This chance rests neither on an agreement about what justice consists of nor on an analysis of how racism, sexism, or class subordination operate. Such arguments and analyses are indispensable. But a politics of conversion requires more. Nihilism is not overcome by arguments or analyses; it is tamed by love and care. Any disease of the soul must be conquered by a turning of one's soul. This turning is done through one's own affirmation of one's worth—an affirmation fueled by the concern for others. A love ethic must be at the center of a politics of conversion. (18–19)

The spiritual idealization and individualization of politics is forcefully expressed here. Perhaps this should come as no surprise. As Hadjor suggests, whatever "their subjective intentions may be, those who help to convert social problems into moral ones will always end up pointing the finger at the individual" (1995:154). Thus, although West begins by critiquing liberal structuralists and conservative behaviorists, indicating that each lacks what the other possesses, he concludes by articulating a theory that is more conservative than liberal. The nihilistic threat can "be conquered by a turning of one's soul . . . through one's own affirmation of one's worth"; that is, social change begins with a change in the individual self. Is this not precisely what conservative social commentators, politicians, religious leaders, educators, and scholars have been saying all along? Is this not the Christian version of Nation of Islam leader Louis Farrakhan's call to African Americans to turn inward and atone for their sins? Is this not what Bill McCartney's Promise Keepers' argue that men must do to restore God's order? Perhaps it comes as no surprise that, having made this argument, West and Sylvia Ann Hewlett cite the Nation of Islam and the Promise Keepers as provocative models (albeit ones limited by anti-Semitism, sexism, and heterosexism) for developing a movement that, as they write in *The War against Parents,* "honors the male yearning to reconnect with wives and children and to harness this energy in a parents' movement that gives new value and dignity to both mothers and fathers" (Hewlett and West 1998:211).[24]

If, however, as West also claims, cultural nihilism is a consequence rather than a cause of the disproportionate amount of capital, power, and influence on society and culture that some factions enjoy—a claim for which the evidence is strong—then it becomes difficult to see how turning one's soul and affirming one's worth are possible for marginalized individuals without distributing resources from the rich to the rest and ultimately without transforming the mode of production that distributes resources unequally. Inasmuch as the capitalist class controls economic, political, and cultural development through its monopoly on productive property, it is difficult to see how blacks who are bereft of resources will find the resources within their own communities, let alone within themselves, requisite to love and care for themselves, affirm their own self-worth, and take control of their destinies in any sustainable manner. If market mentalities derive from and reproduce the capitalist market, then it follows that noncapitalist market moralities can be created only by abolishing the market (unless one assumes that mentality creates materiality) and certainly not by collaborating with the classes that possess an interest in perpetuating the "free-market" system.

Among the most worrisome aspects of West's theory are the following. If nihilism is produced from humanly created circumstances, then representing the nihilistic threat as "a disease of the soul" akin to drug addiction and alcoholism, which West claims can never be completely cured, is tantamount to naturalizing the social relations that generate nihilism (and for that matter, alcoholism and drug addiction)—that is, naturalizing capitalist social relations as "incurable." Furthermore, to the extent that West associates nihilism with being black, he comes dangerously close to assuming an essential relationship between color and condition. One wonders what became of West's radical historicist presupposition that there are no fixed, eternal, absolute, and transcendent conditions, essences, substances, or foundations. Nihilism has apparently always been and will always be a threat. Communities will thrive or not as a function of the institutional resources they have to cope with this threat. West's conception of politics is at this juncture deeply informed by onto-existentialist-theological metaphysics, and it has become more so since *Race Matters.* Rather than think of nihilism as what occurs when the anger and frustration that oppressed individuals and communities feel about their oppression turn inward, are collectively introjected or, in more colloquial terms, "swallowed," West proposes that we understand it as a condition of existence not unlike the natural rhythms of the seasons or biological agents. The nihilistic threat appears to be a condition that derives from the tragic nature of the human plight, the absurd nature of existence, rather than a condition that derives from, as West also suggests, capitalist domination. By naturalizing the nihilistic threat, West's position encourages us to "turn back its deadly assaults" rather than abolish the social, political, and economic forces that assault black and nonblack citizens.

At least as surprising, especially given West's discussions of capitalist domination and determination of values, meanings, and rights, is his claim that to cure "diseased souls" we need neither agree on the nature of justice nor analyze the operation of racism, sexism, or class subordination. Since a small minority of human beings decide virtually all the important questions regarding social development, it is difficult to see how a progressive "conversion" is possible without critiquing the concept of justice that protects this system of development and without analyzing how racism, sexism, and class subordination operate. If, as West indicates, there "is increasing class division and differentiation, creating on the one hand a significant black middle class, highly anxiety-ridden, insecure, willing to be co-opted by and incorporated into the powers that be, [and] concerned with racism to the degree that it poses constraints on upward social mobility," and, on the other hand, "a vast and growing black underclass, an underclass that embodies a kind of *walking nihilism* of pervasive drug addiction, pervasive alcoholism, pervasive homicide, and an exponential rise in suicide" (1993c:90)—if, in short, class domination has everything to do with nihilism—then it seems that ending nihilism depends on critiquing bourgeois concepts of justice.

In fact, West does not fail to emphasize the economic and political structures that set definite limits to the range of possible actions individuals undertake. In *The Future of American Progressivism* he and Unger note that the American religion of possibility is severely constrained by race and class, that "the United States has a relatively well-defined class structure," and that the "basic design of the class system has remained as stable in American reality as it has been clouded in American consciousness" (Unger and West 1998:15 [emphasis omitted]). Nonetheless, Unger and West advance a program that seeks not to transform the property relations that produce and are reproduced by class divisions but rather to narrow the distance between what they call the rearguard and vanguard (16). Under their program the wealth pie would get sliced a little more fairly among Americans, but "how the pie gets baked in the first place," who bakes it, and what gets baked would not be altered in the least (116). In this respect, their critique, as with most post-Marxist critiques, bows before the authority of private property.

5. The Past, Present, and Future of American Pragmatism

I am convinced that the best of the American pragmatist tradition is the best America has to offer itself and the world.
—Cornel West, *The American Evasion of Philosophy*

Give the theory plenty of rope and see if it hangs itself eventually.
—William James, "Humanism and Truth"

WEST BEGINS *The American Evasion of Philosophy: A Genealogy of Pragmatism* by claiming that "the best of the American pragmatist tradition is the best America has to offer itself and the world," adding that he wrote the book "convinced that a thorough re-examination of American pragmatism, stripping it of its myths, caricatures, and stereotypes and viewing it as a component of a new and novel form of indigenous American oppositional thought and action, may be a first step toward fundamental change and transformation in America and the world" (1989:8). Pragmatism's conceptions of knowledge, reality, power, democracy, human nature, and social change support a mode of critical practice that does not shy away from engagement with the crises and challenges that face human beings as they work to create a better life. Although West does not clarify precisely why individuals who are committed to the cause of justice, equality, and fraternity should limit themselves to theoretical resources provided by American traditions or whether he considers Native American traditions, as well as African, Asian, and European traditions that have been developed in the United States, to be "American," he does indicate that even the best of pragmatism "may not be good enough given the depths of the international and domestic crises we now face" (ibid.; see Deloria 1973, 1998; Churchill 1996, 1997). Might there be something about pragmatism as a philosophical outlook that would explain West's guarded optimism regarding its capacity to help us solve these crises?

Perhaps West's cautionary tone derives from his own genealogy of American pragmatism, which demonstrates that pragmatism has been not just "the national philosophy of the American people" but more particularly "the philosophy of middle-class individuals who are caught between capital and labor [and seek] political and ideological positions somewhere between these polar forces in American society," positions that involve the "reforming of capitalism" (Novack 1975:15, 276, 8). Pragmatism has provided policymakers, academic scholars, and political representatives with the philosophical resources they needed to interpret and solve social problems without initiating the fundamental change that West thinks it can produce. Pragmatists have consistently supported reforms that buttressed the ideological and institutional conditions required to reproduce and expand the labor-capital relation and processes of capital accumulation. In *William James: The Message of a Modern Mind* (1950), Lloyd Morris reminds us that the "most significant application of James's ideas was made by President Franklin D. Roosevelt. Pragmatism supplied the philosophy and then helped shape the program of the New Deal," a program that politically co-opted and contained anticapitalist opposition by, among other strategies, offering official recognition to organized labor, mediating labor-capital disputes, coordinating wages and production, and guaranteeing a minimum standard of living for all citizens (Morris 1950:84). The long and short of the New Deal was a new life for capital—a life that was nourished above all by the death and devastation of World War II. It was, after all, this war that rescued capitalism from its global depression and cleared the way for the United States to assert itself as a world political, economic, and military power.

Although some scholars contrast a pragmatic with a principled approach to practical problems, noting that intellectuals who "adopt pragmatism as their 'anti-foundationalist' epistemological theory of choice . . . couple it with a variety of moral and political commitments which owe more or less of a debt to Peirce, James and Dewey," it nevertheless remains the case that virtually all pragmatists have been unified in their opposition to Marxism, class-struggle, and revolutionary socialist politics (Westbrook 1993:2, 11; see Lloyd 1997). Pragmatist categories and concepts have not only sat at the center of ruling-class and, in large measure, working-class politics; they have more than anything else consistently represented the problems, solutions, and interests of what American sociologists refer to as the middle class and West frequently refers to as the professional-managerial class. The "primary social base of Emerson's project," West writes, "consists of the mildly oppositional intelligentsia alienated from conservative moneyed interests, and 'enlightened' businessmen who long for 'culture' as well as profits," that is, who want to enjoy the good life without guilt (1989:39). As it is with Emerson, so too it is with James, for the social basis of his "pragmatism is the professional and reformist elements of the middle class" (62). Although James opposed U.S. aggression abroad, particularly the U.S. war against the Filipinos, his feelings of indignation seldom extended to the oppression of blacks, women, or labor at home. James did not, as did his contemporary Helen Keller, join the Wobblies to fight for workers' rights.[1] Rather, he kept his distance from "the working class, women, and people of color," a posture that derived above all else from the "ambivalent democratic commitments and insecure high-brow elitist allegiances of [his] class" (ibid.). James's democratic commitments were in practice sufficiently flexible and his elitist allegiances sufficiently secure to permit him to advocate "the jingoistic and racist [Theodore] Roosevelt" for Harvard's presidency just three years after condemning the war against the Filipinos as an immoral exercise in "barbaric patriotism" (63).

As with Emerson and James, so too with Dewey. Arriving in Chicago just after the Pullman strike of 1894, Dewey sided with progressive reformers such as Jane Addams and Henry George against the anarchists, socialists, and communists. He joined the Chicago Civic Federation, "a group of businessmen shaken by the specter of class warfare . . . who sought to mediate this and other strikes" and fought with University of Chicago colleagues George Herbert Mead and James Hayden Tufts to defuse socialist politics (Depew and Hollinger 1995:10). Dewey and his colleagues forged a theory of class conciliation, as well as a progressive reform program to lessen socioeconomic inequalities. Following his discussion of the middle-class politics of Sidney Hook, C. Wright Mills, W. E. B. Du Bois, Reinhold Niebuhr, and Lionel Trilling, West notes that most pragmatists have been reluctant to side with the working class because they have been "motivated by a desire to get out from under the smothering parochial anti-intellectualism of the various ethnic, racial, class, and regional groups in American society" (1989:179). Propelled by this desire, they have advanced arguments in defense of the same system that depends on and rewards them for their service as managers of the ideological, political, and technical affairs of the dominant economic class. West notes that the "fundamental difference that pragmatism made to [Hook, Mills, Niebuhr, and Trilling] as persons was to support and strengthen their own volitions and aspirations" (180). This upwardly mobile dynamic may partly explain why pragmatists place more weight on future consequences than past conditions; interpreting the present situation as an effect of past situations might expose realities (e.g., slavery, patriarchy, and class privilege) that would tarnish otherwise optimistic middle-class minds experimentally speculating on their open-ended future. Indeed, an investigation of the concept of "self-reliance" might reveal the "other" selves whose blood, sweat, and tears constitute the material basis for the development of "self-reliant" selves.

According to West's own genealogy, the best of the American pragmatist tradition has generated the following: in the case of Emerson, a mode of criticism that could provide "little substantive opposition" to capitalist expansionism and easily defend "Anglo-Saxon imperialist domination of non-European lands and peoples" (1989:34); in the case of James, a mode of "moral criticism for the preservation of highbrow culture, the election of refined political leaders, and [the] moderate extension of democracy" (63); in the case of Dewey, an "organic intellectual of the urbanized, professional, and reformist elements of the middle class" who advocated progressive change through class collaboration, universal education, and social legislation (76); in the case of Hook, "cold war corporate liberalism" and a vote for that champion of freedom and democracy Richard Nixon (122); in the case of Reinhold Niebuhr, "imperialistic realism" (162); in the case of Trilling, "a tempered rapprochement with the American status quo" (1989:171); and in the case of Rorty, a defense of bourgeois liberalism (205).

Pragmatism has, West explains, time and again spoken to and for "those 'cultured' Saxon gentlemen (and few white women)" who are divided by a "dual allegiance to the conqueror and the conquered," providing them philosophical categories (e.g., improvisation, reconciliation, individualism, and amelioration) that make it possible to negotiate their divided allegiances and to "expiate the 'bad conscience' of moralists who acknowledge the 'inevitability' of American expansionism yet who cannot accept the amoral self-image such acknowledgement seems to imply" (1989:39). This is the unsettling double bind that, as a psychosocially decentering structure, sits at the center of pragmatist philosophy. Indeed, after West strips pragmatism of its myths, caricatures, and stereotypes, we find ourselves inclined to conclude that its open-minded eclecticism and tough-minded affirmation of the unfinished nature of the universe derive as much from the unambiguous commitment of middle-class individuals to protect their position of relative socioeconomic privilege against the destabilizing effects of the sometimes open and sometimes hidden war between labor and capital as they do from those individuals' understanding of the nature of "reality."

The only pragmatists West identifies as having supported anticapitalist politics were Sidney Hook, W. E. B. Du Bois, and C. Wright Mills, and each of these figures supported these politics during periods in which they were influenced by Marxist theory. Moreover, neither "Dewey, Hook, nor Mills grappled in a serious way, in essay or texts, with how racism impeded the development of an Emersonian culture of creative democracy" (West 1989:147).[2] Only Du Bois, who is also the only black figure West includes in his genealogy, fully appreciated that "a racist, sexist, and multinational capitalist America had no potential whatsoever to realize the pragmatist ideals of individuality and radical democracy" and fought against these forces throughout his life (149).

In fact, given West's concern for race matters, it is more than a little surprising that in *The American Evasion of Philosophy* he designates the goal of liberation as an "Emersonian culture of creative democracy." In addition to displaying elitist, aristocratic proclivities, Emerson was, as West admits, not only "blind" to the "social misery of working people"; he was also a "typical nineteenth-century North Atlantic 'mild racist'" (1989:23, 28). What qualifies Emerson as a mild racist? West cites passages from Emerson's writings describing an occasion when he "saw ten, twenty, a hundred large lipped, low-browed black men in the streets" and determined through his self-reliant exercise of a thoroughly socially determined vision that "except in the mere matter of language, [they] did not exceed the sagacity of the elephant. Now is it true that these [black men] were created superior to this wise animal, and designed to control it?" (in ibid.:29). On the basis of this and other experiences with blacks held in bondage by whites, his upper-echelon education, and information gathered from conversations with other members of his class, Emerson surmised that "in comparison with the highest orders of men [i.e., white, wealthy, educated men like himself], the Africans will stand so low as to make the difference which subsists between themselves & the sagacious beasts inconsiderable" (ibid.). Of course, Emerson did support the abolitionist cause and briefly entertained the possibility that blacks have greater intellectual abilities than he initially imagined (i.e., greater than an elephant's), a possibility he contemplated when confronted by the towering intellectual and political achievements of Frederick Douglass and the philosophical acumen and military exploits of Toussaint L'Ouverture. Nevertheless, his position with regard to racism and slavery, like James's with regard to U.S. imperialism, had more to do with their indictment of whites' moral character than with his commitment to human liberation. Said Emerson, "absence of moral feeling in the white man is the very calamity I deplore. The captivity of a thousand Negroes is nothing to me" (20). Whether or not we consider Emerson's racist views "mild," it remains puzzling, if not inexplicable, that West associates the goal of prophetic pragmatism with anyone who promoted racist views of any sort. American history offers many heroic figures whose names might productively be associated with the goal of liberation and who, unlike Emerson, were actively opposed to all forms of oppression. Why not, for example, a Sojourner Truthian culture of creative democracy, Frederick Douglassian culture of creative democracy, or W. E. B. Du Boisian culture of creative democracy? After all, as West clearly indicates, Emerson not only promoted racist views but was responsible for fashioning a mode of cultural criticism that provided "the very ingredients for varying American ideologies that legitimate and rationalize the dominant theme running through these events—the imperial expansion of the American nation principally in the interests of Saxon male elites" (38).

Since West has identified ethnocentric, elitist, racist, sexist, and classist currents running throughout pragmatism's history and highlighted the fact that most pragmatists were at best silent about and at worst supportive of these currents, we might reasonably expect him to draw the following, seemingly unavoidable, conclusion: if pragmatism is the best that America has to offer to itself and the world, then intellectuals committed to creating a genuinely democratic global society will need to look off-shore to find a tradition of theoretical analysis and social criticism that can help them to build such a society. According to his own genealogy, West's failure to draw this conclusion appears to be predicated on his accepting Emerson's antihistoricist declaration: "no Past stands at my back."

Although the spirit of pragmatism may be strenuous, provocative, and revitalizing, as West argues it is, academic intellectuals, business leaders, religious representatives, and professional politicians have strenuously taken a pragmatist approach to revitalize capitalist civilization, often in the name of "freedom," "democracy" and "national well-being," by initiating reforms that seek to ameliorate socioeconomic inequalities and secure worker allegiance to the existing social order. This has so far been pragmatism's unifying project, its historical truth and practical consequence. Making this claim is not merely ad hominem argumentation multiplied. Rather, it is a matter of asserting that the pragmatist tradition represents a coherent pattern of theoretical concepts and claims that express the particular problems, solutions, and interests of the upper layers of the working class. To the extent this is the case, and West's genealogy offers evidence that it is, we are left wondering why, given viable alternatives, West maintains that American pragmatism is the best we have to offer.

Radicalizing Pragmatism's Politics

One way to answer the previous question would be to deny that pragmatism is reducible to those who have so far deployed it or to the particular political purposes for which it has been deployed. Its fundamental philosophical, sociological, anthropological, political, and methodological premises, categories, and values may be used to advance more radical and even revolutionary goals. Assuming as much presupposes that pragmatism's premises, categories, and values are not merely expressions of middle-class intellectuals in search of philosophically sophisticated means for negotiating and ultimately rationalizing their complicated social position. In addition, they are genuine insights regarding the nature of reality. In the light of West's genealogy of the best of pragmatism, it is not difficult to appreciate the ways in which pragmatist philosophy, with its emphasis on amelioration, reconciliation, flexibility, practicality, and eclecticism, expresses the betwixt situation and needs of relatively privileged intellectuals who are both critical of capitalist excesses and yet invested in preserving the social system from which they derive their livelihood. Still, is it possible to be a pragmatist philosophically and a revolutionary politically? Certainly West suggests this possibility in *Prophesy Deliverance* when he names pragmatism as one of the central sources for his development of an "Afro-American Revolutionary Christianity." In *Prophesy Deliverance* and works published prior to *The American Evasion of Philosophy,* however, pragmatism is a distant second to Marxism in terms of contributing to West's project. Although West cites pragmatism as a tradition that led liberationists away from the search for metaphysical absolutes and toward "the search for desirable and realizable historical possibilities in the present" (1982:21), there are only a few scattered references to it in the rest of *Prophesy Deliverance.* The bulk of this work, as with most of the essays written before 1988, were strongly informed by Marxism. The issue, then, is the extent to which the relatively greater weight West gives to pragmatism over Marxism in his post-*Evasion* works supports and is supported by the relatively greater weight he gives in these same works to reforming, rather than abolishing, capitalist property relations. If pragmatist philosophy and reformist politics intrinsically support each other, then advancing revolutionary socialist politics may inescapably require breaking with pragmatism and developing the critical perspective West began to develop in his pre-*Evasion* works.

West suggested why academic intellectuals have difficulty supporting revolutionary politics when, in a conversation with Paul Gilroy and bell hooks, he noted that "one crucial element of the restructuring of this society . . . is the expansion of the professional-managerial class or stratum" and that they and others are "part of it" (1993b:104).[3]

> That means that we're getting a lot of resources that other people are not getting. And some of them are your cousins and my cousins, they're working-class people. They're poor people. Collapsing educational systems, and we get these lectureships and fellowships that are proliferating all the time. I'm in Italy this month, next month I'm in New Brunswick and then California. Where's all the money that *we* get coming from? How come that money is not going to some of the failing educational systems, in Chicago and New York and Houston? I'm not trying to be ugly here; what I'm saying is what critical self-inventory is all about in a Gramscian sense. So the question is how do we fight as progressives and co-opted? (104)

Made in 1991, West's comments were significant precisely because they challenged his colleagues and himself to address the difficulties that derive from their being committed to progressive politics and yet, as relatively privileged workers, also rewarded by the system they critique. By introducing this question, West risked being "ugly" to initiate a self-critical conversation about the ways that class position informs and influences the work of intellectuals who are, as bell hooks writes, "well-paid members of the professional-managerial academic class" and to theorize how they might best contribute to constructing a more humane society (West 1993b:104; hooks 1995:177). The need to secure tenure and promotion often compels professors to produce work that supports the ideological status quo or that has little, if any, relevance to significant societal problems. Although universities and colleges are committed in principle to academic freedom, this freedom is inescapably delimited by individuals who decide the intellectual worth of pedagogy and scholarship on the basis of their intellectual, disciplinary, and political commitments, commitments that frequently support existing social, political, and economic arrangements. Intellectuals who are committed to transforming these arrangements are consequently challenged to remain faithful to their principles in the context of predominantly conservative institutional conditions.[4]

How then might academic intellectuals support radical politics? Among the most provocative responses to this question is West's concept of the critical organic catalyst. Elaborating on Lenin's concept of the professional revolutionary and Gramsci's concept of the organic intellectual, both of which entail that (as Lenin remarked in *What Is to Be Done?)* the division between theoretical and practical labor should "be obliterated," West begins by noting that academic intellectuals who "align themselves with demoralized, demobilized, depoliticized, and disorganized people in order to empower and enable social action, and, if possible, to enlist collective insurgency for the expansion of freedom, democracy, and individuality," are caught "in an inescapable double bind—while linking their activities to the fundamental, structural overhaul of these institutions, they often remain financially dependent on them" (1993d:4). The question they confront is, as West wrote in "Theory, Pragmatisms and Politics," how to advance "a more enabling and empowering sense of the moral and political dimensions of our functioning in the present-day academy" (1993d:94 [emphasis omitted]). The critical organic catalyst is his provisional response.

The critical organic catalyst works "inside the academy, principally in order to survive and stay attuned to the most sophisticated reflections about the past, present, and future destinies of the relevant cultures, economies and states of our time," and maintains links "outside the academy: in progressive political organizations and cultural institutions of the most likely agents of social change in America, for example, those of black and brown people, organized workers, women, lesbians and gays" (West 1993d:102–3). The key to making theoretical work relevant to struggles for justice is, says West, "to fuse the best of the life of the mind from within the academy with the best of the organized forces for greater democracy and freedom from outside the academy" (103). By establishing, maintaining, and developing such alliances, academic intellectuals may make empirical information and theoretical knowledge available to those who otherwise do not have the time, energy, or access to the resources (e.g., information and communication systems) required to acquire this information and knowledge. In this way they may productively empower individuals and organizations to clarify the structural forces generative of their situation by investigating, among other things, the connections between their problems and problems facing other organizations (e.g., between labor and the environment), as well as the connections between their problems and private control of societal planning and development (e.g., the connections between corporate power, low wages, and depleted ecosystems). Establishing alliances with extra-academic organizations also creates the basis for scholars and teachers to maintain greater self-awareness regarding the interests and aspirations they are committed to advancing. Members of these organizations thus have a forum for making their aspirations, interests, and needs known to intellectuals working within the academy and can demand accountability from them. Such alliances establish a mechanism for academic intellectuals to support organizations and movements for social justice, ecological integrity, and human rights.

Indeed, West walks the walk when it comes to working as a critical organic catalyst. He is perhaps the most singularly visible, vocal, and influential progressive academic intellectual among extra-academic communities, organizations, and institutions in the United States today. West provides a provocative model for intellectuals who are concerned with placing their scholarship and pedagogy in the service of human liberation. According to West, fully realizing the political potential of the critical organic catalyst requires overcoming elitism; I believe it requires clarifying the means and ends of critical organic practice as well.

Personal and Structural Adjustments

One of the barriers preventing "co-opted" intellectuals from establishing links with working-class, feminist, antiracist, and gay and lesbian organizations, says West, are feelings of "existential and cultural superiority over and distance from ordinary people," which are reinforced by the ideological and institutional organization of the academy and the general division of manual and mental labor (1989:179). Unfortunately, many intellectuals confuse the task of overcoming their feelings of existential and cultural superiority over less privileged sectors of the working class with eliminating the social relations that produce relations of inferiority/superiority and feelings of guilt in the first place. In short, the step that intellectuals should take first in serving democratic struggles becomes the only step taken. Many become fixated on the problem, as Gates wrote in "Parable of the Talents," of "survivor's guilt," of feeling culpable for being "among the lucky ones" who, through hard work, dedication, and support from enabling communities and government policies, escaped the impoverished circumstances into which they were born (1996:52).

It should perhaps be obvious that the division of labor separating the professional-managerial class fraction from less privileged sectors of the working class is not changed in the least when members of the former overcome their elitist prejudices or guilty feelings—in short, subjective dispositions—about their no longer being members of the latter. Moreover, to the extent that this project leads privileged intellectuals to romanticize less privileged members of the working class or to feel relieved of their guilt, it may also lead them to believe that nothing more needs to be done. While changing intellectuals' dispositions may help to eliminate one of the barriers to radical change, in itself this does nothing to change the existing division of labor that generates social inequalities, elitist prejudice, and feelings of guilt. Those who occupy objectively superior positions may profoundly change their subjective disposition toward those who occupy objectively inferior positions, but this will not overcome relations in which one class or class fraction enjoys greater access to societal and natural resources than does another class or class fraction. Given the nature of academic work, it is difficult to free oneself of the illusion that social life is primarily a product of ideas and in particular a product of the ideas produced by academic intellectuals. Whereas such a view has led some academicians to argue, as poststructuralist feminists Rosemary Pringle and Sophie Watson do, that "'discourse' and 'subjectivity' rather than structures and interests become the key terms" to explain the reality of oppression (1992:65), others who adopt this view have gone so far as to "believe that they have broken free of imperialism through acts of reading, writing, lecturing, and so forth" (Ahmad 1992:11). Mark Lilla notes that Derrida, the figure most closely associated with deconstruction, "is convinced that the only way to extend the democratic values he himself holds is to destroy the language in which the West has always conceived of them, in the mistaken belief that it is language, not reality, that keeps our democracies imperfect. Only by erasing the vocabulary of Western political thought can we hope for a 'repoliticization' or a 'new concept of politics'" (1998:40). That such inflated views regarding the force of language, discourse, subjectivity, and representation in the production of society are pervasive and appear self-evident illustrates not only the degree to which a kind of philosophical idealism pervades academically generated scholarship but also the degree to which the alienating effects of the capitalist division of labor have permeated every sphere of production, including and increasingly intellectual production.

West never argues that reading, writing, and lecturing are enough to end oppression or that oppression may be ended by shedding elitist prejudice;

indeed, he often criticizes those who do argue as much. Nevertheless, to the extent that theorists conceptualize conditions of life as being products of discursive, cultural, or psychological forces, as products, for example, of the "structure of modern discourse," "cultural nihilism," or "managerial greed," they are likely to argue that oppression may be abolished by projects such as deconstructing discursive constructs, dismantling cultural representations, transforming psychological dispositions, or as Gates writes, expiating survivor's guilt by creating a space "to express the desires and anxieties of this new middle class freely and from the inside" without fear of being criticized by the unlucky majority whom structural constraints, not psychological states, consign forever to the outside (West 1982:47–75, 1993a:11–20; Hewlett and West 1998:81–83; Gates 1996:40). If pragmatism theoretically represents the problems of individuals who are divided by a "dual allegiance to the conqueror and the conquered," we perhaps should not be surprised that it is today popular not only among "those 'cultured' Saxon gentlemen (and few white women)" who made it into the ranks of the upper working class but also among those intellectuals who are, as Gates writes, members of "that generation that would tell white folks that we would not be deterred—that, whether they knew it or not, we too were of the elite" (West 1989:39; Gates 1996:49).

What Are We Fighting For?

Going beyond pragmatism's left-liberal bourgeois politics requires formulating clearly postbourgeois goals (e.g., democratic control of the means of social production and distribution). Although intellectuals may form alliances with extra-academic progressive organizations, there is no guarantee that their participation will aid in the theoretical radicalization of these organizations. They may contribute to this end by supporting efforts to combat bourgeois interpretations of and responses to working class social, political, and economic problems, needs, and interests. This requires acting "as tribunes to people impelled by circumstances or enlightenment to vent other, less complicit sentiments" (Lloyd 1997:411). It means challenging bourgeois ideological common sense as it permeates the consciousness and informs the actions of individuals and organizations. But challenging bourgeois concepts in turn requires being clear about the ends one advocates. In this regard, West's post-*Evasion* formulations of the goals that critical organic catalysts ought to advocate do not clearly go beyond the political divide that separates capitalism from socialism. In "The New Cultural Politics of Difference" West writes,

> By [critical organic catalyst] I mean a person who stays attuned to the best of what the mainstream has to offer—its paradigms, viewpoints, and methods—

> yet maintains a genuine grounding in affirming and enabling subcultures of criticism. Prophetic critics and artists of color should be exemplars of what it means to be intellectual freedom fighters, that is, cultural workers who simultaneously position themselves within (or alongside) the mainstream while clearly aligned with groups who vow to keep alive potent traditions of critique and resistance. (1993d:27)

What does West mean by "the mainstream"? What are affirming and enabling subcultures of criticism, and what constitutes a genuine grounding in them? How is the mainstream linked to the dominant structures of economic and political power? How are these cultures linked to the struggle to transform the political economy of capitalism? Perhaps most important, for whom and what are critical organic catalysts fighting as they work to keep alive traditions of critique and resistance or, for that matter, as they aid those individuals and organizations concerned with increasing individual freedom and social and economic democracy? Why not argue, as Lenin and Gramsci argued when they articulated their concepts of the role of intellectuals in the struggle for human freedom, that critical organic catalysts are those intellectuals, both academic and nonacademic, who aim to support, both theoretically and practically, the formation of working-class counterhegemonic movements against global capital? Why not argue, as West did in *Prophesy Deliverance,* that critical organic catalysts support the working class in its efforts to make economic institutions "democratically controlled by the citizenry [because] people should participate in their decision-making process," for only "collective control over the major institutions of society constitutes genuine power on behalf of the people" (1982:114)? Why not argue, as West wrote in 1985 in "Anti-Imperialist Struggle and Black Americans," that left intellectuals should advance "theoretical systemic Marxist-like analyses that link anti-imperialist struggles against common capitalist foes" and, as he wrote in 1986 in "Left Strategies Today," "put forward its socialist, feminist, antiracist, antihomophobic, and anti-imperialist views and programs such that the larger questions of the distribution of wealth and income between groups and the erosion of power of the lower middle class, working class, and poor gain visibility in public discourse" (1998:77, 138)? In "The New Cultural Politics of Difference," however, West does not link the critical organic catalyst to such clearly defined political goals, and in this respect he makes it possible for almost anyone to claim to be acting as one. The ambiguity of West's formulation makes it possible to be entirely flexible—some would say, pragmatic—with regard to one's political commitments. Indeed, this flexibility may be precisely what makes it possible for one to advocate both more democracy and free enterprise or, as is the case with Bill Bradley, to represent, in West's words, "the best of the democratic tradition" (in Goldberg 2000:A7) and yet be, according to the Center for Public Integrity, the presidential candidate who is "closer to Wall Street" than any other (Lewis 2000). Indeed, Bradley is an advocate of universal health care on the one hand and, as a New Jersey senator, a strong supporter of chemical corporations that produce "highly toxic pesticides" on the other (ibid.). He is at once a spokesperson for the poor and a career beneficiary of such financial giants as Citigroup, Merrill Lynch, Goldman Sachs, Morgan Stanley Dean Witter, and Lehman Brothers Holdings (ibid.). In other words, Bradley's critical organic practice has garnered endorsements from folks across the political and financial spectrum: margin to center. Indeed, not just Bradley but also Bill Clinton and Pat Buchanan satisfy West's criteria. Buchanan "stays attuned to the best of what the mainstream has to offer . . . yet maintains a genuine grounding in affirming and enabling subcultures of criticism" (e.g., the militia movements, right-wing libertarians, and radical Christians). In *The Great Betrayal: How American Sovereignty and Social Justice Are Sacrificed to the Gods of the Global Economy* (1997), Buchanan criticizes globalization in the name of "economic justice," yet he does not criticize private ownership of the means of production and their organization for the purpose of profit making. Rather, he argues that globalization itself is the problem facing American workers and that protectionism is the solution. Thus, although Buchanan locates himself principally within the mainstream and maintains ties to certain traditions of resistance, none of those traditions seeks to replace capitalist with democratic globalization. But then, neither do progressive pragmatists. Rather, they are concerned with saving America from decline through the implementation of progressive reforms (see Hewlett and West 1998:93; Unger and West 1998). For progressive pragmatists, as for Buchanan, it is America first and all other nations second—or more accurately, American workers and owners first and all other persons second.

The point is not that West and Buchanan share exactly the same politics. West correctly contends that academic intellectuals ought to "align themselves with demoralized, demobilized, depoliticized and disorganized people in order to empower and enable social action and, if possible, to enlist collective insurgency for the expansion of freedom, democracy, and individuality" (1993d:4). Without such extra-academic alliances, an academician's scholarly work quite often "degenerates into mere accommodation or sheer stagnation, and the role of the 'co-opted and progressive'—no matter how fervent one's subversive rhetoric—is rendered more difficult" (5). Vagueness about precisely for whom and what one is fighting, however, does not make accommodation and stagnation any less likely. Indeed, they are virtually assured.

Speaking Truth to Power

In an interview with Bill Moyers, West explained that he understands "the vocation of the intellectual as trying to turn easy answers into critical questions and putting those critical questions to people with power," adding that the "quest for truth, the quest for the good, the quest for the beautiful, all require us to let suffering speak, let victims be visible, and let social misery be put on the agenda of those with power" (1993c:103). The project of speaking truth to power sounds noble enough and may certainly place the problem of misery "on the agenda of those with power." Closer examination of this strategic proposal, however, raises several questions regarding its potential effectiveness. First, it assumes that if those with power were confronted by the suffering and misery of the powerless, they would not only add these concerns to their agendas but also, for example, rethink policies that create suffering in the first place and perhaps even pursue policies to alleviate this suffering. Although some political leaders have been persuaded to do just this, abundant historical evidence supports Frederick Douglass's claim that power has never conceded anything without a demand. Moral suasion seldom inclines the powerful to pursue social justice. This does not mean that truth should not be spoken to those with power or that efforts to persuade the powerful to give back some of what they took should not be pursued. Rather, it is to suggest that the strategy of speaking truth to power is problematic because it is unlikely to result in any significant transfer of power and especially because it encourages intellectuals committed to supporting progressive politics to orient their "speech" toward those with power rather than those without it. Academic intellectuals who adopt such an orientation are compelled to ask whether the working class and poor are "completely in the dark regarding the reasons for their predicament," "lack self-confidence in every sphere of life or just in middle-class spheres," and are "bereft of cultural agency and a 'capacity for indignation'" (1993b:104), for they are not organically linked to oppressed communities, as West argues they ought to be. In fact, to support struggles against the social conditions that foster oppression, intellectuals should be oriented less by the project of speaking truth to power and more by the project of working to support the efforts of communities seeking to gain power. This does not mean that intellectuals should leave the academy, discontinue writing for academic audiences, or stop "speaking truth to power." Rather, it means that they should, as West argues and does, work to build, maintain, and strengthen progressive academic and extra-academic organizations.

The Past, Present, and Future of Pragmatism

West's concept of the critical organic catalyst provides a provocative strategy for academically institutionalized intellectuals to contribute to progressive agendas and movements. In doing so, it may enable progressive pragmatists to do what past pragmatists have not done: ally themselves with struggles to democratize control of societal production and planning. Pragmatism needs "a mode of cultural criticism that keeps track of social misery, solicits and channels moral outrage to alleviate it, and projects a future in which the potentialities of ordinary people flourish and flower" (West 1993d:140–41). West is clear: "The first wave of pragmatism foundered on the rocks of cultural conservatism and corporate liberalism. Its defeat was tragic" (141). The question that remains is whether pragmatism was defeated or merely realized its true theoretical and material potential as a middle-class philosophy of social reform. If the former, then pragmatism may have the potential to support more radical social goals. If the latter, however, then we should not be surprised if West's prophetic pragmatism results in reform programs similar to those instituted under Roosevelt's New Deal. To the extent that West's prophetic pragmatism is one of the most fully articulated and radical expressions of contemporary progressive pragmatism, we may go a long way toward determining which of these two possibilities is more likely by examining his work. Although I save the bulk of this examination for the last three chapters, I conclude this chapter with a brief overview of West's post-*Evasion* tendency to seek a political middle ground, one that would avoid conflict and unify individuals for common causes on the basis of non-class-based social identities.

Throughout his post-*Evasion* works West attempts to steer a middle course between philosophical, sociological, and political perspectives. West introduced the possibility of pursuing this course in *Prophesy Deliverance* when he argued that the "Marxist conception of historical development leans heavily upon [a] Hegelian notion of determinate negation" that compels us to choose, for example, "between capitalism and socialism, fascism and communism, [or] barbarism and humanism. This choice, though possibly containing a kernel of truth, precludes combinations and amalgamations of the two contending systems" (1982:101). Although it is not clear how one might combine and amalgamate elements of opposed systems such as these, the main point I wish to stress is that, even in his more explicitly Marxist work, the seeds of West's "middle path" are apparent. In fact, throughout much of his work, West develops his ideas by posing what he represented as opposing views, analyzing their strengths and weaknesses, and finally, forging a position that gathers the best of each. In *Race Matters,* as indicated in the previous chapter, West develops his positions by critically synthesizing conservative moralists and liberal structuralist perspectives on race. In *Race Matters, The War against Parents,* and *The Future of American Progressivism,* West and his colleagues propose a new New Deal that tries to include and speak to everyone's needs, from the rearguard/workers/poor to the vanguard/owners/wealthy. It is as if West has come to assume, contrary to his earlier recommendations, that Dewey was correct to believe that "the political left based on class struggle could never win" (West 1993b:94). He thus tends to formulate his theoretical concepts and political ideas so as to please everyone and offend no one. In "The Future of Pragmatic Thought" West depicts the following scenario:

> When you drive through parts of northeast Tulsa it says as much about America as does driving through the suburbs. And that as an American citizen it has as much to do about you as it does me. It is not just a black problem. Not just a poor people's problem. Not just a social pathological problem. It is a symptom of a culture. It is a symptom of a civilization. And we've got to realize this. Because we are all on the same boat. It's got a leak in it. The winds are blowing and the storm is raging. We either hang together or we hang separately. (1993b:68)

Here West represents the problem of the division between the rich (the suburbs) and poor (parts of northeast Tulsa) as one affecting more than just the oppressed. Rather, West claims it to be a symptom of a culture and contends that we must all act together to solve it. But how accurate is West's depiction of the division between rich and poor? To what extent does it conform with the claims he made in *Prophesy Deliverance* and *Prophetic Fragments* that the rich are rich because the poor are poor, that capitalism is a socioeconomic system organized for the purpose of extracting surplus value from and at the expense of workers (see 1982:114–16, 1988a:52, 114–15)? When the arms of criticism are transformed into the criticism of arms, when criticism in theory becomes criticism in practice, what becomes of West's either/or ultimatum regarding how we hang? What happens when criticism of a (capitalist) ship built by exploited shipbuilders becomes revolutionary criticism advanced by the exploited against their exploiters? Should the oppressed "hang together" with their oppressors? Do their interests converge as human beings concerned with salvaging, for example, the ship? If capitalism is, as West argues elsewhere and not infrequently, a system in which the owning class benefits from the exploitation of the working class, then it follows that working-class efforts for democracy will be resisted (as, of course, they presently are) by the owning class and its religious, educational, legal, political, and military servants and allies. Counseling the oppressed to hang together with those who oppress them means, in practice, counseling the oppressed to collaborate with their oppressors to preserve the system that oppresses them.

The claim that we either hang together or hang separately supports the pernicious view that capital and labor, the corporate class and working class, win or lose "as one," when in fact the former class wins precisely because the latter loses (e.g., war is the health of the state). "We are not all in the same boat during hard times," notes Michael Parenti (1995:172); the same can be said for good times, too. The capitalist structure of production and distribution prevents all boats from rising on the high tide of so-called prosperity, for any rise results from the lift some get from others. Record profits and low wages are, in short, coproducing. The incredible gains in wealth and income made by the richest 20 percent of Americans over the past thirty years and the average decline in wealth and income for the remaining 80 percent of the population derive from the relations of exploitation that bind workers and the rich together, or as West wrote in *Prophesy Deliverance,* class divisions "explain the gross disparity between the rich and poor, the immense benefits accruing to the former and the depravity of the latter" (1982:116). "In effect," writes Steve Brouwer, "wealthy Americans have been appropriating part of the national income, about 10 percent, that used to go to other citizens. And their gain has been spectacular: about $700 billion a year in income that once went to others in the form of higher wages for their labor is now being transferred to the very rich every year" (1998:21). In fact, the corporate class's success has effectively meant that "all of the gains won by the working classes in the middle of the twentieth century, and sustained through the 1950s, 1960s, and 1970s, have been lost" (ibid.). Meanwhile, the folks on top could not be more pleased with gushing-up economics. The fact that those who do well often do so at the expense of others is hardly new. Parenti reminds us that "during the depths of the Great Depression, Henry Ford made $30 million and commented that depressions were not all that bad" (1995:172). Sixty years later, "in the last quarter of 1991, a year designated as the worst recession year since 1939, dividend payments to stockholders hit a record high, causing the president to announce that the economy *was* doing fine. In fact, the corporate economy was doing fine; only the ordinary people were suffering" (ibid.). The grossly uneven and ethically unjust nature of development under capitalism has, if anything, increased since 1991.

When Malcolm X was asked to comment on King's nonviolent, integrationist politics, he responded that he and those blacks for whom he spoke did not want to integrate with the enemy; they did not want to live in a burning house (referring to the "white man's" society). From this perspective, it would be more accurate to say that although oppressors and oppressed are all on the same ship—inextricably linked to each other—they are not on this ship in the same way. They are not all confronted with the same problems and motivated by the same purposes. The majority are chained below and struggling to be free, while the rest are on top and enjoying their freedom. The struggle for liberation depends, said Malcolm X, on an absolutely clear understanding of this social difference. When David Walker published *Appeal to the Coloured Citizens of the World* in 1929, he devoted an entire chapter to the issue of black complicity with slaveholders. Walker describes an incident in which a black slave woman, acting on the basis of white Christian morality, aided a slave driver who had been wounded by blacks fighting for their freedom. By assisting her oppressor, she showed that she had failed to appreciate the nature of slavery, which compels slave drivers, regardless of their individual dispositions, religious or otherwise, to "think nothing of murdering us in order to subject us to the wretched condition" (Walker 1965:25). The struggle for emancipation takes a tremendous leap forward, wrote Walker, when the oppressed break free of the ideological chains of so-called common interest or, today, the American myth of classlessness and the siren call of shared moral, national, or parental interests. The narrative that all Americans are in the same boat and that if we go down, we go down together, a narrative essential to preserving the rule of the few over the many, conceals the incompatible interests separating those who build from those who own and control the boat. Twenty-five years into a period that has witnessed a historically remarkable upward transfer of wealth from the wealth-producing class to the wealth-appropriating class, West no longer defends the interests of any particular class; rather, in the tradition of the great reformer John Dewey, he now promotes the ideals of "democracy," "freedom," "America," and even "civilization." Meanwhile, most working parents and children in the United States and virtually every other nation are drowning in the rising waters of the free market while a small minority enjoy (at least for the time being) swelling portfolios from the sunny decks of their luxury yachts.

Although West introduces strategies for overcoming pragmatism's characteristic politics and certainly lays the theoretical groundwork for overcoming its racist, sexist, and elitist prejudices, his own work, as representing the best of American pragmatism, does not break with the essentially ameliorative orientation of the American pragmatist tradition. Unlike Emerson, James, Dewey, Trilling, Niebuhr, and Mills, and like Du Bois, West makes the struggle against racism, sexism, and elitism central to his own work. At the same time, however, he remains faithful to pragmatism's dominant historical position on capitalist property relations. Whether West's shift from his earlier Marxist revolutionary socialist politics to his current pragmatist left-liberal reform politics reflects changes in his own circumstances (his move from Union Theological Seminary in New York City to Princeton University and subsequently to Harvard University and his increasingly prominent position as a member of what he calls the "professional-managerial class") is of less concern for my project than is determining prophetic pragmatism's contribution to the development of revolutionary theory and practice. Although determining the nature of West's contribution necessitates further examination of his application of prophetic pragmatism to concrete social, political, and economic matters, it is possible at this juncture to suggest that intellectuals committed to supporting working people who seek to control societal planning and ensure that every boat rises when each boat rises ought seriously to consider West's own suspicion that even the "best of the American pragmatist tradition . . . may not be good enough given the depths of the international and domestic crises we now face" (1989:8).

6. Saving the Nation in the Era of Transnational Capitalism

> First, we must fight racism (including anti-Semitism) and Eurocentrism within the anti-imperialist movement. . . . Second, we must practically ground ourselves in particular anti-imperialist struggles in light of theoretical systemic Marxist-like analyses that link anti-imperialist struggles against common capitalist foes. . . . Last, we must strive to bring together black and white anti-imperialist groups for dialogues, discussions, and demonstrations.
>
> —Cornel West,
> "Anti-Imperialist Struggle and Black Americans"

> The work of progressives is to speak, within and outside the Democratic party, for a clear alternative. Not for some impossible, romantic dream of a different "system." Not for the last-ditch defense of every part of the New Deal compromise in American politics. Not for the Republican agenda—or the doctrine of the one true way—with a human face. Not for the humanization of the inevitable. But for a practical view of how, step by step, and piece by piece, to democratize the American economy and reenergize American democracy.
>
> —Roberto Mangabeira Unger and Cornel West,
> *The Future of American Progressivism*

The Future of American Progressivism

IN THE PREVIOUS CHAPTER I reviewed West's genealogy of American pragmatism and explored some of the important ways in which his own work enriches its progressive dimensions. I not only concurred with West's own evaluation that pragmatism has been marked by elitism, ethnocentrism, racism, sexism, and a consistent, almost universal reluctance to side with the working class; I also suggested that, as West intimates in *The American Evasion of Philosophy* (1989), even the best of pragmatism may prove to be inadequate as a *theoretical* means for interpreting our profound social, political, economic, and environmental problems and as a guide for solving them.

"At its worst," notes West in *Keeping Faith* (1993d), pragmatism has been "a mere ideological cloak for corporate liberalism and managerial social engineering which served the long-term interests of American capital; at its best, it survived as a form of cultural critique and social reform at the service of expanding the scope of democratic process and broadening the arena of individual self-development here and abroad" (103). For the most part, however, West fails to explore the real possibility that the best of progressive pragmatism has served and currently does serve the long-term interests of American capital precisely by way of its concern for social reform. James and Dewey provided vital philosophical and political support for the articulation and implementation of Roosevelt's New Deal social contract, which contained anticapitalist forces within the limits established by capitalist political economy. Is West contributing to a similar end through his elaboration, with Sylvia Ann Hewlett, of a parents' "Bill of Rights" and, with Roberto Mangabeira Unger, of a reoriented American progressivism (Hewlett and West 1998; Unger and West 1998)? If so, does this mean that West's political philosophy is no longer doing what West previously argued it should, challenging a society he described in *Prophesy Deliverance* as an "anti-democratic mode of socioeconomic organization," "racist and sexist at its core and based upon class exploitation and imperialist oppression," in which "the profit-maximizing activity of a few is integrally linked to the dehumanization of the many" (1982:122, 125)? In short, does prophetic pragmatism remain within or transcend the political limits that have characterized American pragmatism? In this chapter I consider these questions by examining West's formulation of the concepts of democracy, freedom, individuality, and the nation-state.

Democracy: Formal and Substantial

In *The Ethical Dimensions of Marxist Thought* (1991), West recalls that he was a student at Princeton University when he "became convinced that the values of individuality—the sanctity and dignity of all individuals shaped in and by communities—and of democracy—as a way of life and mode of being-in-the-world, not just a form of governance—were most precious" (xx). In an interview with Bill Brown, West identified himself as "a radical democrat." Said West, "I am a proponent of individuality in terms of the uniqueness, the irreducible and irreplaceable character of individuals shaped by groups and communities; so I do in fact want to argue that certain cultures—to the degree they conform to radical democratic principles and radical libertarian principles—are preferable to other kinds of cultures" (1993c:126). West describes his reader as containing texts that embody "a certain kind of musical life that painfully pursues a compassionate individuality and courageously struggles for a more free and democratic world" (1999b:xx). Indeed, the categories of individuality and democracy, the value of individual freedom within community, and the centrality of radical democratic and libertarian principles are central to prophetic pragmatism.

As I began to argue in the previous chapter, however, West invokes, even while he sometimes criticizes, one of bourgeois society's fatted calves: the concept of democracy abstracted from and purified of the class antagonisms that structure its actualization. In *Prophesy Deliverance* West argued that "capitalism is an *antidemocratic* mode of socioeconomic organization in that it requires the removal of control of production from those engaged in production" and that "genuine power on behalf of the people" requires production to be "democratically controlled by the citizenry" (1982:122, 114). In his post-*Evasion* works, however, West defines democracy less in terms of the relationship that citizens have to the means of production and more in terms of bourgeois rights. In *The War against Parents* Hewlett and West even use the category of democracy as a substitute for capitalism when they write that the "GIs who fought in World War II were vitally important in maintaining America's national security, risking their lives to defeat fascism and in so doing making the western world safe for democracy" (1998:230). West's criticisms of U.S. capital's post–World War II domination of the world economy in the name of "democracy" do not inform their narrative. It is as if U.S. imperialism never existed. Also absent is any discussion of why, if "Americans who were children in the 1950s and 1960s grew up with an optimistic and generous take on the future" (63), blacks and women, among many other groups, protested in the streets over their living conditions in the United States.[1] What is missing from West's concept of democracy that might explain the 1960s revolution? Martin Luther King Jr. offers a clue in his discussion of the relationship between democracy and economics:

> We must ask the question, "Why are there forty million poor people in America?" And when you begin to ask that question, you are raising questions about the economic system, about a broader distribution of wealth. When you ask that question, you begin to question the capitalistic economy. And I'm simply saying that more and more, we've got to begin to ask questions about the whole society. We are called upon to come to see that an edifice which produces beggars needs restructuring. It means that questions must be raised. You see, my friends, when you deal with this, you begin to ask the question, "Who owns the oil?" You begin to ask the question, "Who owns the iron ore?" You begin to ask the question, "Why is it that people have to pay water bills in a world that is two-thirds water?" These are the questions that must be asked. . . . Now, when I say question the whole society, it means ultimately coming to see that the problem of racism, the problem of economic exploitation, and the problem of war are all tied together. These are the triple evils that are interrelated. (King 1986:250)

King understood the necessity of thinking about democracy in terms of working people's control over the social, political, and economic institutions that govern their lives.[2] Unlike King, West has increasingly abstracted the concept of democracy from the property relations that mediate democratic practice, thereby allowing him to evaluate social formations via prophetic pragmatism's democratic and libertarian principles with little regard for the material difference property relations make to the actualization of these principles. The "black freedom struggle is a species of the radical democratic tradition," West said at Le Moyne College in a lecture entitled "Race Matters." How "rare it is in the history of the human adventure that there are citizens rather than subjects . . . , persons who are capable of ruling and being ruled, that facilitates the possibility of the alternation of rule and the rotation of rulers" (1993e:n.p.). West then turned his attention to the specific social formations of Cuba and the United States and suggested that "some folks don't know how to rotate. It's time for Mr. Castro to rotate and be a citizen. We know a fellow citizen [former president George Bush] who just rotated and lives in Houston right now" (ibid.). Cuba is less democratic than the United States even though the latter, as West indicates in many of his writings, has yet to realize fully its constitutional commitment to the ideals of liberty and justice for every person. Although this comparison of Cuba and the United States employs only part of West's concept of democracy, it nevertheless demonstrates a tendency to advance a formal, rather than substantial, concept of democracy—in short, a concept abstracted from "class matters." Whereas a formal definition of democracy highlights the rights to vote, assemble, and speak, a substantial definition highlights, for example, rights to health care, education, and employment, as well as the provision of resources required to ensure that everyone has the opportunity to realize formal political rights. The difference between formal and substantial democracy is, to paraphrase King, the difference between having the right to sit at a lunch counter but no money to buy lunch and having both the right *and* the money. Political scientist Claude Ake clarifies the difference this distinction makes as he discusses human rights in Africa:

> Where is this freedom, this right? I cannot read, I cannot write. I am too busy trying to survive[.] I have no time to reflect. I am so poor I am constantly at the mercy of others. So where is this right and what is it really? Granted, I have the right to seek public office. That is all very well. But how do I realize this right? I am a full-time public servant who cannot find the time or the necessary resources to put up the organization required to win office. If I take leave from my work, I cannot hold out for more than one month without a salary. I have no money to travel about and meet the voters, even to pay the registration fees for my candidature. If I am not in a position to realize this right, then what is the point of saying that I have it? Do I really have it? . . . The Western [capital-

ist] notion of human rights lacks concreteness. It ascribes abstract rights to abstract beings. . . . what is needed is the empowerment[,] by whatever means, of the common people. This is not a matter of legislation, although legislation could help a little. It is rather a matter of redistributing economic and political power across the board. That means that it is in the final analysis a matter of political mobilization and struggle. And it will be a protracted and bitter struggle because those who are favored by the existing distribution of power will resist heartily. (1994:39, 36, 40)

By distinguishing formal from substantial democracy, I am not suggesting that formal rights are unimportant. Rather, I am arguing that formal and substantive democratic rights ought to be understood as structuring each other's concrete realization. Although formal democratic rights are essential to a society based on rule by the people, they should be taken not as the goal of the struggle for democracy but rather as vital means to establishing democratic management of society's productive powers. For example, no one can exercise the right to free expression in a society in which the means for developing and exercising this right are privately owned, controlled by and concentrated in only a few hands. Universal realization of a rich individuality presupposes that all members of society have equal and adequate access to the resources they need to develop their abilities and aspirations. This goal can be more fully and progressively realized only if working citizens are able to plan production to minimize the time, energy, and resources consumed producing the goods required to satisfy their material needs and to maximize the time, energy, and resources available for individuals to develop their interpersonal, athletic, artistic, and scientific potentials. On the basis of the distinction between formal and substantial democratic rights, King, Maynard, and Woodyard offer a notably different evaluation of democracy in Cuba from that made by West:

When wealth and income are so heavily concentrated, sharing offers a real possibility for improving the conditions of the masses. The standard of living of the masses of Cuba before and after the 1959 revolution point to the possibility that a different vision of who owns what can have a startling impact on the well-being of the mass of the population even when the overall economy is not performing particularly well. In 1975, sixteen years after the revolution, the gross domestic product per person in Cuba was the same as it was in 1952. Measured in terms of the traditional economic output measure, Cuba was clearly not doing well. On the other hand, the percentage of the secondary school age population actually enrolled rose from 14% to 74% during the 1960–83 period. For the college age population, the enrollment percentages rose from three to twenty. In 1960, there were slightly less than 1,100 people per doctor. By 1983, that figure had improved to 600 people per doctor, about the same as in Australia, Canada, and the United States. In the years since the revolution,

> average life expectancy has risen from sixty-three to seventy-five years. Even these limited data indicate that quality of life has been improving significantly for the masses in the Cuban population. (1988:76–77)

Although the United States is characterized by a regular rotation of political leaders, American workers do not enjoy many of the substantial democratic rights that Cuban workers enjoy. Cubans enjoy almost universal access to sanitation, education, health care, housing, and employment. Infant mortality dropped from 60 per 1,000 in 1960 to 9.7 per 1,000 in 1991. Contagious diseases such as smallpox, malaria, tuberculosis, typhoid, and polio, once common on the island, have been largely eradicated by improved living standards and health services. Cuban literacy rates are higher than those found in other poor nations and better than what is found in most wealthier nations. Cubans also enjoy access to the arts, sports, and various recreation facilities, including, of course, access to some of the most beautiful beaches, mountains, and countryside that, previous to the revolution, were privately owned by foreign nationals and the small minority of elite Cuban families (see Parenti 1997:38–39).[3] In "Race, Culture, and Social Change," Gayle L. McGarrity indicates that in terms of redressing racial inequalities, the

> Cuban revolution took a monumental first step, unique in the Americas, by transforming the nation's economic structure. Other political regimes and social movements, which have emphasized the racial aspect of oppression to the minimization or exclusion of the class issue, may have succeeded in promoting the self-esteem, sense of pride, and dignity of peoples of African descent, who had been demoralized and humiliated by the slave and colonial experience. However, by not transforming the class structures and the exploitative apparatus of societies concerned . . . these movements did little . . . to end the economic victimization of the majority. Those accustomed to the de facto racial segregation in the United States, the legalized apartheid of South Africa and Namibia, or the brutal economic exploitation elsewhere of peoples of African descent . . . have to be impressed with the contemporary Cuban panorama. (1992:194)

The revolutionary socialist Cuban government advanced a project similar to the one West articulated in *Prophesy Deliverance* and *Prophetic Fragments,* recognizing that class contributes as much as, if not more than, race does to the powerlessness of those individuals whom society designates as "black" and that abolishing the racial division of society is at once a cultural, political, and especially economic project. This does not mean that there is no longer a race problem in Cuba or that Cuba is without significant social, political, and economic problems. This could hardly be the case in a world as socially, politically, and economically divided as ours now is and in which the ruling economic class is as hostile to the development of noncapitalist modes of production as it now is (Landau 1999). Rather, my discussion of West's remarks regarding democracy and Cuba is concerned with highlighting the way in which his post-*Evasion* formulation of democracy and freedom increasingly excludes consideration of what he earlier argued was key: worker control over the processes and products of production.

Not only do substantial democratic rights play a less significant role than do formal rights in West's conception of democracy (although they are certainly not absent from his social analyses, particularly the proposals for a parents' Bill of Rights in *The War against Parents* and the progressivist agenda in *The Future of American Progressivism*), but his method of comparison leaves out the concrete historical differences (e.g., the difference between an imperialist nation and a nation fighting to liberate itself from imperialism) and social relations (e.g., the U.S. blockade of Cuba) that bind Cuba and the United States together and shape their respective social development. Taking these concrete differences seriously, one would begin by noting, as Aijaz Ahmad does, that Cuban performance has so far been much "better than that of comparable countries in the Caribbean and Central America—all this with no imperialist loot, no Marshall Plan, and under conditions of extreme duress" (1992:24)—even as the U.S. embargo, which was declared illegal and inhumane by both the pope and the United Nations and tightened by Clinton when he signed the Helms-Burton Act, continues into its fourth decade (1992:24).[4]

Social relations under capitalism, relations in which the interdependent nature of personal existence is concealed through the individual exchange of commodities in the marketplace, encourage us to think according to a *nonrelational* mode of analysis in which various "parts" of reality are considered in abstraction from the whole in which they are constituted.[5] We interpret classes, nations, regions, states, cities, communities, neighborhoods, individuals, and even individual traits as self-generating rather than cogenerating phenomena. It is precisely this nonrelational, one-sided, abstract—in a word, "bourgeois"—mode of interpretation, one encouraged by capitalist theory and practice, that inclines citizens to defend capitalism by pointing out that, for example, "our system is better than the Mexican system." In doing so, interpreters fail to appreciate the extent to which "our" system is both a product *and* producer of "their" system, that developed nations are a product and producer of underdeveloped nations, that the so-called cycle of poverty is a product and producer of the cycle of wealth, that conditions for whites are a product and producer of conditions for blacks, that the rich are the products and producers of the poor, and so on. In short, such an analysis fails to appreciate the relational determinations that structure society. Life in Cuba results not only from forces within Cuba but also from forces outside of and, in the case of the United States, antagonistic to

Cuba's efforts to build a society based on noncapitalist principles of development. A historically and socially concrete evaluation of Cuba's situation should include a discussion of the U.S. government's ongoing efforts to destroy Cuba's noncapitalist development through assassination, sabotage, invasion, disinformation, and embargo and by threatening nations friendly to Cuba (e.g., Mexico, Brazil, Costa Rica, Nicaragua, Grenada, Japan, France, Canada, Germany, and England) with cultural, political, and economic sanctions. Although the leaders of the self-declared leader of the free(-market) world do indeed rotate on a regular basis, they all, whether Democrat or Republican, nevertheless share the view that the Cuban Revolution, which has produced remarkable achievements by virtually any measure and especially so given the belligerent policies of the United States, must be terminated by any means necessary. The irony of West's claims about Cuba is that some of the policies he and Hewlett advocate in *The War against Parents* and that he and Unger advocate in *The Future of American Pragmatism* have already been at least partially achieved by the "undemocratic" nation of Cuba.

West's evaluation of Cuba, like his and Hewlett's narrative of American history, accords well with the evaluations advanced by Senators Jesse Helms and Dan Burton, exiled Cuban rich, and the corporate-owned and -controlled media. A casual remark about Cuba's being undemocratic, particularly when made by someone with as much public authority and influence as West enjoys, not only contributes to the belief, pervasive among American workers, that socialism's failures are, like their own, *self*-produced, a sort of Horatio Alger myth writ large. It also buttresses a discourse that, as West wrote in *Prophesy Deliverance* and *Prophetic Fragments,* functions as an ideological cover for U.S. imperialism. To invoke the concepts of democracy and freedom as if they stand above property relations and class struggle amounts to supporting the dominant theory and practice of democracy and freedom.

Abstracting democracy and freedom from these realities allows West to theorize progressive social change as the quantitative addition of, as he says, "more democracy and freedom" rather than a qualitative change in the socioeconomic basis of democracy and freedom. This is not to say that West avoids discussing the role that class plays in determining individual and collective life conditions and opportunities. He quite frequently does so, which is one of his works' major strengths. In both *The War against Parents* and *The Future of American Progressivism,* West and his coauthors discuss how class inequalities differentially determine conditions of life for different individuals and classes in the United States. Indeed, in *The Future of American Progressivism* Unger and West note that "the United States has a relatively well-defined class structure," that "the basic design of the class system has remained as stable in American reality as it has been clouded in American consciousness," that the United States "has seen increasing inequality of wealth and income, driving the life chances of individuals apart," and that we as a nation must be willing to loosen this structure a bit if we hope to create greater social mobility within the context of this system (1989:15, 16 [emphasis omitted], 24, 34). They go on to propose legislative and extralegislative loosening measures so that "the grid of class, gender, and race weighs less heavily upon our life in common" (60). Their multifarious measures constitute "a broad-based and market-friendly effort to lift up the rearguard" (77).

But can the rearguard be lifted up without transforming the property relations that generate rearguards and vanguards? Can democracy be expanded without transferring power to those who produce wealth? How can substantive democracy be realized if the means for producing, distributing, and consuming the wealth are controlled by a few individuals who employ the working majority to accumulate private capital? King, Maynard, and Woodyard elaborate on the relationship between democracy and economic power:

> In 1974 the top 100 manufacturing corporations in the United States owned 56% of all manufacturing assets. Assume there is an average of ten top-level managers in each of these corporations. Then 1,000 people controlled better than 50% of the productive assets in America. That is five ten-thousandths of 1% of the population! Those corporate managers make decisions every day that affect all of us. They can close a plant and move operations to Taiwan, as in the recent decisions of a microchip manufacturer in Silicon Valley, instantly eliminating thousands of jobs. Their decisions can lead to a Sunbelt that blooms while the Northeast dies. (1988:82–83)

This picture represents the distribution of wealth and power over twenty-five years ago, well before Reagan and Bush began their all-out assault against labor and well before the present era of megacorporate mergers. Over the past twenty years, especially the past ten, wealth and political power have become monumentally concentrated. In addition, substantial evidence indicates that wealth inequality is growing at a faster rate than it did during the 1980s as the Clinton administration continues to cater to its transnational (that is, international) corporate sponsors by implementing policies Reagan would have thought unattainable, though no doubt desirable (Marable 1997a:153). Between 1983 and 1995 the richest 1 percent of the American population increased its control of wealth from 33.8 to 37.6 percent, while the poorest 80 percent of the population saw its wealth share decrease from 18.7 percent in 1983 to 15.7 percent in 1995. The richest 20 percent now control 84.3 percent of the wealth (Mishel, Bernstein, and Schmitt 1999:262). Wealth inequality in the United States is as great today as it was in 1929. In *Global Village or Global Pillage,* Jeremy Brecher and Tim Costello note that in 1994, of "the top 100 economies in the world, 47 [were] corporations—each with more wealth than 130 countries" (1998:18).

With productive assets being concentrated in so few hands, a process that is accelerating, political power and the capacity to control even the most intimate aspects of human life are concentrated as well. Although the scandalous inequalities resulting from capitalist exploitation are certainly morally offensive, capitalism's antisocial nature rests in the fact that a minority of human beings owns, controls, and organizes social and natural resources for the purpose of producing and accumulating capital rather than for ensuring universal satisfaction of material needs and fostering universal enrichment of individual abilities. As Tom Athanasiou indicates in his brilliant and sobering work *Divided Planet: The Ecology of Rich and Poor* (1996), the World Trade Organization, which, like the World Bank and International Monetary Fund, oversees international capital investment, is made up of nonelected officials whose decision-making criterion is the rate of return on capital invested.

> In the new global economy, the TNCs [transnational corporations] dictate the overall terms. The wild capitalism of the East is certainly more brutal, and the "crony capitalism" of the Marcos dictatorship was more devastating, but in these and all other cases, TNCs, with their routine and rationalized imperatives, set the stage. While the planet slides toward the cliffs, the TNCs are simply doing business. They are, as Alfred Sloan, president of General Motors, put it in 1935, "continuously exploring and capitalizing the secrets of nature, making it possible to create new luxuries to be turned into new necessities." What is crucial about the TNCs is that they pursue this imperative with organizations, tools, and methods that far surpass the power of either community resistance or governmental regulation. They are regional and global actors in a world broken into nations and tribes. They play country against country, ecosystem against ecosystem, simply because it is good business to do so. Low wages and safety standards, environmental pillage, ever-expanding desires—all are symptoms of economic forces that, embodied in TNCs, are so powerful they threaten to overcome all constraint by the society they nominally serve. (196)

Prophetic pragmatists, says West, invest their philosophical "capital" in the historically concrete realities of social, political, and economic life. Nevertheless, he does not consistently advance a socially, politically, and economically concrete concept of democracy and as a result risks supporting a belief he correctly identifies as an essential component of capitalist ideology: "the myth of classlessness," a myth promoted, West adds, "especially among those guilt-ridden about their upward mobility or ashamed of their class origins" (1993c:42). In *The American Evasion of Philosophy* West describes prophetic pragmatism's political goals as "more democracy and freedom"; in *The War against Parents,* as "more equity and fairness"; and in *The Future of American Progressivism,* as a more democratic free market (West 1989:4; Hewlett and West 1998:87; Unger and West 1998:93). For West, the problem is not class divisions and capitalist exploitation *as such* but rather, as he wrote in the foreword to Mumia Abu-Jamal's *Death Blossoms* (1997), "the forces of our *unregulated* capitalist market, which have yielded not only immoral levels of wealth inequality and economic insecurity but also personal isolation and psychic disorientation" (West 1997b:xi [emphasis added]). As West said in an interview with Henry Louis Gates Jr., it is possible "to humanize capitalism" and to create greater class mobility within and less inequality between the classes that make up the American class system (West 1998; Unger and West 1998:24).

West's position implies that more freedom and greater democracy can be achieved by instituting (assuming that this could be accomplished within one nation) regulations that compel capitalist corporations to invest in a more socially responsible manner rather than by supporting working people around the world in their efforts to redistribute economic and political power. The problem of democracy is not so much "that we're experiencing a breakdown in democratic processes," as West suggested to Ruth Simmons, the president of Smith College (1996–97:14). Rather, the practice of genuine democracy as West characterized it in *Prophesy Deliverance,* is that it has yet to be tried.

Individuality, Property, and Freedom as Strategies of Containment

To maximize profits capital must, on the one hand, organize workers collectively and, on the other hand, prevent them from acting on the basis of common interests. As I have described in previous chapters, the productive capacities of an unprecedented number of human beings are now combined and organized for the primary purpose of producing value in the form of commodities. By socializing production, capital not only dramatically increases the overall rate of value production but also places workers in a position to assume democratic control over their own productive capacities, the products of their capacities, and the social and natural forces they employ to produce these capacities. From the point of view of capital, there is always the danger, one that is regularly and increasingly being realized around the world, that the same workers it organizes to produce surplus value will transform their fragmented positions as individual workers into a unified position as members of the working class and act to advance their collective interests (e.g., by demanding universal child care, health care, and housing; an end to wage discrimination; and ultimately a transfer of political power so that working people may control their own individual and collective development).

Maintaining the dominance of capital within relatively wealthier capitalist nations during the post–World War II era has not, by and large, involved direct violence, although violence is hardly unknown within these nations and is likely to become more frequent as living conditions worsen for the majority of human beings. The dramatic expansion of police forces, prison construction, and criminalization of the unemployed and underemployed indicate that the state is arming itself for just such necessities. For the most part, however, the ruling class remains the ruling class because members of the ruled class accept the existing society as the way things must be. Ruling-class ideas support the ruling class by encouraging workers to accept existing social relations and conditions of life as natural, inevitable, and if at all possible, desirable.[6]

The ruling-class ideas of individuality, freedom, and property are key in this regard, for they help to prevent members of the working class from recognizing and acting on shared class interests. The bourgeois ideas of individuality and freedom presuppose commodity exchange relations in which commodity owners are legally free to dispose of their respective commodities as they see fit. As is well known, however, the purportedly equal and free exchange of commodities in the marketplace presupposes a system of economic compulsion in which one class owns nothing but the capacity to produce value while another class possesses the means for purchasing and employing the commodity of value producers. Workers bring their capacity for labor to market just as owners bring money to purchase workers. There is a difference, however. Unlike the parties to other commodity transactions, in which owners exchange their commodities and then go their separate ways, workers who sell their commodity—labor power—must then subordinate themselves to the authority of the buyers, the money owners, for a specified period of time; in short, they must surrender themselves and the products of their labor to the owners of the means of production. The legal equality of commodity owners at the level of exchange is premised on and compromised, if not contradicted, by substantial inequality at the level of production. The bourgeois concept of the individual mystifies the relationship between formal equality and substantial inequality by abstracting individuals from the social relations that determine their respective control over the resources required to exercise their "freedoms." Bourgeois ideology may claim that individuals are equally free to pursue their own ends, but to the extent that realizing that freedom depends on having the resources to achieve these ends, this freedom is most fully realized by those who own the means of producing value, namely, the capitalists. Arguing that individuals are equally free, as in the claim that America is a free country, results from a process of abstraction in which the freedom enjoyed by those who possess capital to invest in those whose labor produces capital, that is, those who derive their living from other people's labor, is represented as being more or less equally available to both groups. From this perspective, the mass media mogul Ted Turner and a single mother raising children on poverty-level wages are equally free to make of their lives what they want.[7] Individuals either do or do not possess the will power to act on their "inalienable" freedom to produce themselves, to be all they can be, as the U.S. Army commercial echoes Heidegger in urging. This explains why bourgeois biographies of the rich and (in)famous emphasize personal characteristics and capacities rather than access to other people's labor and lives in explaining their "success." The law reflects the abstraction of class from the categories of freedom, individuality, and property, for it makes few important distinctions between private ownership of the means of production and personal ownership of the products of production.[8] There is no legal difference between the property rights of Nike Corporation and Toys "R" Us and those of a child who owns a pair of Air Jordan's and a backyard basketball hoop. Yet there is a significant difference in their capacities to shape the world they inhabit together. Whereas the child has the power to decide how he or she might win a basketball game and whom to invite over to play, Nike CEO Philip Knight and Toys "R" Us CEO Michael Goldstein have and exercise the power to decide issues that affect living conditions in communities both here and abroad. Thus, whereas private property, in personal and corporate form, is sacred, private control and planning of society ensures the reproduction of socioeconomic inequalities and the inability of humanity to solve many of its most basic problems. In short, it is a structural condition rather than, as Hewlett and West contend in *The War against Parents,* a psychological disposition or sociocultural condition that impels individuals to behave immorally.

Once the difference between private ownership of the means of production and personal ownership of the products of production is rendered illegible, proposals to subordinate societal planning to collective authority appear to violate individual liberty and freedom when in practice they would negate the liberty and freedom of those who own the means of production to exploit labor. As Greider points out, in "the global marketplace defined as free trade, everyone is free, it seems, but the people. Multinational enterprise can come and go from one market to the next, investors may insist upon terms for the use of their capital, [and] governments may demand concessions in exchange for commercial opportunities" (1997:388). Nevertheless, these "contractual rights do not extend to the citizens . . . in large portions of the global system. In many developing countries, people are rigorously regulated by the state as a commodity—wage labor—and often forcibly deprived of the most basic individual freedoms—the right to speak one's mind or associate freely with others" (ibid.). Private property rights always trump human rights, for a relatively small percentage of individuals control the conditions of labor and life for the vast majority, from the ideas they are fed to the food they eat—indeed, whether they have any food at all.[9]

To combat the accumulating concentration of economic and political power, it is necessary to advance the idea of human rights against the absolute right of individuals to dispose of property without considering how their actions affect society and the environment. Private ownership of productive property not only undermines the universal realization of justice, equality, and democracy; it also increasingly conflicts with capitalism's socialization of the forces of production. Socialization of production creates the structural basis for organizing the economy in response to questions such as the following: How much food must be produced, and how should it be distributed? How many homes must be built to provide housing for everyone? How much wealth should be devoted to scientific research relative to that which is devoted to meeting primary, secondary, and tertiary needs? What levels of production are necessary to meet these needs and maintain good stewardship with the Earth? Human rights, the legalized expression of substantive democracy, oppose the right of private ownership of the means of production, the legalized expression of the capitalist system of property relations. To advance the cause of human rights we should, first, expose the incompatibility of human rights with the existing socioeconomic system and, second, show how realizing substantial human rights is necessary for fully realizing formal democratic rights. With regard to the first task, for example, the decision to grant China favored nation trade status may be exposed as evidence of the current economic system's structural incompatibility with the realization and protection of formal and substantial human rights. With regard to the second task, it may be argued that only democratic planning of the economy can ensure the possibility that all individuals will enjoy access to the cultural, social, and economic resources required to exercise their right to free expression. Although criticizing private ownership of the means of production is, according to prevailing orthodoxy, sacrilegious, this task remains essential to concretizing the struggle for democracy as a struggle for democratic control of economic resources and social planning.

A historically progressive concept of democracy, one that would constitute a *qualitative* extension and deepening of the realm of freedom, would inescapably entail establishing public determination of the resources, capacities, and powers necessary to satisfy and develop, consciously and democratically, the needs, wants, and desires of all human beings in a manner that replenishes the natural basis of all existence. It would mean, in short, making the principle that capitalist society has already made for the majority of human beings around the world—namely, propertylessness—the principle for society as a whole.

Saving the Nation in the Era of Transnational Capitalism

In *Prophesy Deliverance* and *Prophetic Fragments* West argued that an international framework is absolutely essential for grasping the causes of the oppression of blacks in the United States. It would be impossible, said West, to account for the hell that blacks catch in this country without comprehending the global social relations that separate, connect, and reproduce their situation and the situation of oppressed classes in maldeveloped countries. Marxism, with its emphasis on totality, supports this project because it brings the "relationship of black oppression in America to black and brown oppression in Third World countries . . . to light in an extremely clear and convincing way" (1982:115). In "Left Strategies Today," an essay originally published in the March-April 1986 issue of *Socialist Review,* West wrote that the "task of the American left in this period is to gain a foothold in the public discourse of the nation in order to articulate both a moral vision and an economic program" (1988a:137). During a period when Reagan's dismantling of the New Deal social contract was in high gear, and in concert with his brother in faith and comrade in arms James Cone, West argued that advancing this vision and program "requires that the left engage in a more explicit *class politics.* The present class offensive by the business community must be met by a counter-offensive by the organized victims of pro-business policies. Class politics must be the prism through which black politics are elaborated" (ibid.). Moreover, West added, this class-based counteroffensive must be international (77).

West's analysis was based on his understanding of capitalism's realities. Although capital has been global for over five hundred years, revolutions in communication, transportation, and information technologies have made it possible for transnational corporations to move their production operations around the world and invest capital more quickly than ever before. The fact that large corporations are increasingly liberated from domestic captivity, that they no longer pledge allegiance to their home nations, and that they can move production at the drop of a hat or the sign of a strike constitutes a principal weapon in capital's war against workers.[10] Today corporations not only outsource low-skill manufacturing jobs but are increasingly outsourcing high-skill technical jobs to relatively underdeveloped capitalist nations (see Brouwer 1998:72–75). Indeed, the design, production, and marketing of virtually every kind of product is now subject to exportation to lower-wage sites, even though producing commodities in low-wage regions and selling them in high-wage regions lowers the wages of workers in every region, a fact that is presently generating overproduction and underconsumption. Corporations pit workers in different nations against one another and in so doing are able to divert attention from their own efforts to maximize profits at the expense of every worker.[11] The fact that corporations increasingly have the entire global labor market at their disposal, a market made available by authoritarian governments and U.S. military forces, means that workers from one nation cannot easily protect their wages, benefits, and securities without acting in solidarity with workers from other nations. Capital has the power of moving whenever workers from one nation, region, or state demand too much (which is to say, increasingly, anything at all). Capital's international mobility and labor's national captivity place owners in a powerful position vis-à-vis workers (see Burbach and Robinson 1999:27).

Today nation-states increasingly function much as South African Bantustans did and largely still do. Under this system, national governments often act as international capital's "local" administrator, implementing policies that weaken the position of workers and strengthen the position of capital. The World Bank, International Monetary Fund (IMF), and World Trade Organization (WTO), institutions that operate above and against the laws of all nations, coordinate the flow of money and direct politicians, under the threat of divestment, to implement structural adjustment programs (SAPs) in order to ensure the highest rates of return on capital investments. Although such policies have been the norm in relatively underdeveloped nations for quite some time, international finance capital is now demanding similar adjustments in relatively developed nations. Welfare reform, deregulation of labor and capital markets, and reduced government spending on programs that benefit working people are local manifestations of transnational capital's global assault on labor and nature (see Sciacchitano 1999). In *Dark Victory: The United States, Structural Adjustment and Global Poverty,* Walden Bello, Shea Cunningham, and Bill Rau indicate that capital's "war against the South is accompanied by another war on the home front, this time against the work force inside the United States" (1994:xi). The dismantling of New Deal legislation, cuts on capital gains taxes, and corporate subsidies constitute domestic versions of the structural adjustment programs initiated by the World Bank, IMF, and WTO in Third World nations. In the post–New Deal, post-Marxist, post-socialist, free-market era, Democrats have proven themselves equal to the Republicans as allies in capital's war against the working class. The Clinton administration, working under the guise of building a bridge to the twenty-first century, has in large measure enacted the death sentence Reagan passed on the New Deal.[12] The North American Free Trade Agreement (NAFTA) and the General Agreement on Tariffs and Trade (GATT), protectionist treaties designed to ensure U.S. capital's supremacy over labor and resources, facilitate the flow of technology, factories, equipment, and money—but not labor—across national borders. It is not so much that, as Unger and West write, politicians have proven themselves "unable to deliver the goods" as it is that they have been completely dedicated to delivering all the goods to the richest individuals, households, and corporations in the United States (1998:55; see Mishel, Bernstein, Schmitt 1999). With the possible exception of the period during which the slaveholding class, led by Thomas Jefferson, dominated federal politics, the state has never worked as well for the propertied few as it has over the past twenty-five years.

In the era of transnational capitalism, nationalist politics that do not challenge transnational capitalist powers inhibit workers' capacity to build alliances around the world and render workers in every nation more vulnerable to corporate exploitation. The growing dominance of a thoroughly transnational bourgeoisie, a bourgeoisie whose financial interests are advanced by politicians, the World Bank, IMF, WTO, and global military forces, weakens the sovereignty of nation-states through trade agreements that supersede national laws that protect the rights of workers and the environment (e.g., WTO decisions have significantly compromised the Endangered Species Act and efforts to curtail the growth of sweatshop labor). The fact that individual capitalists from all nations increasingly pursue productive and financial investment opportunities around the world also further weakens the idea that they share common interests with workers from their own nation. Capitalists do not hesitate to fire workers from their "own" nation and hire workers from other nations if doing so increases their profit margin.

Yet workers from every nation are encouraged to think and act in terms of national interests. In doing so, they continue to cover the costs of worker education, research done at public universities, societal infrastructures maintenance, and military expenditures, as well as the staggering costs associated with paying for a global police force to protect the processes of capital accumulation. In addition, they are prevented from thinking and acting as members of the international working class.[13]

In a global system in which nationally based corporations and financial enterprises have become thoroughly international, entering into strategic alliances and forming international conglomerates, activists who limit their framework to the category of the "nation" risk assisting capital's ongoing efforts to *domesticate* the working class. The struggle to improve living conditions for workers in any particular nation can succeed only if it becomes a struggle to improve life for workers in every nation. This is not a metaphysical claim regarding the inescapable oneness of humanity but rather a practical truth. Inasmuch as capital operates transnationally, the struggle for democracy may be and perhaps must be advanced through globally coordinated efforts among workers, students, and citizens. Without such efforts, improvements in living conditions for citizens in one nation may well be gained through the degradation of living conditions in other nations. This does not mean abandoning the nation-state as a site of political struggle. Nor does it mean forgoing the articulation of progressive political agendas that demand state intervention to improve living conditions for working citizens. In fact, as I have suggested, the nation-state remains a principal institution for creating the conditions necessary to ensure that capital investors enjoy lucrative access to labor and consumer markets at home and abroad. Supporting the development of revolutionary democratic consciousness and political movements, however, requires examining nation-states in terms of the specific role they play in buttressing transnational capitalism. Social movements seeking to institutionalize democratic globalization ought to challenge individual nation-states and transnational institutions to be more responsible to the needs of working people and the environment. The key is not to abandon the nation-state but rather to articulate progressive agendas that foreground the struggle for socialist democracy so that workers do not fall prey to the ideological notion that what is good for their exploiters is good for them. Only in this way will workers be able to succeed in their coordinated national efforts to build democratic transnational institutions.

Interestingly, such efforts are clearly under way. The anti-WTO protests that occurred in November 1999 announced to the world that corporate-organized and -controlled globalization will not go unchallenged. Although the protesters represented diverse national and international labor, environmental, and human rights organizations and, as indicated in my introduction, diverse political perspectives, they nevertheless demonstrated remarkable concern for one another's issues. Corporate globalization has in this way not only made it possible for transnational corporations to reap enormous profits; it has also fostered among those whose lives it transforms a growing awareness that nation-based politics are not sufficient to challenge transnational capitalist power.

> The laboring classes in the North and the South have begun to realize that their struggles against the adverse effects of globalization must take on a transnational perspective and that they may even need to engage in transnational organizing. Moreover, most of the new social movements, from the women's rights and gay movements to the environmental and indigenous movements, have a transnational perspective and can even be characterized in many ways as transnational movements or ideologies. In the long term the question is whether these movements can begin to coalesce and build a transnational platform to challenge capital and to make the new global economy serve the needs of the many rather than the interests of the rich and powerful, as it currently does. (Burbach and Robinson 1999:37–38)

In this regard, West's post-*Evasion*, post-Marxist, prophetic pragmatism may provide little assistance. Although West indicated in 1994 that he "loathed nationalism" (1994:70), his post-*Evasion* political work has become almost completely U.S. centered. In the context of capital's ratcheting down of labor and the Democratic and Republican anti–New Deal consensus (a one-party state?), West now places the aim of unifying a nation divided by class at the center of the programmatic essays in his *New York Times* best-seller *Race Matters, The War against Parents,* and *The Future of American Progressivism.* Whereas West was previously concerned with building an internationally based working-class movement against global capital, he is now concerned with creating a "freer, more efficient, and stable America"; with "furthering the public interest of the nation"; and with restoring "America's stock of social and human capital," "recaptur[ing] the American dream," "democratiz[ing] the American economy and reenergiz[ing] American democracy" (West 1993a:7, 24; Hewlett and West 1998:53, 87; Unger and West 1998:93). As far as living conditions in other countries are concerned, Hewlett and West say that there is little we can do to help and, in terms of our own lives, not much reason to try, for growing class inequalities in the United States have more to do with "the overwhelming greed of American managers" than with capital's pursuit of cheap labor and lives in other nations (1998:80). It is precisely in his efforts to "save" the United States from social balkanization, however—a task that must send shivers through parents and children around the world who make the goods required to realize the American Dream and who suffer the violence of U.S.-sponsored warfare and repression—that West's postsocialist/liberal/conservative politics do not break with the project of reforming capitalist ideologies and institutions in a manner that serves the dominant factions of American capital.[14]

In *The Future of American Progressivism* Unger and West argue that "to understand your country you must love it. To love it you must, in a sense, accept it. To accept it as it is, however, is to betray it. To accept your country without betraying it, you must love it for that in it which shows what it might become" (1998:93). What it might become, however, is something that can be fully achieved only if Americans identify fully with citizens around the world struggling to create a global economy that actively promotes, rather than constantly subverts, human rights, justice, and peace.[15]

West's nationalist framework, as well as his tendencies to abstract the categories of democracy, individuality, and freedom from the class relations that determine their practical realization, to transform political and economic problems into cultural and psychological problems, and to seek a middle path between fundamentally opposing social, political, and economic alternatives, is expressed in the programmatic essays contained in *Race Matters,* essays I examined in chapter 4, and in *The War against Parents* and *The Future of American Progressivism.* These books represent the clearest articulation to date of West's post-Marxist progressive pragmatist politics. It is with an examination of these works that I conclude my study of prophetic pragmatism.

7. Prophetic Pragmatism and the American Evasion of Class Struggle

> Class politics must be the prism through which black politics are elaborated.
> —Cornel West, "Left Strategies Today" (1986)

In *The War against Parents,* Hewlett and West continue to develop the post-Marxist, post-liberal/conservative politics West initially formulated in *Race Matters.* In *The War against Parents* Hewlett and West describe the problems facing parents in America, explain the factors they contend have created these problems, and propose a program to support the "ultimate non-market activity" of raising children (1998:35). As was indicated in chapter 1, *The War against Parents* has received widespread praise from politicians, businesspersons, social scientists, religious leaders, psychologists, and community activists for making a vital contribution to our understanding of and response to the increasing difficulties many parents face in raising psychologically, intellectually, and ethically well-developed children who are able to contribute to society. Hewlett and West tell us that, although many factors have been cited "to explain why Americans are newly isolated, distrustful, and depoliticized, newly 'bowling' alone rather than in leagues, . . . no one has gone upstream to the source of the problem—the huge erosion of the parental role. When parenting breaks down, the mechanism that transmits self-love is shattered, and this seriously compromises society's ability to pass from one generation to the next the values of compassion and commitment to others, which are the essential raw material of community-building and citizenship" (51). The costs associated with poor parenting are not only personal and familial but also national.

> If the center of this nation is to hold, we have to learn to give new and self-conscious value to the art and practice of parenting. It can no longer be left to invisible female labor or the tender mercies of the market. Make no mistake about

> it: the work of moms and dads is of utmost importance to our nation. . . . By tapping into the latent strength of our democratic processes, we craft a parents' movement that will send America's 62 million parents to the polls. This will have the magical effect of tilting our entire political culture in a direction that supports and values adults raising children. . . . The project of giving new status and support to mothers and fathers has extraordinary potential because of the ways in which the parent-child bond is the most fundamental building block in human society. When this is hollowed out, the wellspring of care and commitment dries up, and this has a huge impact beyond the home: community life shrivels up, and so does our democracy. America's stock of social and human capital becomes dangerously depleted. If we can produce this magical parent power, we can go to the very heart of our darkness and make the center hold. . . . What better project to revitalize our republic than giving strength and succor to parents so that they can weave the web of care that is so vital to our nation. (41, 53, 258)

After Hewlett and West describe "the grim economic reality that profoundly debilitates American parents and their children," they proceed to analyze various factors that social scientists claim are responsible for this reality (1998:87). Following the mode of argumentation that West initially developed in *Race Matters,* they investigate the causes of the problems facing American parents by examining the respective strengths and weaknesses of liberal and conservative perspectives. On the one hand, liberals rightly identify corporate downsizing, declining wages, and government cutbacks to social programs that benefit low- and middle-income families, but they wrongly emphasize personal freedom to such an extent that, for example, liberal feminists now place career aspirations over mothering responsibilities (37). Liberals have contributed to the destruction of the nuclear family, a mode of reproduction that Hewlett and West identify as fundamental to society, by creating bureaucratically dominated child-care centers that remove children from their biological parents, media that represent parents as fools and celebrate single parenthood, and social programs that discourage fathers from participating equally with mothers in the task of raising children. On the other hand, conservatives rightly identify some of the problems with liberal political theories, but they wrongly believe that the market provides, on its own and without regulation, all the financial, educational, and environmental resources that parents need to raise their children well.

There is, however, one factor that Hewlett and West contend is key to understanding why American families have fallen on hard times. The real cause of the declining wages and social insecurity is neither international capitalist competition; the drive to secure higher rates of return on investments by gaining access to cheaper resources, especially cheaper labor; the organization of productive and consumptive relations for the purpose of capital accumulation; nor heterosexism, racism, nationalism, or militarism. Although these factors may in some ways and in some instances have contributed to the dissolution of the American Dream and to the dramatic growth in inequalities over the past thirty years, they are not the most important factors:

> Yes, there is a new, fiercely competitive global economy and this has the potential of producing downward pressure on wages. However, despite this logical connection, it turns out that the central cause of falling income levels and heightened insecurity is the overweening greed of American managers, not Korean textile workers or Russian scientists. In fact, all the cruel belt-tightening, all of the new stress and fear, have had absolutely no impact on America's competitive position in the world. Smaller paychecks for 80 percent of workers have surely shaved an enormous amount off the wage bill, but this huge savings has merely been transferred to the pockets of managers. From the important vantage point of competitive strength, the entire debilitating exercise has been irrelevant. (80)

Managerial greed, pure and simple, is dissolving the American Dream. Indeed, there is no question that American managerial and CEO greed has fueled the generally downward trend in wages and wealth for American workers: "CEO wages (cash payments including bonuses) grew 44.6% from 1989 to 1997, far exceeding the growth in any other occupation. These CEO wages grew 36.6% just in the recovery years from 1992 to 1997 (Mishel, Bernstein, and Schmitt 1999:209). Moreover, "the growth of CEO pay has been even larger when one includes all of the components of direct compensation: salaries, bonuses, incentive awards, stock options exercised, stock granted, and so on. The full compensation of CEOs actually doubled over the 1989–97 period, growing 71% in the 1992–97 recovery. Even lesser-paid CEOs at the 25th percentile saw a 48.8% compensation growth in the recovery" (210–11). By 1997 the average "CEO worked half a week to earn what an average worker earned in 52 weeks" (211).

What is the solution to the specific problem of American managerial greed and the consequent problems associated with falling incomes and rising insecurity? Hewlett and West propose what they call "A Parents' Bill of Rights." A parents' movement could mobilize a bloc of 62 million voters that would have the power to move this country toward policies supportive of raising healthy children. Parent power, they write, "can be a powerful healing force in American society. The deep and desperate concerns of parents cross the usual divides of gender, race, and class and thus feed a common vision and seed a common ground in ways that are rare and precious in our centrifugal society" (Hewlett and West 1998:53). Hewlett and West model their "Parents' Bill of Rights" on the GI Bill, a government-sponsored program that played a vital role in supporting the unprecedented expansion of the middle class after World War II.

> The GI Bill is a powerful model for parents because it encompasses several important principles. First, it was constructed as a set of *universal benefits* that were available to all veterans—women as well as men, blacks as well as whites—who had fought for their country during World War II (and, later, the Korean and Vietnam wars). Second, these benefits were *enormously generous.* The idea was to pay homage to the significance of what these veterans had done by risking their lives for their country. Third, the individual benefits that made up the programs were tremendously *enabling and empowering:* the educational benefits enhanced earning power, and the housing benefits encouraged veterans to buy their own homes. GIs were not warehoused in public projects; instead, they were given the tools to build lives they could be proud of. Finally, when all was said and done, the GI Bill was a stunningly successful investment that immeasurably *boosted the nation's economic well-being.* In concrete terms, the government received eight dollars back for every dollar spent, and who can quantify the value of ten Nobel prizes? (229)

Drawing from the reciprocally supportive principles that informed the GI Bill, Hewlett and West propose a parents' Bill of Rights that specifies a combination of tax adjustments, wage increases, voting rights for parents, child care, health care, regulations on the media, and changes in the legal structure that support the preservation of the two-parent, heterosexual nuclear family. As their programmatic categories indicate, their bill is designed to ensure that these parents enjoy the following benefits through the corresponding provisions: first, more time with their children, provided by paid parental leave, family friendly workplaces, and a safety net; second, economic security, provided by living-wage laws, job opportunities, and housing assistance; third, increased voting power, provided by incentives to vote and votes for children; fourth, increased legal support for heterosexual marriages and adoption assistance; fifth, a nurturing environment, including quality schooling, and violence- and drug-free neighborhoods; and finally, honor and dignity for parents, provided by creating an index of parent well-being, a National Parents' Day, and sundry social and political advantages. Hewlett and West recognize that achieving these goals will not be easy, but they hope that their

> book will provide the spark to ignite a tinderbox of passion in the hearts and minds of parents—that it will give moms and dads the urgent energy to pull together, to cross those rifts of color and class and find the collective strength to ask for and take what is their due. For it is only with a groundswell of grassroots support that our Parents' Bill of Rights will become a reality. When the voices of America's 62 million parents unite and grow into a roar, then and only

> then will parents obtain the support they yearn for and so richly deserve. If parents can mobilize behind our Bill of Rights, it will vastly improve the circumstances of their lives, but it will also transform our democracy, for we are not talking about narrow interest-group politics here. We are all stakeholders in this critical endeavor. (1998:257)

Hewlett and West mark out what they admit is an ambitious program for rebuilding American communities. They have correctly and carefully described the increasing difficulties that a growing proportion of working-class Americans face in making ends meet and in creating the quality time, acquiring the personal resources, and enjoying the societal support that have been and remain key to raising children well. Their parents' Bill of Rights certainly would, if implemented, improve the ability of most working-class Americans to raise their children. Hewlett and West rightly note that "American moms and dads are expected to do a stellar job without the benefits of a living wage, medical coverage, decent child care, or parenting leave" (1998:28), a situation quite different from that in most wealthy capitalist nations, where parents see a much greater percentage of their tax money returned in the form of programs that are responsive to their needs.

Nevertheless, their post-liberal/conservative politics begin to dissolve on closer analysis. For example, although Hewlett and West make what amounts to a liberal critique of conservatives and a conservative critique of liberals, in the end their program is thoroughly liberal; indeed, it is a conservative's nightmare of government spending and tax cuts that, from a conservative perspective, benefit the wrong people—that is, the economically lower 90 percent of the population. Of course, this is one of their program's strengths; if anything, their policies do not go far enough to redistribute wealth that is currently concentrated at the top. Any redistribution of resources to working-class citizens constitutes a step in the right direction, that is, to the left. However, the real problems with their analyses and proposals, as I will elaborate, run much deeper than the fact that they advance a mild-mannered liberal agenda. Moreover, the real problems do not lie in their view of parents as a potentially significant voting bloc, which, as Joan Walsh indicates (1998:11), ignores the fact that parents' interests are divided, as are the interests of all citizens, by opposing class interests, a point to which I return later. Nor do these problems lie in the proposal that Walsh correctly designates as thoroughly antidemocratic: giving parents the right to cast votes for their children, a proposal that raises, among other questions, the matter of "who gets to cast the votes, mom or dad? And why not extra votes for grandparents, or people who work with kids?" (ibid.). The issue is even thornier, however. What about parents under eighteen? Would they get to cast a vote for themselves and their children, while their own parents would cast a vote for them? And what about adults who remain dependents beyond the age of eighteen? Nor do these deeper problems lie in Hewlett and West's proposal for a compulsory ten-day paternity leave to "give" fathers time to bond with their newborn sons and daughters—apparently whether they want to bond or not. As Walsh notes, "the fact that they have to make it compulsory will probably cheer skeptics of the fathers' rights movement, because it implicitly acknowledges that the vast majority of men don't take the parental leave provisions currently available to them" (12). Finally, these deeper problems do not arise because, as Walsh writes, "the something-for-everybody solution they craft to address these problems is muddled, self-contradictory and ultimately unconvincing," because "their moral diagnosis will enrage liberals, [while] their policy prescription will drive away conservatives," or because "the book leaves us no closer to a family agenda than before they began" (13), although these assessments are accurate. For example, in one section Hewlett and West evoke Rush Limbaugh by criticizing unnamed feminist texts, individuals, and organizations for encouraging "women to clone the male competitive model in the marketplace," even though in another section they argue that one goal of their project is to enable women "to stay on their career ladders during the childbearing years" (1998:37, 39). They contend that culture has contributed to increasing rates of teen pregnancy even though they also note that these rates have decreased over the last thirty years. They criticize feminists, psychologists, sociologists, and social workers for overstating the problem of child abuse, but they also point out that in 1996 "there were over 3 million reported cases of child abuse and neglect—a figure that is up 367 percent since 1976" (166), numbers that make it difficult to see how one could "overstate" the personal and societal significance of this problem.

Rather, the most serious problems with *The War against Parents,* as well as with *Race Matters* and, as I will elaborate, *The Future of American Progressivism,* derive from the unexamined presuppositions that inform its analyses, arguments, and proposals. These presuppositions involve the following: first, Hewlett and West's conception of the immediate post–World War II era as America's "Golden Age"; second, their conception of the heterosexual nuclear family as the foundation stone of society and their justification of this conception on the basis of sociobiological and essentializing psychological arguments and presuppositions; third, their emphasis on redistributing wealth rather than reorganizing the mode of its production; fourth, their focus on the United States as the fundamental framework for their articulation of progressive politics; fifth, their failure to address the role that racism plays in the degradation of socioeconomic conditions for black and nonblack workers and the importance of fighting racism to improve these conditions; and finally, their claim that liberals and conservatives represent significantly different political perspectives when in fact they are unified in affirming the free market as the foundation of freedom.

The Politics of Nostalgia

In discussing the problems currently confronting America's parents, Hewlett and West establish their argument largely through reference to the "Golden Age" of American history, the period immediately following World War II. Not only did this period see the greatest expansion of the middle-class in American history; in addition, they argue, it was characterized by, among other things, a culture that did not trash parenting, with the "traditional" family enjoying a positive image in movies such as *April in Paris* (1952), *Calamity Jane* (1953), *A Bundle of Joy* (1956), *The Pajama Party* (1957), and *The Teacher's Pet* (1959) and in television shows such as *Father Knows Best, I Love Lucy, Ozzie and Harriet, The Donna Reed Show, The Life of Riley,* and *Good Times.* Hewlett and West also note that these movies and television programs were quite often sexist and thus uncritically represented and supported a gendered division of labor, property, and power. In terms of their project, however, the important point is that these narratives "gave tremendous honor and respect to the roles of mom and dad" and that their "praise of parents created a kind of public affirmation of the parental role that served to enhance the authority accorded to mothers and fathers" (Hewlett and West 1998:130). Indeed, the work of raising children found generous support not just in culture but also in government programs, most notably the GI Bill, tax relief to married couples with and without children, and business-labor contracts that included regular wage increases, job security, health care, and retirement benefits. Today, however, businesses show little if any allegiance to workers as they downsize, outsource, and cut back workers, leaving fewer and fewer with the kind of socioeconomic stability they previously enjoyed. Government legislation, programs, and taxes do not provide anywhere near the kind and quality of support that parents received for almost thirty years following World War II. Moreover, business and government are not the only sectors that no longer support working parents; culture, too, has turned its back. Movies such as *Honey, I Shrunk the Kids* (1989), *Home Alone* (1990), and *House Arrest* (1996), not to mention *Thelma and Louise,* as well as television shows such as *My So-Called Life, Married with Children,* and *Party of Five,* all denigrate parenting, and as Hewlett and West continually remind us, they are especially hard on fathers. They are part of what Hewlett and West believe is a father-bashing culture (a claim that is prima facie curious since fathers—men—do almost all the physical bashing of women, children, and other men). The bottom line is that from roughly 1945 to 1970 culture, government, and business did something they by and large no longer do: support parents in their efforts to raise children. Given how Hewlett and West view this period, it comes as no surprise that their work is permeated by a nostalgic desire to "regain," "recover," and "reestablish" what used to be.

Of course, all was not well during this era, despite what the media, television, and movies suggested and what Hewlett and West argue. For many, life was far from golden during this "Golden Age," which is why blacks, women, gays and lesbians, as well as Native American, Asian, and Hispanic citizens, demonstrated in the streets and took over mainstream institutions, organizing militant opposition to the existing socioeconomic order of things. The latter part of this period saw this dissatisfaction manifest itself in several movements and organizations, including the civil rights movement; the Black Power movement; the Student Non-Violent Coordinating Committee; feminist, environmental, antiwar, antimilitarism, antinuclear, anti-apartheid, vegetarian, counterculture, and back-to-the-land movements; the Chicano/a movement; La Raza; the push for Puerto Rican independence; Students for a Democratic Society; the American Indian Movement; the United Farm Workers; and the Dodge Revolutionary Union. In addition, America's "Golden Age" was predicated on precisely what is most problematically absent from Hewlett and West's analyses, arguments, and proposals: the U.S. military subjugation and corporate exploitation of parents and children all over the world, an absence that is evident in their cold war claim that the "GIs who fought in World War II were vitally important in maintaining America's national security, risking their lives to defeat fascism and in so doing making the western world safe for democracy" (1998:230).[1] Of course, hundreds of thousands of U.S. soldiers fought and thousands died fighting the Axis powers, but Hewlett and West's claim that they did so to maintain something called "national security" and to ensure a place for democracy in the Western world is true only if we define national security as the security of U.S. capital, the Western world as global capitalism, and democracy as the right to vote, speak, assemble, bear arms, look for work, and pay state and federal taxes. But Hewlett and West do not clarify the social meaning of these concepts. What is clear, however, is that West no longer assumes, as he explicitly did in *Prophesy Deliverance,* first, that whereas "the American and French Revolutions did contain allusions to the norms of individuality and democracy," their "self-understanding [of these claims] constitute[d] the liberal vision within capitalist civilization," a "vision [that] was—and remains—the grandest vision capitalist civilization has to offer," and second (and most significantly for my point here), that this liberal capitalist vision of individuality and democracy was and "is, for the most part, limited to the sphere of government affairs, corrupted by the institutionalization and legitimation of white male supremacy, and rendered nearly obsolete by unaccountable economic power principally in the form of private multinational corporations" (1982:125). Again, in *Prophesy Deliverance* West contended that capitalism is "an *antidemocratic* mode of socioeconomic organization" because it removes control over the means and fruits of production from those who actually use and produce them; that capitalism "is inseparable from imperialism"; and that the United States has been since World War II and remains to this day the principal financial, political, and military power supporting the international capitalist system (122). If these claims are true, however, then on the basis of West's own former politics, his claim about U.S. soldiers' having fought for democracy appears to be ideological cover for capitalist operations. Of course, Hewlett and West do not view it as such, and we are left to conclude that their narrative is, just as bourgeois versions of individuality and democracy were, "the liberal vision within capitalist civilization" (125).

The Politics of Biological Determinism

Feminism is one of the numerous social movements that sought to expand the realm of democracy during the post–World War II "Golden Age" of American history. Feminism, a movement that in many respects grew out of and drew deeply from the civil rights movement, has criticized the same political, economic, and cultural arrangements that Hewlett and West say can improve life—or could do so, if divested of their sexism, heterosexism, religious chauvinism, ethnocentrism, and racism. After quoting a passage from a book by the evangelical leader Dr. Tony Evans, *Seven Promises of a Promise Keeper,* in which Evans asserts that men should not ask their wives' permission to assume their divinely ordained role but rather should simply take back this role, Hewlett and West reply that it "is difficult to read this passage without picking up a strong undertow of male arrogance" (1998:198–99). Certainly this and other related statements exhibit at least an "undertow" of male arrogance. Following their praise of the Promise Keepers and the Nation of Islam as serious, though deeply flawed, attempts to recover empowering "traditional" family values, they argue that "if the leaders of the Promise Keepers were to affirm homosexual and women's rights and stay out of the abortion wars, and if the leaders of the Nation of Islam were to repudiate anti-Semitism and patriarchy, it would be a giant step forward" (211). We might add that if they were to reject capitalist political economy, racist theories of humanity, militarism, consumerism, individualism, and neocolonial domination, then all would be fine. As will be come clear, Hewlett and West's rather generous, if not antimaterialist and utopian, reading of the Promise Keepers and the Nation of Islam derives from the fact that the authors share much in common with both organizations regarding matters of gender and class. Although both organizations provide powerful channels through which working-class white and black men have been able to express their frustrations over worsening social conditions and to find solace in facing them, the fact remains that these organizations are highly unlikely to break from their individualist, patriarchal, procapitalist biases. Indeed, I concur with Manning

Marable that they are much more likely to coalesce around right-wing agendas, if not protofascist populist ones (1998:161–82).

So committed are Hewlett and West to the "traditional" nuclear family as the most productive and nourishing structure within which to raise children that they dismiss the sexism that has "traditionally" characterized this historically particular mode of raising children with little more than a shrug of disapproval, downplaying the limitations and violence of this structure for women and children. Following presidential candidate Dan Quayle's lead, they criticize the fictional Murphy Brown and the real-life Madonna and Rosie O'Donnell for setting bad examples by choosing to raise children without the helpful hand of a father. They criticize child-care programs and nontraditional family structures, arguing that "whether we are talking about toddlers or teenagers, children desperately need a parent—preferably two of them [preferably male and female]—who will give them unconditional, devoted care over a long period of time" (1998:110). In addition, although they criticize the sexism and heterosexism promoted by the Promise Keepers and the Nation of Islam, their proposals, which they claim are based on the GI Bill's principle of *universality,* say nothing about supporting the legal right of gay men and lesbian women to marry, adopt, and raise children. In "Pro-Family Legal Structure," section 4 of their Bill of Rights, Hewlett and West indicate that they "are firmly convinced that most children benefit from the sustained loving attention of two parents," and they argue that "the best way of ensuring an increase in the number of two-parent families is to bolster the institution of marriage" (241). Throughout this entire section and the subsection on "adoption assistance," however, they say absolutely nothing about extending marriage and parental rights to gays and lesbians. Their democratic "sin" of excluding gays and lesbians from enjoying the same rights as every other citizen, rights that their own principles imply ought to be universal, may be one of omission, but it remains a sin just the same. The problem facing gays and lesbians is not merely a matter of preserving laws that protect their rights to marry and raise children, as responses to Hewlett and West's questionnaire suggest (222). Rather, it is a matter of establishing these laws in the first place. Hewlett and West's indifference, their virtual silence, to the matter of gay and lesbian civil rights, particularly rights of marriage and adoption, reveals their heterosexist difference. Their conservative anthropology truncates the universality of their proposal.

Perhaps this silence regarding gay and lesbian efforts to secure constitutional rights should come as no surprise. Hewlett and West defend the heterosexual nuclear family not through divine design, as the Promise Keepers and the Nation of Islam do, but through sociobiology, the "work by a group of scholars called the 'New Darwinians'" (1998:166). On the basis of this research, Hewlett and West contend that children develop best when raised by their biological parents, preferably both mother and father. Indeed, biology explains why "the parent-child bond is the strongest and most primeval of all human attachments" and why male and female children need both the nurturing and compassion of a mother and the strength and authority of a father (41).

Hewlett and West cite the animal psychologist Harry F. Harlow's experiments with monkeys and surrogate wire-mesh and terry-cloth "mothers," concluding from these experiments that the love of biologically unrelated adults and children is no substitute for the love of biologically related parents and children (1998:41). They then ask, "Should we be surprised by the connection between father absence and child abuse?" (166)—assuming, of course, that there is a causal connection and not merely a correlation; after all, children may be abused more frequently in the absence of a father because the adults left to raise that child are poor and the frustration of being poor is often taken out on those who are within reach. Nevertheless, Hewlett and West maintain that there is a direct causal connection, in fact a series of them: "Recent work by a group of scholars called the New Darwinians reminds us that as a species, we are grounded in genetic self-interest. Biological parents have unique genetic investments in their children and as a result will care much more profoundly for them than [will] substitute parents" (ibid.). Citing a single study, they argue that surrogate parents are more likely to commit acts of abuse than biological parents. A "society that relies increasingly on substitute parents is one that veers increasingly toward violence" (ibid.). It's that simple. They conclude by quoting from *Family and Nation* (1986), in which Daniel Patrick Moynihan reverses his earlier argument that family dissolution is primarily caused by poverty and argues instead that impoverishment is primarily caused by the absence of a father. Without the father's authoritative presence, a community "asks for and gets chaos," a rather ominous justification for police occupation, incarceration, and the rollback of the Bill of Rights (in Hewlett and West 1998:167).[2]

Hewlett and West's claims regarding the biological basis of good parenting and children's developmental needs for a father are thinly supported and weakly explained, but their proposals for, among other things, compulsory paternity leave to "enable" fathers to bond with their children and sanctions on noncustodial parents to "encourage" their participation in raising their own biological progeny strongly suggest that, contrary to the claims made by New Darwinians, "genetic self-interest" and "unique genetic investments in their children" fail to ensure that biological parents will commit themselves to raising their "genetic investments." If parents, especially the male parent, must be bribed and coerced to raise their own offspring, then there appears to be little reason to suppose that biological parents will be superior to substitute parents. Indeed, the evidence marshaled in support of their claim regarding biological versus surrogate parents does not strongly support claims for a causal relationship between biology and parenting. Even though some studies may show that children raised by biologically unrelated parents are more likely to be abused than children raised by biologically related parents, this may tell us more about the average socioeconomic differences between these two parental categories and the relative support that each receives from society than it does about the presence of "genetic investment."

The notion that individuals possess a genetic interest in the perpetuation of their own "individual" genes is problematic for several reasons. First, it does not explain why individuals who mistakenly believe they are raising their own offspring (e.g., when hospital workers mistakenly give children to the wrong parents) relate to their children *as if* they had a real genetic investment—that is, as if the children were their "own." Second, if, as Hewlett and West and the New Darwinians contend, the genetic investment that biological parents have in their children tends to make them much more caring parents than substitutes are, then we might ask why many biologically related parents, especially fathers, psychologically abuse, physically injure, or simply abandon responsibility for raising these "investments." How are such widespread acts explainable on the basis of sociobiological presuppositions? Assuming that most parents who mistreat their biologically related children are not suffering from genetic abnormalities that compel them, on the one hand, to perpetuate their own genes by having children and, on the other, to commit "genetic suicide" by terminating their genetic heirs, then we may surmise that nonbiological factors matter as much as, if not more than, biological factors with regard to raising children. Third, this claim about biological parents' genetic investments assumes that reproduction of the individual assumes priority over reproduction of the species. To argue as much is to engage in the kind of biological reductionism that characterizes both the old and new social Darwinism and that has been used to justify social relations of the most oppressive kind (see Lewontin, Rose, and Kamin 1984; Lerner 1992; Lewontin 1991). Assuming that individuals have a genetic interest in reproducing not the species but their own individuality provides a sound basis for arguing not only that the nuclear family is the most "natural" institution for raising one's own children but also that competition between individuals—and by extension, competition between privately owned corporations to accumulate and appropriate private property—is a "natural" condition. Indeed, the entire regime of capitalist relations of production and consumption, the war of all against all, is nothing other than a social expression of a genetic compulsion to reproduce one's particular genes. It does not take much reflection to appreciate the thoroughly conservative, even reactionary, nature of this argument and, in political terms, its thoroughly antisocialist, procapitalist bias. If we are genetically predisposed to reproduce our individual genes, as Hewlett and West contend, if we are fundamentally motivated by genetic self-interest, then any attempts to organize our social relations on the basis of nonindividualist, nonaccumulative, nonegoistic principles would require us to swim against our genetic disposition (a choice Hewlett and West attack in their defense of heterosexual parenting). Finally, and perhaps most important, even if it were proven that adults who are biologically related to the children they raise are more likely than others to care for and not abuse those children—in short, even if, as Freud once remarked, "biology is destiny"—the question before humanity has been and remains whether and to what degree biology should determine our destiny.

According to Hewlett and West, the answer to this question, at least with regard to raising children, decidedly favors biology (or at least their interpretation of the meaning of biology, especially genetics). Not only do they argue that children are best raised by their biological parents, but they also suggest that there is something like a "natural" division of capacities between males and females that explains why children will develop the highest level of maturity if they are raised by a father and a mother. Citing psychologist Carol Gilligan, they write that "men gravitate toward the instrumental and the impersonal and emphasize abstract principles, while women lean toward intimacy and caring and give priority to human relationships" (1998:37). Just as Moral Majority leader Jerry Falwell and Nation of Islam leader Louis Farrakhan contend that the divinely designed gendered division of labor does not mean that women's roles are any less valuable than men's roles within the political economy of this division (men and women are still equal in the eyes of God), Gilligan is also quick to note, as Hewlett and West approvingly report, that "the female 'care' voice is not inferior to the male 'instrumental' voice, as it is often treated in psychological theory; it is simply different—different and enormously important" (ibid.; see also Farrakhan 1993:58, 59). The "voice of care," Hewlett and West write, "has played a critical role in producing a healthy equilibrium between individual and community in American society. Because it balances self with other and tempers market values with nonmarket values, it has gone some distance toward redeeming the urgent greed that is the spirit of capitalism" (ibid.). Women have been and generally remain society's backbone, "offering," gratis, the labor required to produce the elemental ingredient of all societies, human beings, as well as the tenderness, compassion, and care needed to soothe and console sons, daughters, and men ravaged by the less than tender, compassionate, and caring operations of the market. "At least in the middle classes, a clear division of labor between the sexes allowed women to devote huge amounts of time to nourishing and nurturing: they read bedtime stories, helped with homework, wrapped presents, attended parent-teacher conferences, and taught Sunday school" (ibid.). By the late 1960s and early 1970s, however, this "traditional" gendered division of labor, property, and power "went by the board as American society underwent a sea change" (ibid.).

What produced this change? According to Hewlett and West, the most notable causes were a "liberation movement that often encouraged women to clone the male competitive model in the marketplace" and "a new set of economic pressures that increasingly required both parents to be in the paid labor force to sustain any semblance of middle-class life" (ibid.). They admit that these changes were in many respects enormously progressive seen against the rigidity of the traditional—that is, patriarchal—division of labor, property, and authority. The "invisible labor of women comprised nothing less than the bedrock of America's prosperity and power" (Hewlett and West 1998:38). Although the "female voice of care" is important, indeed essential, to the creation of family and community, "it is clear that relying on free and invisible female labor as the wellspring of our social and human capital no longer works. Modern women are intent on a fair measure of self-realization, and besides," they add in a nod to necessity that amounts to a naturalization of the decline in worker's power, "the economic facts of family life preclude a return to traditional structures" (38–39).

Hewlett and West do not, however, say anything about wage compensation for the work of raising children, whether that work is done by a male or female. Nor do they consider that what they identify as the "female voice of care" might not reflect women's ontological nature but rather indicate their subordinate position in the domestic division of labor. Rather, Hewlett and West want to show that each family needs both an adult male and an adult female because each brings particular qualities to the project of raising children. They criticize Madonna, Rosie O'Donnell, and Diane Keaton for having made single motherhood "a chic thing to do—the ultimate liberated act of a strong woman"—and argue, again without much in the way of empirical substantiation, that although "Madonna may not want to deal with a male partner . . . [,] most children do much better in life when they can count on the loving attention of both a mother and a father" (1998:34, 35). The women's movement, too, is culpable for the degradation of fathering.

> Over the past three decades, important segments of public opinion have become convinced that fathers don't matter—a point of view encouraged by modern feminism, which for all its enormous value has indulged in some excesses. Most damaging has been a set of attitudes that center on the expendability of men. Ideas that women don't need men, women can do whatever they want without men, men are responsible for all the evil in the world, children need only a loving mother, and men only teach children how to be patriarchal and militaristic have become standard fare on the cutting edge of the women's movement. (161)

Interestingly, though perhaps not accidentally, given Hewlett and West's New Darwinian analysis of gender, this is precisely what Falwell, Limbaugh, Farrakhan, and Evans also contend.

Ultimately Harlow's monkey experiments, Gilligan's essentializing psychology, the little-known scientific studies, sweeping generalizations, biological reductionism, and simplified causal explanations are all deployed in support of one claim: David Popenoe's assertion that "on the whole, two parents—a father and a mother—are better for the child than one parent'" (in Hewlett and West 1998:164), although, curiously, they do not consider how children raised by more than two adults might fair. The main point, however, the point around which everything Hewlett and West write in *The War against Parents* pivots, is that our nation's well-being depends on having mothers and fathers raise their own biological children.

Nevertheless, it is far from "overwhelmingly" evident that children must be raised by a female/mother and a male/father to develop into mature adults. Although Hewlett and West say little regarding what men specifically bring to the work of raising children and less regarding what men *ought* to bring, they do suggest, by way of Gilligan and Moynihan, that men bring "instrumentality" and "authority" to the parent-child relationship, capacities women presumably lack as a result, again presumably, of their "biological constitution." But evidence abounds that women, heterosexual or homosexual, are perfectly capable of embodying, modeling, and teaching all the skills and abilities children need to learn to become loving, compassionate, self-confident, and competent friends, partners, workers, citizens, and even parents. Evidence also abounds that women are, just as the "male-bashing feminists" contend, as capable as men of being aggressive, competitive, and assertive. Interestingly, Hewlett and West concede as much (no doubt unintentionally) when they contend that modern feminists have encouraged women to imitate the male competitive model in the working world, in other words, that biological females can act just like biological males. It short, it is not biology but education, not genetic codes but social relations, that really matters when it comes to the organization and division of labor, property, and authority.

I make these points not because I think men should not be involved in raising children. Indeed, men should be as involved as women in raising children, although simply passing Hewlett and West's proposed compulsory paid ten-day paternal leave law probably will not ensure such involvement. Rather, I raise these points, first, because I am highly suspicious of Hewlett and West's return to biology as the purported basis for determining the proper order of our social relations, institutions, and practices; second, because I am not persuaded that the two-parent, heterosexual family is the only, let alone the best, means for raising what Hewlett and West call America's "human capital"; and third, because their argument is quite straightforwardly heterosexist and contrary to the principle of universality on which stands or falls any political agenda worthy of the title "progressive." Assuming that men and women are equally capable of developing the full range of human capacities, would it not be better for children if all adult citizens were enabled institutionally to participate more fully in the work of raising children? Would it not be better if, to paraphrase Hillary Clinton, the entire tribe were to assume responsibility for raising children?

The Politics of National Redistribution

Hewlett and West's post–World War II narrative and New Darwinian arguments are not the only problems with *The War against Parents.* As indicated previously, Hewlett and West contend that the most significant cause of growing social insecurity and economic instability for most Americans is not private ownership of the means of production, international capitalist competition for increased profits, militarism, nationalism, racism, or sexism. Rather, the fundamental cause of the American Dream's dissolution is "managerial greed" (Hewlett and West 1998:61). In short, it "all seems to boil down to pure, unadulterated [managerial] greed" (83), a claim they also share with Farrakhan (1993:29–35).

To establish this claim, Hewlett and West compare the United States to other rich capitalist nations and quite rightly report that its distribution of financial wealth is by far the most unequal, a claim supported by the Economic Policy Institute's study *The State of Working America: 1998–99* (Mishel, Bernstein, and Schmitt 1999). And certainly the cultural peculiarities of the United States have much to do with the fact that U.S. managers and CEOs feel much less guilty, if they feel guilty at all, than do managers and CEOs from other nations about milking every last drop of value from workers (212–14). There is certainly a strong case to be made that the U.S. ruling class exploits "its own" workers at least as ruthlessly as any other rich First World capitalist ruling-class leaders exploit "their own" workers (of course, this reveals more than a little about the organizational and ideological weaknesses of American workers). Even assuming that American CEOs are especially or even exceptionally greedy, however, arguing that the main cause of economic decline for workers is managerial greed rather than private ownership of the means of production and the organization of production for the purpose of making capital makes reversing this decline and improving everyday conditions of life seem to be a matter of redistributing wealth more equitably rather than a matter of reorganizing the mode by which wealth is produced in the first place. The source of the difficulties that most parents in America now face trying to raise their children well thus becomes not exploitation of the international working class but the unfair exploitation of U.S. workers by U.S. managers and CEOs. If we could manage managerial greed and distribute wealth more equitably, if only we could, as Hewlett and West contend, "reintroduce notions of fairness and equity in the labor market," we might then "reinvent the social contract and recapture the American Dream" (87). And what of this dream for parents and children in China, Russia, and Mexico whose labor and lives are consumed producing jackets for Liz Claiborne, computer chips for Intel, sweaters for Kathie Lee Gifford, Air Jordans for Nike, and Christmas toys for Toys "R" Us?

Even assuming a democratic redistribution of wealth along the liberal lines of Hewlett and West's proposals, conditions of labor and life for parents and children around the world would not merely remain unchanged; if the United States continues its current levels of consumption at home and its financial and military policies abroad, these conditions will probably worsen. In an age in which corporations employ beleaguered parents and children worldwide to produce commodities for sale around the world, Hewlett and West concern themselves only with beleaguered parents and children in the United States. If implemented, Hewlett and West's parents' Bill of Rights, like Unger and West's progressive agenda, would certainly improve living conditions dramatically for most working-class parents here, though certainly not all. Arguing for and institutionalizing agendas that call for the state to spend more tax-payer money on programs that benefit the majority of tax payers rather than only the wealthiest 10 percent of U.S. citizens ought to be a key component of any progressive political agenda. Although President Clinton's fiscal year 2000 budget specifies $262 billion for defense (with a projected increase to $301 billion by 2004), health and human services are to receive only $42 billion; housing and urban development, $34 billion; education, $32 billion; labor, $11 billion; and environmental protection, $7 billion. Clearly the quality of life for most working-class citizens would be significantly improved by shifting spending from the military to these other categories. Moreover, increasing taxes on the wealthiest Americans, the richest 1 percent, even a couple of percentage points would greatly increase tax revenues available for programs beneficial to workers and nonworking poor.

Such "reforms," implemented within the limits of private property, are in fact key to replacing "the whole system" (Unger and West 1998:29). As I have argued throughout this work, reforms ought to be seen not as revolution's "Other," to borrow from pop deconstruction, but rather as its political prerequisite. The important political dividing line is not between reform and revolution, between piecemeal improvement and total replacement. Rather, the deep political dividing line is between reform toward socialism versus reform toward preservation of the existing system of private property. Alternatively, as West argued in *Prophesy Deliverance,* the line stands between those who presuppose "the existing system of production" as the unsurpassable transformative horizon and those who believe that capitalism negates democracy because it denies workers the right to control the social conditions of their own production (112). Social agendas that increase the control working people exercise over the conditions of their own lives and improve the quality of these conditions ought to be supported. What remains key, however, is to link such agendas to the larger struggle to reorganize capitalist political economy, a political economy that can be successfully challenged only by a united international movement against private control of collectively generated wealth.

Unfortunately, Hewlett and West's narrative of the post–World War II era conveniently excludes any analysis of the relationship between the "bad life" that people around the world endured as they labored in hellish sweatshops, mines, and plantations to create a large portion of the wealth that supported the good life here. According to their narrative, the good old days were made possible primarily by a war that made the Western world safe for democracy, by hard work, and by the GI Bill, which rewarded soldiers for their service to America. Their narrative fails to tell how the middle-class expansion in the United States was in no small measure made possible by U.S. military subjugation and corporate exploitation of people around the world. It thus comes as little surprise that when Hewlett and West make their proposals for improving the lives of parents, they not only remain silent about living conditions for parents in other countries, but they explicitly disavow themselves and their readers of any responsibility for these conditions, saying that we "clearly cannot control wage levels in Korea, Mexico, or Russia" (1998:87). As with Unger and West's *Future of American Progressivism*, Hewlett and West's *War against Parents* says little more than this about the links between rich, developed nations and poor, underdeveloped ones, between the American Dream here and the nightmare there.

In *One World, Ready or Not*, William Greider describes the May 10, 1993, fire that consumed a Kader Industrial Toy Company factory just outside the city limits of Bangkok: "The official count was 188 dead, 469 injured, but the actual toll was undoubtedly much higher since the four-story buildings had collapsed swiftly in the intense heat and many bodies were incinerated. Some of the missing were never found; others fled home to their villages. All but fourteen of the dead were women, most of them young, some as young as thirteen years old" (1997:337). The Kader fire was among the worst industrial disasters in the history of capitalism, but similar incidents are occurring with increasing frequency as capital seeks to lower production costs by avoiding the expenses associated with ensuring workers' health and safety. Not surprisingly, the fire and deaths received almost no attention from the corporate-owned and -controlled media and produced no "meaningful political responses or even shame among [First World] consumers. The indifference of the leading [U.S.] newspapers merely reflected the tastes of their readers, who might be moved by human suffering in their own communities but were inured to news of recurring calamities in distant places" (338). The rule seems to be something like "If it did not happen to me (or to those whom I know), it did not happen."

Perhaps, adds Greider, the Kader conflagration would have touched more citizens if they had seen photos of the charred bodies among such recognizable household dolls as Bugs Bunny, Bart Simpson, Big Bird, and the rest of the Sesame Street Muppets and labels for toy companies such as Toys "R" Us, Fisher-Price, Hasbro, Arco, Kenner, Gund, and J. C. Penney. But they did not. These images remained as invisible to American consciousness as the voices of the dead remained silent (Greider 1997:338). In its relation to the "big gun" transnational corporations, the "Third World" Kader toy factory typified all the factories in the export-processing zones of all the underdeveloped nations: it provided TNCs with the cheapest possible labor and protected the "good name" and "public reputations" of the ironically named "parent" companies.

> Globalized civilization has uncovered an odd parochialism in the American character: Americans worried obsessively over the everyday safety of their children, and the U.S. government's regulators diligently policed the design of toys to avoid injury to young innocents. Yet neither citizens nor government took any interest in the brutal and dangerous conditions imposed on the people who manufactured those same toys, many of whom were mere adolescent children themselves. Indeed, the government position, both in Washington and Bangkok, assumed there was no social obligation connecting consumers and workers, at least none that governments could enforce without disrupting free trade or invading the sovereignty of other nations. The toy industry, not surprisingly, felt the same. (Greider 1997:338)

Hewlett and West's work not only does absolutely nothing to change this odd American parochialism, the peculiar inability to extend care for anyone who belongs to another national Bantustan; worse, it helps to solidify this parochialism. By extending the principles of fairness and equity only to heterosexual men and women and their own biologically related children, Hewlett and West seriously compromise the principle of universality they maintain is central to their program to improve the quality of life for all. By extending the principle of fairness and equity only to *American* heterosexual men and women and their biologically related children, Hewlett and West further compromise this principle. Either all parents and children are equally deserving of social goods such as sanitation, health care, housing, education, employment, recreation, and a safe environment, or they are unequally deserving. To be realized universally, a genuinely democratic project must affirm the former. As Joan Walsh writes, "almost no one is articulating a universalist vision for all children," not just American children, but for all children (1998:5). Unless we "figure out ways to make people care about kids who don't look like their own," she adds, "conditions for [all] children will remain dire" (6). Hewlett and West's American-centered program is highly unlikely to foster such care.

Moreover, by focusing on redistributing wealth rather than on reorganizing the power to control its production and by focusing on the well-being of citizens in one's own nation rather than on the well-being of people everywhere, Hewlett and West advance a program that is unlikely to have political power sufficient to force any kind of serious redistribution from the "top" downward, that is, a democratic redistribution from those who appropriate to those who generate wealth. The New Deal was instituted under tremendous pressure from working-class organizations as a strategy to appease workers who were threatening to reorganize the economy along noncapitalist lines. Organized and militant workers were able to compel representatives of the ruling economic class to cede to some of their demands in part because U.S. capital depended largely on U.S. workers to produce its goods. Today, as is well known and as I have been elaborating throughout this work, the working class is ideologically underdeveloped and politically disorganized, while the dominant factions of the capitalist class do not only depend on labor and consumers from their "home" nations to produce and sell commodities and, most important, to realize profits. In addition, the shift from productive to finance capital has further internationalized surplus-value appropriation. Hewlett and West's proposals are not likely to get as far as the New Deal–era workers' demands did without a similarly organized working-class opposition, and it is not clear that this opposition can be mobilized on national grounds or, and perhaps especially, on the grounds of a parents' Bill of Rights. Indeed, there is good reason to believe that, if instituted, such a bill would drive a new lever between the parental and nonparental members of a working class that is already significantly divided by ethnic, racial, gender, sexual, and national identities. In this way, their parents' Bill of Rights would do little to democratize capitalist society and might well support the expansion of capitalist power.

Interestingly enough, although Hewlett, Unger, and West argue for a great many changes, they never mention redirecting military spending toward more socially beneficial and beneficent projects. This is curious, to say the least. Although they call for the creation of violence-free neighborhoods, they do not challenge the militaristic nature of U.S. state policies (in this respect they differ from Farrakhan, who *does* call for such cuts). This silence regarding the military-industrial complex, U.S. armed intervention, and exportation of arms around the world seems to be inexplicable for a couple of reasons. First, military spending represents almost half of all discretionary spending and therefore remains the best source from which to draw funds for programs to benefit working people and the poor. Second, Martin Luther King Jr., the person West claims represents the best of the prophetic black Christian tradition, argued that such spending constitutes a war against the people of the United States, for it robs them of precious resources just as wars rob them of precious lives. Yet their silence seems inexplicable only if one fails to recall that Hewlett, Unger, and West are concerned above all else with preserving the well-being of U.S. citizens and with rejuvenating our collective potential to compete with other capitalist nations (Hewlett and West 1998:93). Without a doubt, possessing the most powerful military forces in the world not only constitutes an enormous source of publicly funded, government-guaranteed private profits for some of the wealthiest individuals and richest corporations in the world; it also provides a distinct advantage to corporations seeking to extend their domination of world labor, resource, and product markets. One never knows when U.S. forces will be called on, as Hewlett and West write, to make "the Western world safe for democracy" (230).

Not only does Hewlett and West's American-centered program fail to address living conditions for parents and children worldwide, however. If their program were implemented, it would actually make matters worse for them. Indeed, it is possible, though admittedly unlikely, that U.S. capitalists might back a program like Hewlett and West's to avoid the crises deriving from overproduction and underconsumption. After all, someone must buy the products produced if someone else is to make a profit. Just as Henry Ford understood why increasing wages for U.S. workers was necessary to ensure high rates of profit, so too might CEOs today support a proposal to increase U.S. workers' wages so that they would be able to continue to profit from the exploitation of workers laboring in factories, mines, and plantations around the world. As Toys "R" Us CEO Michael Goldstein contends, Hewlett and West go "to the heart of the matter—what our society must do to support mothers and fathers so they can come through for their children" (in Hewlett and West 1998:i). Someone must be able to purchase the toys made for Toys "R" Us, among other "family-friendly" corporations, in the "dark satanic mills" by women and, increasingly, children who cannot afford to purchase what they make or, for that matter, to exchange what they are paid (if they are paid at all) for goods sufficient to meet even their basic needs (Greider 1997:359). Hewlett and West may find widespread support from corporate "visionaries" who, seeing ever so slightly beyond tomorrow's earnings' report, understand that to avoid the catastrophe of overproduction, a catastrophe that haunts the international economy like the specter of democracy, some workers must have enough cash to buy the commodities produced by other, relatively more exploited workers in, for example, Korea, Mexico, Russia, Indonesia, and China.

One solution to this crisis, which is shredding life around the world, is to divide the booty gained through the exploitation of foreign labor a little more equitably and fairly with U.S. workers. U.S. workers could thus buy the commodities produced, and the companies that organize their production and consumption could continue to profit. The current practice of producing in low-wage dictatorships and selling to high-wage democracies could then continue apace. Moreover, to the extent that U.S. workers are guided by such a classless-nationalist politics and thus unified to save their own nation above all else, they are positioned to support the same forces that increasingly reduce the vast majority of people around the world to wage slaves and, in the case of an increasing proportion of women and children, to outright slaves (see Meltzer 1994; Ross 1997). To encourage workers to identify first and last with the abstract political concept of the United States, as Hewlett, Unger, and West do, is to encourage them to be willing to pay for and send their children around the world to help maintain their country's "national security" and make the Western world "safe for democracy," that is, make capital safe from those other mothers, fathers, and children who are struggling to liberate themselves from the utopia of endless exploitation. Seen in a global context, Hewlett and West's parents' Bill of Rights asks only that wealth derived from the exploitation of the international working class be distributed more equally and fairly among the population of one nation, the Bantustan known as the United States of America. In this respect, their program not only leaves in place the socioeconomic system currently devastating living conditions for parents and children around the world; it may serve to buttress this system. Indeed, this explains why such programs find support among CEOs such as Goldstein, who understand that you sometimes have to give a little to keep a lot.

When Hewlett and West's proposals are situated within the context of the bipartisan project to dismantle the New Deal social contract and to forge New World Order ideologies (free trade), treaties (GATT), and institutions (the WTO) that support the interests of American capital, it becomes evident that "some form of large-scale public intervention to ensure access to basic social goods" could occur only if the same corporations that have benefited and continue to benefit from gutting resources previously under public control give back some of what they have because they "*care* about the quality of our lives [as human beings and as Americans] together" (West 1993a:6). To imagine that such a possibility has any chance of becoming a reality assumes that morality, nationality, and parental identity matter in corporate investment decision making as much as international competition for profits does. Unfortunately there is little evidence to support the claim that corporate owners have been, are, or might be persuaded by an ethics of care to return any portion of the resources that are presently under their control, let alone the tremendous resources required to ensure universal access to basic social goods. Believing that corporations might invest in nonprofitable production, for example, to ensure that all human beings enjoy access to basic social goods, mistakenly assumes that corporate directors are able to chose to make less profit if doing so would be good for their nation, parents, blacks, and so on. In other words, it assumes, as Hewlett and West assume in *The War against Parents,* that although global capitalist competition and the drive to generate the highest rates of return on capital investments may "have the potential of producing downward pressure on wages," they are not the culprit responsible for class inequalities (1998:80). Nevertheless, although certain factions of the capitalist class may attempt to stave off economic collapse and political unrest by forming a strategic alliance to enact a mild-mannered redistribution of wealth from the 10 percent who, as of 1997, control 71.6 percent of the nation's productive assets to the 90 percent who work for them (Mishel, Bernstein, and Schmitt 1999:263), it is more likely that global competition will prevent such an alliance from ever being formed (the recent breakdown of WTO talks is a case in point). West's call in *Race Matters* for massive public intervention to ensure universal access to basic social goods and in *The War against Parents* for a parents Bill of Rights that would redistribute socioeconomic resources to heterosexual parents to assist them in raising children may not fully appreciate the probability that "national regulation of capital allocation in the global context may simply be ineffective in maintaining or enhancing the position of the working class" (Ross and Trachte 1990:214). "Sooner or later," says Greider, "as the global system progresses . . . , people will begin to grasp that enormous economic power is becoming concentrated in a very few hands and on a plane beyond national systems of accountability" (1997:191), that because transnational capitalist corporations operate above and beyond national borders and have already developed transnational legal, juridical, financial, and military forces to ensure the continuing reproduction of their operations, the struggle to create, for example, investment principles that support the realization and protect the reality of human rights will have to be waged transnationally. As I suggested in chapter 6, crafting neo–New Deal contracts *within* the parameters of nation-states may prove difficult, if not impossible, for capital is no longer limited to national labor or consumer markets. In short, the basis of nation-based contracts between labor and capital may now rest in the garbage heap of history. Within the transnational context, calls for cross-class national solidarity are no substitute for international working-class solidarity.

Racism and Reform

Among the most remarkable aspects of Hewlett and West's work is the fact that it pays only passing attention to the problem of race, which assumes central importance throughout virtually all West's other works, from *Prophesy Deliverance* (published in 1982) to *The Future of American Progressivism* (published in 1998). Although Hewlett and West offer pro-parent proposals they believe will "overcome the usual divides of gender, race, and class" (1998:53), they fail to examine the insidious ways in which politicians have used race as a cover for their assault on workers' wages, benefits, and securities. This theoretical and political lacuna is particularly conspicuous because no other issue has received greater public and private attention over the past ten years. Even President Clinton wants us to talk about it. Nonetheless, Hewlett and West mention race only five times: in West's recollections of what life was like in the 1950s (14–15); in their brief discussion of racial bias in child abuse investigations (115–16); in their chapter on the Promise Keepers and Nation of Islam (185–211); in their discussion of welfare reform's impact on black families (77); and in their survey suggesting that parents across races share similar concerns (220). Other than that, not a word. There is no discussion of the ways politicians manipulate race as a strategy for securing white working-class support for conservative socioeconomic policies (see chapter 3). There is no discussion of the role that white supremacist ideas and practices have played and still play in preventing white and black workers from uniting to fight for shared socioeconomic ends. As Joan Walsh notes, the

> toughest barrier to forging pro-family or pro-child policies is race. It's no accident that the most racially diverse [and divided] Western nation has the thinnest safety net on every issue, not just family policy. Racial divisions split the labor movement, blocking the formation of a constituency for an expanded welfare state. Later, they brought about the defeat of another so-called war, the War on Poverty. Today those divisions are reflected in the fact that most of the states with the most generous provisions for education have the most homogeneous—read white—student populations. Certainly in California it's difficult not to notice that the state's ranking in per-capita education funding has plummeted as California's white population has declined. And while many groups of color have mobilized for programs and policies to help their children, almost no one is articulating a universalist vision for all children. If there's a war against anyone in this country, it's a war against children, and until we figure out ways to make people care about kids who don't look like their own, conditions for American children will remain dire. (1998:5–6)

Although Hewlett and West are concerned with advancing just such a universalist vision, albeit one constricted by its exclusion of gays, lesbians, and non-American families—that is, the majority of human beings—they do not address the problem of racism or sexism in a manner that recognizes how much these forces weaken the potential for building a movement that could realize even the rather mild-mannered proposals they make as part of their parents' Bill of Rights. Seeking to forge a political agenda across the "usual divides of gender, race, and class," that does not engage with the superstructural and structural realities of sexism, racism, and class exploitation, is pure utopianism.

Interestingly, Unger and West do speak to these realities in *The Future of American Progressivism*, making Hewlett and West's omission all the more peculiar. Unger and West write that "racial antagonisms hurt American democracy twice: first by the evils of racial discrimination and segregation; and, second, by the obstacles they create to the redress of class injustice" (1998:71). The "most important complication of the American class system is the unique way in which it has combined with racial prejudice. Race has always been America's rawest nerve and most explosive issue—as manifest in our Civil War and uncivil urban uprisings" (16). Nevertheless, their discussion of "the first constraint upon the American religion of possibility," that is, "the poisonous mixture of race and class" (18), remains strikingly reticent about the fact that, as West previously argued, "racism (especially white racism) and sexism (especially male sexism) are integral to the class exploitative capitalist system of production" (West 1982:106), especially when compared to West's earlier analyses and arguments in *Prophesy Deliverance* and *Prophetic Fragments*. Unger and West admit that "the antidiscrimination laws we now have may be too little to combat the hardened, substantial forms of racial prejudice that remain" (1998:72). They suggest that we "need a policy of active preferment in education and jobs in favor of those caught in entrenched situations of social disadvantage and exclusion from which they cannot escape, readily or at all, by their own initiative. However, we should not base this preferment solely on race, for race is typically just one element, although often a major one, of the social disablement we seek to repair" (73–74). Unger and West call for prolabor legislation, tax reforms, government-brokered partnerships between private and public entities, and nongovernmental citizens' actions councils that would have the power to make decisions about neighborhood development, as well as investments in child-centered support programs and "the broadening of access to finance and technology, through the establishment of independently administered venture-capital funds, chartered to invest in the rearguard and to conserve and grow the resources by which they would be endowed" (78). After all their proposals have been articulated, Unger and West do not link their agenda to a class-based politics. Although they indicate that racism "excite[s] resentments that prevent the formation of a progressive majority of working-class people of all races" (17), their goal is to narrow the gap between rather than end the conditions that create vanguard/rich and rearguard/poor.

West has shifted away from a Marxist conception of class as defined in terms of individuals' relationships to the means of production and toward a more Weberian conception of class as defined by income, status, and privilege differentials. Whereas a Marxist conception of class emphasizes control over productive property as key to expanding the quality of life for all persons, a Weberian conception of class emphasizes increased income. Although West maintains elements of the Marxist approach to class he used in *Prophesy Deliverance* and *Prophetic Fragments* (e.g., by describing growing economic disparity and the ways in which class position impedes the realization of individual potential), he no longer advocates abolishing private ownership and the anarchic planning that results from competition among private owners and building a society based on democratic planning. Unger and West address race matters, but their approach emphasizes how race compromises class mobility. In other words, the issue is not West's failure to discuss race and class but rather the specific manner in which he and other non-Marxist, progressive pragmatist scholars address these matters. According to Henry Louis Gates Jr., the interactions of race and class remain an organizational research focus of the Harvard Dream Team (Trescott 1999:42). Nevertheless, as Gates clearly indicates, the goal of their research "is to get more Black people to the middle class" (ibid.), or as West and Unger write, to reform political and economic institutions step by step and piece by piece so that gradually "the grid of class, gender, and race weighs less heavily upon our life in common" and more individuals will thereby be able "to climb the ladder of class distinctions" (Unger and West 1998:60, 24). In this regard, West's reoriented American progressivism does not transcend the fundamental socioeconomic limitations that capitalist property relations impose on the realization of democracy as people's control over social, political, and economic institutions.

It Takes Two Right Wings (Liberals and Conservatives) for Capitalism to Fly

West is certainly right to contend that we must go beyond the limits of liberal and conservative perspectives in order to address the problems associated with socioeconomic inequality and a society driven by market values and structures of production and consumption. Nevertheless, West's post-liberal/conservative progressive pragmatism does not challenge, let alone go beyond, the fundamental premise that informs both liberal and conservative interpretations of and responses to these problems. The fundamental premise is not that blacks are "a problem people" who must change themselves or be changed (although liberals and conservatives often share this premise). Nor is it that nihilism, even as West defines it, is not a problem that warrants serious consideration (indeed, many conservatives and most liberals are quick to point out that blacks suffer from despair, depression, and personal worthlessness). Rather, the assumption that unifies liberal, conservative, and post-liberal/conservative interpretations of race matters and class issues is that private ownership of productive resources and their organization for the purpose of capital production and accumulation are principles of social development whose ethical legitimacy is beyond question. The "murky waters" into which neither liberals, conservatives, nor post-liberal/conservatives (including West; Hewlett; William Julius Wilson; Senators Bill Bradley, Edward M. Kennedy, and Daniel Patrick Moynihan; and President Bill Clinton) dare to delve is not the culture of nihilism itself or the problem of managerial greed but rather the capitalist political economy that generates nihilistic conditions within working-class and nonworking poor U.S. communities and genocidal ones within most Third World nations. Although West identifies "market institutions" as responsible for creating a nihilistic culture, he does not identify the political economy of transnational capitalism as the primary culprit behind the problems associated with racism. In this way his analysis is more similar than dissimilar to the analyses of racism advanced by the same liberals and conservatives he endeavors to supersede. West, notes Stephen Steinberg, "presents social breakdown and cultural disintegration as a problem sui generis, with an existence and momentum independent of the forces that gave rise to it in the first place" (1995:130). He quite "explicitly divorces nihilism from political economy, thus implying that moral redemption is to be achieved through some mysterious 'turning of one's soul'" (132), and in so doing, he ultimately fails to exceed the fundamental socioeconomic assumption regarding the legitimacy of private property that politically unifies liberals (Bradley), conservatives (George W. Bush), and centrists (Al Gore).

I am not suggesting that progressive political agendas should not fight for, as Hewlett, Unger, and West do, large-scale government-sponsored interventions to ensure universal access to basic goods, the expansion of public control over assets, and a democratic redistribution of wealth and power. To the extent that such policies and programs would improve life for most working people and, perhaps as important, raise expectations that life should by characterized by more or less continuous improvement, they place the working class in a better material and psychological position from which to struggle against private control of societal planning. What is problematic is not so much West's call for public intervention to reinvigorate the public square after a period in which it has been gutted, or Hewlett and West's call for a new social contract in their parents' Bill of Rights (apart from its significant problems already discussed), or Unger and West's call for a redistribution of national income. Rather, what is problematic is their combined failure to link their proposals to the kind of internationally based working-class counter-offensive West earlier argued is necessary to advance a progressive political agenda. West now appears concerned, as John Dewey was during the 1930s and 1940s, to avoid class conflict at all costs by articulating a politics based on our identity as "people of good will," as Americans, or as parents (West 1989:235; Unger and West 1998; Hewlett and West 1998).

Without exposing and explicating the problem of class domination, any coalition among government, business, and labor is likely to result in the goal of meeting human needs' being subordinated to the goal of accumulating of private profits. Perhaps the best examples of such plans are the enterprise zones intended to encourage capital investments in urban and rural areas with high levels of unemployment and thus, as Clinton explains, help put "America back to work."[3] Because intellectuals have failed to promote a Marxist analysis of class exploitation and struggle, organizations that might otherwise be radicalized through their participation as critical organic catalysts have been left vulnerable to business, political, and religious leaders' claims that what's good for corporate America is good for every American. Following the 1992 Los Angeles riots, leaders from the Bloods and the Crips street gangs called a truce and developed a plan for mobilizing their considerable resources to improve their communities. The "most striking thing about the Bloods and the Crips' plan," notes Hadjor, "is its conservatism" (1995:167), a fact that should perhaps come as no surprise, inasmuch as most gangs are guided by the entrepreneurial ethics of individualism, competition, conquest, and profiteering.

> The central economic demands of the Crips and the Bloods were for more assistance for Black businesses in the inner cities. They asked for low-interest loans to be made available to minority entrepreneurs, in exchange for which the new Black and Latino businessmen would have to hire 90 percent of their employees from within the community. The gang leaders also asked for more investment in the community, in return for which they would "request the drug lords of Los Angeles to take their monies and invest them in business and property in Los Angeles." Aside from the bizarre proposal to turn crack dealers into socially responsible investors, perhaps the most dramatic (and dramatically conservative) proposal in the Bloods and Crips' plan concerned their view on welfare benefits. "We demand that welfare be completely removed from our community and these welfare programs be replaced by state work and product manufacturing plants that provide the city with certain supplies—The state and federal governments shall commit to expand their institutions to provide work for these former welfare recipients." That sounds pretty much like "workfare for welfare," a major slogan of the conservative campaign to make the inner city poor work for their miserly welfare checks. The striking thing about the gangs' proposal for work schemes is that it made no mention of poverty, or of how much people should be paid in government jobs. As such, it seemed to accept the basic premise of the elitist workfare argument: that it is welfare itself, rather than the poverty that it perpetuates, that is the problem in the ghetto. (168)

Thus two powerful organizations representing as many as several thousand individuals came together and developed what amounts to a Milton

Friedman/Louis Farrakhan solution to the problems confronting blacks living, laboring, and dying in America's inner cities, a solution that would almost certainly have placed members of both gangs in a position to dominate their local economies. Their proposals illustrate the extent to which right-wing ideology has permeated society, as well as the extent to which leftists have failed to promote a revolutionary analysis of race and class among the poor and oppressed.

By linking social reform policies to the development of an international movement for democratic globalization, the problem of inequality can be seen as a matter of control over the means of production and the principles governing this control. For the post-Marxist, postsocialist West of *Race Matters, The War against Parents,* and *The Future of American Pragmatism* and others who advance similar analyses, arguments, and agendas, the main problem is how to divide wealth more equally among U.S. citizens. For the Marxist/socialist West of *Prophesy Deliverance* and *Prophetic Fragments,* however, the problem is not principally one of dividing the fruits of production more fairly but rather one of democratizing control of the means of production.

Us versus Them and the American Pragmatist Evasion of Class Struggle

The "Los Angeles upheaval" may have been "an expression of utter fragmentation by a powerless citizenry," but contrary to West's assertion, that citizenry does not include "all of us." America is not only fragmented but also divided between a small number of economically and politically powerful individuals and organizations and a vast majority of economically and politically powerless ones, between a class of haves that transcends cultural, racial, ethnic, sexual, and gender lines and a class of have-too-littles and have-nothing-at-alls. A narrative that ignores the structural roots of these divisions, proposing that the propertyless and the propertied might overcome their differences by working together to create a "freer, more efficient and stable America," obscures the actual conditions of struggle by reproducing a myth of classlessness that, as West himself often notes, has time and again delivered workers into the hands of those who exploit them.

If, as Frederick Douglass, Martin Luther King Jr., and Claude Ake contend, genuine democracy involves control over productive property and cooperative planning to ensure satisfaction of basic needs and support for individual development, then we may expect that the struggle for democracy in America and around the world will involve not "mak[ing] the center hold," as Hewlett and West write in *The War against Parents,* but rather displacing the center of class power (1998:53). To put matters in the terms that Unger and West use in *The Future of American Progressivism,* the rearguard must displace the vanguard if we are to build a society that does not divide human beings into the wealthy and poor, propertied and propertyless, vanguard and rearguard (1998:41). The rich/propertied/vanguard do not view kindly any political actions, even peaceful ones, that challenge the structures that divide society into warring classes and the institutions that maintain their centralized authority over societal resources and planning. Capital's political and military representatives are quick to repress virtually any form of opposition to corporate power and thus ensure that democratic globalization will not be achieved without destabilizing actions.

Yet West seeks to avoid such unsettling possibilities in his post-*Evasion* works. In *The American Evasion of Philosophy* West seeks to unify people of goodwill to build an Emersonian culture of creative democracy. In *Race Matters* he seeks to unify American citizens to save America from disintegration. In *The War against Parents,* West seeks to unify citizens regardless of gender, race, or class, in an effort to enable them to do the best parental job they can. On the basis of moral, cultural, and psychological categories (goodness, nihilism, and greed), rather than social, economic, and political ones (state, class, and class struggle), West weaves the concepts of "humanness," "Americanness," and "parenthood" into a narrative in which the United States is depicted as having fallen from its "original" democratic or moral essence, an essence embodied by Thomas Jefferson, David Walker, Abraham Lincoln, Frederick Douglass, Chief Joseph, and Martin Luther King Jr. We have fallen by maintaining a "racial hierarchy [which] dooms us as a nation to collective paranoia and hysteria—the unmaking of any democratic order" and allowed personal greed to get in the way of collective well-being (West 1993a:4; Hewlett and West 1998:83). Social transformation is then conceptualized as a problem of personal conversion, of motivating "the better angels of our nature," of reducing greed, and of making "some form" of large-scale public intervention that will provide universal access to social goods or instituting a parents' Bill of Rights that will provide the resources required to produce the "magical parental power" that might allow us to "go to the very heart of our [nation's] darkness and make the center hold" (West 1993a:7; Hewlett and West 1998:53). West's project is precisely opposite to that which Ward Churchill argues is key to liberation, namely, getting "the United States—at least as we've come to know it [as the most powerful representative of the rule of capital]—out of North America altogether" and "banished from the planet" so that "we can join hands to create something new and better" (1996:89).

The Los Angeles riots were not, as West claims, a transclass phenomenon, even if those who participated represented various racial, ethnic, national, and religious groups. Indeed, the pleasureful, propertied, and powerful "communities" looked on with fear and trembling as pleasureless, propertyless, and powerless individuals expressed frustration at their worsening conditions of existence, at the fact that their own quest for pleasure, property, and power has been and is continuously thwarted by the antisocial logic of capital accumulation, a logic that remains largely incomprehensible among those who lack the resources to critique the ideologies that mystify how this logic determines their lives. Indeed, despite West's claims, their "quest for pleasure, property, and power" was no more "empty" than the concentration of pleasure, property, and power in the hands of a few citizens is simply a product of managerial greed (1993a:5). The upper middle class and wealthy in Los Angeles and around the country became increasingly hostile toward the working-class and poor rioters as the fires and looting spread toward what West, borrowing from the musician George Clinton, describes as their secure "vanilla suburbs"—which are today more accurately described as "chocolate chip" (5). Meanwhile, the corporate-owned and -controlled media reinforced ethnic and racist stereotypes, fostering hatred, ignorance, and fear among white working- and non-working-class citizens. Although twenty-five African, nineteen Hispanic, and ten European Americans were killed during the riots, only the attacks on Reginald Denny and Matthew Haines received continuous attention. Almost immediately after the fires were extinguished, public discussions shifted from questions concerning the best ways to address the social and economic factors fueling the unrest, that is, from the old Moynihan perspective, to the reasons the police did not act more swiftly and with greater force to restore "law and order," that is, the law and order of capital. Then presidential candidate William Jefferson Clinton, never slow to seize a public relations sound bite, promised that, if he were elected, he would put 100,000 more police on the street to prevent further such "uncivil uprisings"—one of the few promises he has since kept, along with instituting welfare reform, brokering international treaties in the interests of corporate power, keeping military spending at cold war levels, and zealously bombing into oblivion any powers that threaten U.S. military and corporate power.[4] In *Black Liberation in Conservative America* (1997a) Marable notes:

> The primary response of the U.S. government, elected officials, and corporate elites to the growing crisis of inequality has been the massive expansion of public and private security forces, and the incarceration of literally millions of black, Hispanic, and poor people. Between 1980 and 1990, the number of police in the United States doubled. As of 1995, 554,000 officers were employed by local and state police forces and legislation signed since then promises 100,000 more. Beyond this, an additional 1.5 million private security officers are currently employed to guard office buildings, stores, affluent neighborhoods, and corporate headquarters all over the country. Private patrol cars now cruise entire communities of middle- to upper-class Americans, whose streets

are closed off to outside traffic. Much of the new suburban housing being built today in "planned communities" is surrounded by walls and gates, wired for electronic surveillance, and guarded 24 hours a day by private security personnel. (43)

The U.S. National Guard, police, armed forces, and other security agencies are not the only forces busy restoring and reinforcing the existing capitalist legal and socioeconomic order in the United States and around the world. Over the past twenty-five years liberals and conservatives, seeking to survive in the age of transnational capitalism, have reached a bipartisan, post–New Deal consensus, fabricating an ideology designed to keep a racially, ethnically, nationally, linguistically, sexually, and culturally heterogeneous U.S. working class both loyal and subordinate to the dictates of capital. This ideology constitutes a necessary response to the problem of revitalizing "America"—that is, securing the legitimacy of private determination of human development in the context of increasingly transparent social, political, and economic inequalities—by arguing, against the outmoded, explicitly racist, sexist, ethnocentric, and religiously chauvinistic "vision" of such right-wing dinosaurs as Rush Limbaugh, Pat Buchanan, and Jesse Helms, that, as West wrote in *Race Matters,* "whoever *our* leaders will be as we approach the twenty-first century, their challenge will be to help Americans determine whether a genuine multiracial democracy can be created and sustained in an era of global economy and a moment of xenophobic frenzy" (1993a:7–8). As West contends, to accomplish this goal, they must invoke "ideals of freedom, democracy, and equality" and involve "all of us, especially the landless, propertyless, and luckless" (7). We should work together as morally good, nationally committed, parentally concerned U.S. citizens.

West's call has not gone unanswered. President Clinton has made the project of forging a post-conservative/liberal agenda the guiding principle of his efforts to build a capitalist bridge to the twenty-first century. He and other more "enlightened" representatives of the transnational bourgeoisie affirm the values of diversity, tolerance, freedom, democracy, and equality; place a small number of blacks, Latinos/as, Asians, and others who represent historically marginalized social groups into highly visible administrative positions; and call on all Americans, especially the landless, propertyless, and luckless (the rich heed their own call), to work together to realize America's potential as a great nation. Clinton has even gone so far as to call for something like the institutionalization of an international New Deal contract between international capital and labor. At the November 1999 WTO talks in Seattle, Washington, Clinton suggested that WTO leaders should consider legislation guaranteeing certain basic labor rights and work standards (a suggestion Third World bourgeois representatives rejected as "unfair" and labor advocates saw as little more than a cynical effort to appease the concerns of WTO protesters). Whereas West's post-socialist/liberal/conservative (prophetic) pragmatist political discourse seeks to establish a "reasonable" middle ground between the liberal extremes of the 1960s and conservative excesses of the 1980s, Clinton argues that we must transcend conservative and liberal "labels" to formulate bipartisan solutions to the problems that confront "America" (i.e., American corporations), in what amounts to the constitution of what Gore Vidal called "one party with two right wings" (in Wood 1997b:8). Since his defeat in the 1988 presidential election, Jesse Jackson has (dis)pleased conservatives and liberals alike with his "it takes two wings to fly" sermons. Much to the delight of conservative Republicans, Nation of Islam leader Louis Farrakhan now calls blacks to atone for their sins by undergoing an inner spiritual transformation.

Now Cornel West, one of the most influential intellectuals in the United States today, takes up a similar call. He argues that the "major enemy of black survival in America has been and is neither oppression nor exploitation but rather the nihilistic threat." He urges labor, government, and business to work together to build an "Emersonian culture of creative democracy," a "multiracial democracy," "a freer, more efficient, and stable America." He tells us that the oppressed must undergo, even if or perhaps especially because they are completely "bereft of resources," a "psychic conversion" by means of self-love, while CEOs and shareholders must show how much they care for the other 90 percent of the American population by divesting themselves of capital resources so that the basic needs of every person can be met; that is, they must become socialists for capital. He affirms that we can redress the inequalities in the United States, remake the social contract, recapture the American Dream, and fuel a great and glorious national endeavor by forging a parents' movement that unifies citizens across race, gender, and class divisions. By thus allying himself with other "Reaganly" reformed Marxists, West remains within the postsocialist "fold," that is, among those procapitalist "progressives" who accept that "the best we can do is liberate a little more space in the interstices of capitalism, by means of many particular and separate struggles—the kind of struggles that sometimes go under the name of identity politics"—and by way of proposals to redistribute wealth generated through capital's exploitation of workers in, for example, Korea, Mexico, or Russia more equally among U.S. workers (Wood 1997b:9).

Political balkanization and social demonstrations in the United States do not reveal an "us-versus-them" mentality and a nation plagued by contempt for the "common good," which West claimed the 1992 Los Angeles riots demonstrated. Nor do they reveal the fact that managers and CEOs are too greedy, although capitalism certainly institutionalizes greediness as essential to humanity's well-being. Rather, they reveal the extent to which the working class and poor have yet to liberate themselves "from the mythologies of spurious appearances and turn away from false idols—so better to struggle toward real democracy"—and, correspondingly, the extent to which intellectuals who are in a position to aid in this liberation have failed the task (Parenti 1995:173). In short, they indicate that oppressed and exploited Americans by and large still view reality through the lens provided by the ruling class, that is, according to the dominant ideology, even if they do so while living, laboring, and dying in South Central Los Angeles or Cambridge, Massachusetts. The auto worker uprisings in South Korea; the student uprisings in Indonesia; the peasant uprisings in Mexico; the citizen uprisings in France; the women workers' uprisings in the Philippines; the poor people's uprisings in Los Angeles; and the ongoing struggles of the Ogoni in Nigeria, the Banaba in the South Pacific, and the Hopi in Arizona to protect their traditional ways of life and the Earth, as well as the United Mine Workers strike at Pittston Coal Company, the United Auto Workers strike at Caterpillar, the United Rubber Workers strike at Bridgestone/Firestone, the Teamsters strike against United Postal Service, and most notably the anti-WTO protests in November 1999—all these actions and many more reveal not the "end of ideology" and certainly not the "end of history." Rather they reveal the extent to which human beings around the world are voting with their hearts, minds, and bodies against the inhumane rule of international capital. In the case of the United States, such protests often, though not always, reveal the extent to which working-class citizens have not developed what they need to advance the struggle for genuine democracy, namely, a class-conscious, anticapitalist us-versus-them mentality that understands at least as well as do members of the capitalist class and their political, intellectual, educational, and religious representatives that the struggle over power is an *us*-versus-*them* struggle.[5] And they reveal the degree to which the postsocialist, post-Marxist, progressive American left has, in the name of going beyond Marxist theory and revolutionary socialist politics, which have yet to be fully developed in the United States, evaded class struggle, the central dynamic of capitalist society and the political weapon by which, as West argued in *Prophesy Deliverance,* the battle for a genuinely democratic global society must be advanced.

8. The Future of Revolutionary Democratic Politics

> Those who speak of class struggle do not "advocate" it—as some would say—in the sense of creating it out of nothing by an act of (bad) will. What they do is to recognize a fact and contribute to an awareness of that fact. And there is nothing more certain than a fact. To ignore it is to deceive and to be deceived and moreover to deprive oneself of the necessary means of truly and radically eliminating this condition—that is, by moving towards a classless society. Paradoxically, what the groups in power call "advocating" class struggle is really an expression of a will to abolish its causes, to abolish them, not cover them over, to eliminate the appropriation by a few of the wealth created by the work of the many and not to make lyrical calls to social harmony. It is a will to build a socialist society, more just, free, and human, and not a society of superficial and false reconciliation and equality. To "advocate" class struggle, therefore, is to reject a situation in which there are oppressed and oppressors. But it is a rejection without deceit or cowardliness; it is to recognize that the fact exists and that it profoundly divides men, in order to be able to attack it at its roots and thus create the conditions of an authentic human community. To build a just society today necessarily implies the active and conscious participation in the class struggle that is occurring before our eyes.
>
> —Gustavo Gutiérrez, *A Theology of Liberation*

IN 1994 ANDERS STEPHANSON asked Cornel West about the difficulties and dilemmas that intellectuals who are committed to progressive politics encounter working within the academy. West answered, "You do get 'mainstreamed'"; in other words, there is "a selective appropriation of certain motifs in your work that are considered safe and acceptable" (West 1994:67). West's comments productively refer us back to one of the main problems that, drawing from West's own reflections, I posed in the first chapter: the problem of attempting to critique and support democratic struggles from within an institution whose mission, increasingly determined by corporate interests, is to provide the education and workforce required to maintain and further develop the existing socioeconomic order. As West asked in a discussion with Paul Gilroy and bell hooks about the consequences of attempting to restructure the economy and academy while being a member of the professional-managerial class, "How do we fight as progressives and co-opted?" (1993b:104). Fighting as both progressive and co-opted requires charting a path that is on the one hand responsible to the established criteria of good scholarship and teaching, criteria frequently dressed in the garb of academic freedom, political impartiality, rational inquiry, and objective analysis, and yet on the other hand is able to challenge the existing ideological, political, and economic order of things, relations, and people. Those who emphasize the first course risk retreating into status-quo acceptability; those who emphasize the second risk marginalization within and sometimes even exclusion from the academy.

This does not mean that one must avoid investigating, analyzing, and even strongly criticizing capitalist society to secure a position within higher-education institutions. West's work demonstrates that it is possible to generate such critical scholarship and secure a position, indeed, a relatively privileged one, within the academic hierarchy. Scholars may write and teach about the social and natural problems associated with global capitalist society—in fact, they are encouraged to do so—as long as they assume that these problems can and will be solved once "normal" capitalist operations are permitted to develop. It is generally acceptable to discuss economic inequalities, ecological destruction, militaristic policies, sexism, racism, ethnocentrism, and nationalistic chauvinism and even to argue that we ought to legislate against these problems and to implement social, political, and economic reforms that redress them. It is generally acceptable for academicians to argue for progressive agendas along the lines of those articulated by Hewlett, Unger, and West and even to argue, as West did recently, that "the Marxist tradition . . . tells some fascinating stories about our historical conditionedness, the crucial role of how the dynamics of power at the workplace curtails potential, the crucial role that banking and corporate elites play, given their wealth and power, in making it difficult for working people actually to fulfill their potentiality" (1999b:558).

There are, however, certain boundaries at which the ideological-intellectual border guards draw no uncertain lines with regard to the established criteria of academic acceptability. Although talk about creating a global community that would make possible the universal satisfaction of basic needs and realization of individual aspirations is certainly acceptable (e.g., the recent "Gang of Eight" Nobel Peace Prize winners talk eloquently about the need to create such a society), what remains less acceptable is challenging the moral and social right of capitalist property relations (e.g., these same Nobel Prize winners by and large do not talk much about these relations, let alone explicitly argue that they are incompatible with human rights; rather, they assume human rights can be realized without transforming a mode of production that daily negates their realization). Although it remains acceptable to declare oneself a Democrat, Republican, or Libertarian and to argue for tax cuts on capital gains, trade agreements that benefit corporations, and increased military spending to protect "American" interests around the globe, what is less acceptable, as West indicates, is to challenge the existing regime of property relations and support the "revolutionary transformation of capitalist societies" (1993c:181).

Academic scholars and teachers are less likely to be warmly received and generously supported if they develop analyses and arguments like those that West developed in *Prophesy Deliverance* and *Prophetic Fragments.* In these works, as I have elaborated, West argued that "capitalism is a historically transient system of production which requires human beings to produce commodities for the purpose of maximizing surplus value (profits)" (1982:108); that "racism (especially white racism) and sexism (especially male sexism) are integral to the class exploitative capitalist system of production" (106); that "capitalism is an *antidemocratic* mode of socioeconomic organization in that it requires removal of control of production from those engaged in production" (122); that "capitalism is inseparable from imperialism in that the latter is an extension of capitalism across national borders and political boundaries" (ibid.); that, as a result of its global pursuit of profits, capitalism is leading to the "violent destruction of the biosphere, nature, and potentially the planet" (1988:48-49); and that, in response to capitalist realities, "we must practically ground ourselves in particular anti-imperialist struggles in light of theoretical systemic Marxist-like analyses that link anti-imperialist struggles against common capitalist foes" (1988:77). Indeed, West's shift away from systemic transformation to ameliorative modification, from class struggle to the struggle to rebuild America, is precisely what makes it possible for liberal and conservative corporate leaders and politicians such as Senator Edward M. Kennedy, president and CEO of the NAACP Kweisi Mfume, Toys "R" Us CEO Michael Goldstein, and former U.S. senator Bill Bradley to praise West as someone whose prolific contributions to public discourse on race and racism, as Bradley wrote of *Race Matters,* "should give hope to all of us who believe that America's racial diversity is our strength" (cover material). It is difficult to imagine mainstream political figures and academic intellectuals offering similar praises to the Cornel West of *Prophesy Deliverance,* who argued that private ownership of the societal means of production is essentially antidemocratic and the source of human misery and planetary degradation. West's shift from his previous socialism to his present position of accepting capitalist property relations as the framework within which to advance the struggle for democracy and his shift from an internationalist to a nationalist perspective made it possible for *Race Matters* to become a *New York Times* best-seller and for *The War against Parents* to be celebrated by liberals and conservatives alike. Hewlett and West, says Toys "R" Us CEO Michael Goldstein, go "to the heart of the matter—what our society must do to support mothers and fathers so they can come through for their children" and, as Hewlett and West write, thereby increase "America's store of human capital and help this nation compete with the Germans and Koreans" (in Hewlett and West 1998:i, 93). Nonetheless, it is highly unlikely, to say the least, that CEOs such as Goldstein would pay similar tributes to the West who argued in *Prophesy Deliverance* that we should build a counter-hegemonic working-class movement that challenges U.S. imperialism and global capitalism.

The fact that West has largely abandoned his earlier commitment to such revolutionary projects as being "some impossible, romantic dream of a different 'system'" and has embraced what he and Unger identify as "the truth about political possibility," that is, "a practical view of how, step by step, and piece by piece, to democratize the American economy and reenergize American democracy" (Unger and West 1998:30, 93), may best explain why West and those who share his post-Marxist, left-liberal progressive pragmatist theory and politics have been so well received and strongly supported by corporate executive officers, Democratic and Republican politicians, and advocates of neoliberal social, political, and economic policies. If Goldstein, Bradley, and Clinton are right, West's project is good for capitalism or at least poses no serious threat to those who defend and benefit from the "free-market" system of exploitation.

Prophetic pragmatism, one of the most fully elaborated and progressive expressions of post-Marxist politics in the present era, appeals to academicians, politicians, and business leaders precisely because it poses no serious threat to the class of individuals who control and appropriate the lion's share of the Earth's resources and humanity's collectively generated wealth. If implemented in the form of a new social contract, West's reoriented progressive theory and politics would certainly improve the quality of life for most working-class citizens, but implementing the proposals made by Hewlett, Unger, and West would not in the least alter the system that denies most human beings the possibility of enjoying dignified, peaceful, and fulfilling lives. Progressive pragmatism poses no serious threat to the ruling economic class for at least three reasons: first, it seeks to implement a reform agenda that attempts to address the needs of both rulers and ruled by establishing cross-class alliances on the grounds of shared moral, parental, or national identity; second, and closely related to the first reason, it seeks to solve human problems without challenging the moral legitimacy and social consequences of privatized control of production and planning of societal development; and third, the ruling class is highly unlikely to implement Hewlett, Unger, and West's agenda, or any version thereof, if they are not compelled to do so, and they can be compelled to do so only by an organized and militant working class.

Although Unger and West represent their reoriented progressivist politics as "the alternative" to the "one true way and its companion, the humanization of the inevitable" (1998:3), its realization would at best result in the neo–New Deal social contract among business, government, and labor that guarantees a kinder, gentler, more equitable capitalist society for American workers; at worst it would distract those who might otherwise commit themselves to working in solidarity with people around the world to create a genuine alternative to the current system, a genuinely just, free, and human system, keeping them preoccupied with innocuous and probably unrealizable social agendas. The new transnational robber barons, as well as their educational, political, bureaucratic, and military defenders, will never bow to an agenda that requires even the slightest redistribution of wealth unless, to paraphrase Frederick Douglass, those who produce this wealth demand they bow. To expect otherwise assumes that the ruling class, which consciously and methodically poisons, robs, plunders, and murders people around the world, will demonstrate how much it cares about these same people by divesting itself of capital resources to ensure their basic needs and spiritual aspirations are satisfied. We should not hold our breaths but rather build a socioeconomic system that puts people before profits. Because the postsocialist left has by and large abandoned the reality of class struggle, however, it has forfeited the basis for building a life-enhancing alternative to capitalist-controlled globalization. Because they have jettisoned this project as "hopelessly romantic," they have consigned humanity to a ruthless struggle for survival rather than a cooperative project of living. Yet we need to dream of a radical alternative to the existing international order of privatized ownership of the means of production, privatized competition for profits, production for capital, the fetish of consumerism, and violence to maintain social order, because anything less is utopian.

The Rightward Drift

Although I have detailed the theoretical, philosophical, and sociological aspects of West's transition from his earlier socialist to his present progressivist politics, I have only briefly attempted to explain what forces may have contributed to this shift, a shift that has been characteristic of the political drift (for some, rightward tack) of many post-Reaganite leftists. West's transition reveals among other things the capacity of dominant institutions to contain the radical potential of even the most energetic and committed intellectuals. The relatively successful incorporation of new social movements (feminist, antiracist, ecological, etc.), "radical" theories, and individuals whose socially defined characteristics, if not their politics, link them historically to marginalized, subjugated, and exploited populations within the mainstream and mainstreaming institutions demonstrates these institutions's power to appropriate motifs that are not only sociopolitically acceptable but also useful to the reformation of capitalist institutions and discourses and the preservation of transnational processes of capital accumulation. I intended my extended critical analysis to demonstrate some of the principal limitations of prophetic pragmatism, but it remains vital to understand these limitations as a product of social forces not of West's own making. The material effectiveness of theories, oppositional or otherwise, always depends on social, cultural, political, and economic conditions that establish the general parameters of theoretical production, distribution, and implementation, even if these forces do not mechanically determine the specific content of the theories produced. Whether radical theories become material forces depends on organizations that are receptive to these theories and able to develop them. Socialism's discreditation following the experience of the Soviet Union and the Eastern Bloc nations and their subsequent collapse and the working class's organizational and ideological weaknesses go a long way toward explaining why non-class-based theories flourish within the academy. The possibility of advancing revolutionary theory was and in large measure is connected to and dependent on the existence and development of working-class organizations and consciousness; their limited existence renders even empirically well-supported and logically persuasive arguments for such theories seemingly "out of touch" with the truth about political possibility. So, as capital battered workers during the last quarter of the twentieth century, the left retreated from the working class and proceeded to advance, with generous poststructuralist support, anything-but-class theories. More than a few successful academic careers were made by scholars who invested their time and brains debunking Marxism, socialism, and class struggle in the name of other, more "radical" and more sophisticated theories. Indeed, no small number of academicians argued that calls for fundamental structural change repressed the intrinsic heterogeneity and incompatibility of social identities, struggles, and goals.

The fact that West's theoretical and political development is conditioned by circumstances not of his own making does not make this transition inconsequential. Indeed, his post-*Evasion* politics tend to obscure "where [and who and what] the enemy is" precisely by formulating programs that attempt to speak to the needs of both the exploiters and exploited (West 1994:68). Such politics derive in part from individuals who feel, as West wrote in *The American Evasion of Philosophy,* "a dual allegiance to the conqueror and the conquered" (1989:39). Like the petty-bourgeois socialists that Marx and Engels critiqued in their work, progressive pragmatists argue for an agenda that seeks to improve living conditions for all by having both more governmental activism and more free-market economics: "Hence, they habitually appeal to society at large. . . . they wish to attain their ends by peaceful means, and endeavor, by small experiments, necessarily doomed to failure, and by the force of example, to pave the way for the new social Gospel" (Marx and Engels in Tucker 1978:498). As Gutiérrez writes in *A Theology of Liberation,* such postsocialist progressives "make lyrical calls to social harmony," "reconciliation[,] and equality" without working to eliminate the class divisions—in effect, private ownership of the means of life—that prevent human beings from building "an authentic human community" (1973:274). Yet, says Gutiérrez, "to deny the fact of class struggle is really to put oneself on the side of the dominant sectors. Neutrality is impossible. It is not a question of admitting or denying a fact which confronts us; rather it is a question of which side we are on" (274–75). It is precisely in relationship to this political question that progressive pragmatists remain unresolved as they advance agendas that seek to expand and enrich democracy without challenging class domination. They seek to build what has never existed and, as West correctly argued in *Prophesy Deliverance,* structurally cannot exist: a democratic capitalist market. The market cannot be both democratic and capitalist precisely because the latter mode of control excludes the former. A democratic market can exist only if those who produce society's wealth control the means of producing and distributing wealth; as West himself explained in a 1994 interview with Anders Stephanson published in *Art Forum,* "the rule of capital stands in the way of democratization" (1994:70). Capital represents the negation of democracy, just as democracy can be fully realized only through the negation of capital as a socioeconomic relation of alienation.

Like Dewey's projects, those of the post-Marxist left are likely to find support from individuals who believe, either because it serves their interests or because they have been misled into believing it does, that our social and natural problems can be solved within the framework of the capitalist market. This may explain why Bill Bradley supports West and West supports Bill Bradley. Although Bradley may have represented the most progressive politics among the Republican or Democratic presidential candidates, he nevertheless remains fully committed to the capitalist market and is not about to rock any major corporate powers, especially those that so generously funded his campaign (e.g., Citigroup, the world's largest financial services firm; Merrill Lynch, America's largest brokerage firm; Time-Warner, one of the largest multimedia conglomerates in the world; Prudential Life Insurance, the largest provider of life insurance in the country; and Walt Disney Company). Proponents of the kind of postsocialist, progressive pragmatist politics that West supports will no doubt be institutionally authorized, recognized by enlightened supporters of neoliberal policies as speaking "the truth about political possibility," and financially, socially, and politically rewarded for their contributions as long as they do not explicate the links between suffering and, as West wrote in *Prophesy Deliverance,* "the internal dynamics of liberal capitalist America, how it functions, why it operates the way it does, who possesses substantive power, and where it is headed" (1982:113). Perhaps they will be rewarded even more generously if they argue, as Unger and West do in *The Future of American Progressivism,* that such a "system out there—'capitalism'—with its driving laws, its inner logic, and its indivisible unity" does not exist (1998:29). Meanwhile, West and other similar progressives will no doubt continue to receive, as West noted that they do, "a lot of resources that other people are not getting" (1993b:104). Moreover, West's version of progressivism is likely to receive widespread support from citizens outside the academy who have been generously encouraged to see reality through corporate eyes, that is, to interpret their own experiences through concepts that support their oppressors. And this raises a strategic question about which projects are possible given the conservative nature of the American political context.

Strategies and Goals

Does West's transition from a more explicitly Marxist, revolutionary socialist analysis and politics to his current, more pragmatist, progressive reformist analysis and politics indicate a change in his political goals rather than simply a change in strategies, and if so, to what extent? Might it be the case, as I suggested in the introduction, that West's reoriented progressivism engages more profoundly and therefore productively than does Marxism with the objective and subjective conditions of struggle and thus more accurately appreciates political possibilities? Do left progressives understand something that Marxists do not, namely, that "to indigenize socialist thought and practice," a project West contended in *Prophetic Fragments* the left must undertake if theory is to become a material force (1988:48), requires translating this thought and practice into the idiom of progressive reform? Has West's search for currently realizable projects led him to conclude that the best we can hope for at this moment is to ameliorate exploitative relations and redistribute wealth and income more democratically? Does he correctly understand that because American workers enjoy bourgeois political rights and relatively high standards of living, attempts to develop socialist thought and practice are inevitably doomed to fail and that consequently the best we can hope for is to democratize the free market?

Clearly most Americans do not use socialist vocabulary, and fewer use Marxist theory. For many citizens, as for much of the left, the ideas of exploitation, class struggle, state power, and socialism have never been relevant to the United States and are not relevant in our postcommunist world. The free market, many Americans believe, may not be the best world we can imagine, but inasmuch as socialism did not work, we are left with little other choice than to do the best we can under capitalism.

Although such thoughts may be widely shared, there are growing signs of resistance to the established global capitalist order among labor, environmental, and human rights organizations. Moreover, the fact that only a small portion of American citizens are familiar with Marxist theory stems less from its irrelevance to conditions of labor and life in the United States than it does from the failure of those who are committed to create "authentic human community" to encourage its development through their scholarship, pedagogy, and community engagement (Gutiérrez 1973:274). What remains unknown is the extent to which the development of Marxist thought might help labor, environmental, and human rights organizations succeed in their efforts to construct a coordinated transnational movement against capitalist-controlled globalization. There is, of course, no way to know in advance whether Marxist thought would foster the development of a global movement to replace capitalist globalization with democratic control of the economy. If, however, "to build a just society today necessarily implies the active and conscious participation in the class struggle," then failure to develop the theoretical means for comprehending the nature of and participating in the class struggle will certainly impede the collective work of building such a society (ibid.).

In fact, resistance to capitalist domination of human and planetary existence is on the rise around the world, as students, citizens, church organizations, indigenous peoples, and workers of all faiths, ethnicities, races, and nationalities courageously combat neoliberal capitalist policies. Still, although capital has been waging an assault against American workers, downsizing wages and benefits, degrading workplace and environmental safety, and destroying the social safety net, a self-consciously antineoliberal political movement has yet to develop among workers in the United States. Furthermore, given the U.S. state's pivotal role in promoting, propping up, and protecting the global capitalist disorder, U.S. workers possess an obvious potential to make a vital, indeed key, contribution to the collective human work of building a just, peaceful, and humane way of life.

The Future of Revolutionary Democratic Politics

> I look forward confidently to the day when all who work for a living will be one with no thought to their separateness as Negroes, Jews, Italians or any other distinction. This will be the day when we bring into full realization the American dream—a dream yet unfulfilled. A dream of equality of opportunity, of privilege and property widely distributed; a dream of a land where men will not take necessities from the many to give luxuries to the few; a dream of a land where men will not argue that the color of a man's skin determines the content of his character; a dream of a nation where all our gifts and resources are held not for ourselves alone, but as instruments of service for the rest of humanity.
>
> —Martin Luther King Jr.,
> Address to AFL-CIO Convention, 1961

So where do we go from here? Contrary to West's claims regarding political possibility, the most fruitful course for advancing the struggle for justice lies not in Hewlett, Unger, and West's progressive pragmatist politics, which reject the "dream of a different 'system'" (Unger and West 1998:93), but rather in politics inspired by a vision of a qualitatively different mode of human society. The articulation of such a vision and the elaboration of strategies to realize it do not require abandoning all the social reforms that Hewlett, Unger, and West outline in their work. Rather, it means formulating worker-friendly reforms as integral steps toward what ought ultimately to be a qualitative transformation of the property relations—the system of capitalist relations—that presently structure human labor, leisure, and life and our relations with one another and the planet. We need to think beyond the ideological boundaries imposed by neoliberal politics and the fetters of capitalist property relations to imagine a world in which human beings are not simply remunerated better for producing commodities for those who employ them, a world in which human beings are no longer systemically reduced to commodities that are bought and sold, no longer subordinated to the authority of a minority and reduced to working to produce for someone else's profit, a world in which all human beings would have the opportunity to enjoy fully dignified, secure, fulfilling, and holistically enriching lives. To imagine such a society is not to engage in romantic speculation. Rather, it is to confront candidly the extent to which the existing system of global socioeconomic organization is killing life around the world and to appreciate fully the extent to which we cannot afford to limit ourselves to tinkering with this system. Instead, we owe it to ourselves and future generations to build a life-enhancing global society. Nothing is more unrealistic and utopian than to believe that it is possible to build such a society without democratizing control of societal planning.

Along these lines I suggest that the revolutionary socialist perspective that West articulated in *Prophesy Deliverance* and the essays contained in the collection *Prophetic Fragments* provides a productive starting point from which to advance this project. West's pre-*Evasion* work is provocatively suggestive with regard to this collective human task. Indeed, I cannot emphasize sufficiently the extent to which my own critique of West's prophetic pragmatism, arguably the best of left liberal progressive politics, and my own commitment to creating a genuinely life-enhancing world society are theoretically informed and ethically inspired by West's early work. In this regard, I conclude by making several suggestions regarding work that the left may undertake to contribute to the development of revolutionary democratic theory and practice.

First, we ought to critique all claims regarding capitalism's potential to satisfy humanity's biological needs and diverse spiritual aspirations. Contrary to those who would have us believe that capitalism is capable of realizing these goals once all its "kinks" are worked out, once capitalism is finally, after more than five hundred years, permitted to develop "naturally," we should vigorously argue that regardless of the moral disposition of the agents running it, capitalism is structurally incapable of achieving these goals. No amount of tinkering, no change of the political guard, no enlightened corporate leaders, and no social compacts between labor and capital will result in the universal satisfaction of basic needs, the all-around spiritual development of humanity, or the continuous replenishment of the Earth. These goals can be achieved only by organizing production to meet them, and doing so means negating the antisocial goal of producing capital for private accumulation. We should, as West argued in *Prophesy Deliverance,* work to "uncover the systematic misunderstanding of capitalist society by bourgeois thinkers; to show how this misunderstanding, whether deliberate or not, supports and sanctions exploitation and oppression in this society; and to put forward the correct understanding of this society in order to change it" (1982:110). We must debunk the myth that, given sufficient time, capitalism will eventually satisfy humanity's needs and aspirations in a manner that is responsible to the natural basis of human life. This myth must be debunked so that working people are able to act, both individually and collectively, with a clear understanding of what must be done to achieve genuine equality, democracy, fraternity, and peace. Our choice remains either socialism or barbarism—or, given that life on this planet is now at stake, socialism or death.

Second, and related to my first suggestion, the left should develop politics that oppose in principle cross-class alliances, even though it may form such alliances to advance the struggle for democracy. The left should not mislead people into believing that those who are rich from their exploitation and oppression are "in the same boat." No effort to create a genuine human community by abolishing class divisions can proceed through political agendas that seek to please everyone on both sides of the class divide. Michael D. Yates notes that although post-Marxist progressive pragmatists, along with labor leaders such as AFL-CIO president John Sweeney, make much "of the long-term decline in real wages and the growing inequality in income and wealth," as well as "the destruction of the social safety net and exorbitant CEO pay," such claims remain "woefully inadequate as a basis for waging class struggle" (1999:4). Workers not only deserve a greater portion of the wealth they produce but should exercise authority over the means of its production. Not only is the capitalist class parasitical; it also constitutes a structural obstacle to creating a mode of socioeconomic organization made by, of, and for people, not capital. To ignore class struggle (e.g., by calling for "healing," "reconciliation," "harmony," and "making the center hold" without transforming the social relations that injure, separate, alienate, and shatter the bonds of genuine human affection, caring, relationship, and community) "is to deceive and to be deceived and moreover to deprive oneself of the necessary means of truly and radically eliminating this condition—that is, by moving towards a classless society" (Gutiérrez 1973:274). What we need are politics that understand, as United Mine Workers Association vice-president Cecil Roberts does, that "this is class war. The working class versus the corporate rich and their allies in state and federal government" (in Brecher 1998:332).

Third, the left should synthesize the old, class-based left and the new, issues-based left. This project does not involve a simple addition of the old and the new, however. Rather, it requires investigating and explicating the connections between issues raised by new left social movements (e.g., feminist, gay and lesbian, antiracist, environmentalist, antimilitarist, and peace movements) and the global operations of transnational capitalism. Engaging in this work does not mean placing less stress on sexist, heterosexist, ethnocentrist, nationalist, and racist practices; rather, "these practices [must] be linked to the role they play in buttressing the current mode of production, concealing," for example, "the unequal distribution of wealth," weakening the overall power of the working class, and dividing workers against one another (West 1982:114). Eliminating racism, sexism, and heterosexism is not secondary to the work of eliminating exploitation; rather, such efforts are integral aspects of the struggle to democratize global society. Ensuring that everyone enjoys access to sanitation, health care, child care, education, housing, employment, recreation facilities, a safe natural environment, and a society free of intolerance and prejudice is, as I argued in chapter 3, a fundamental dimension of this struggle. Interestingly, the task of recognizing how these issues are related to democratic globalization was discussed quite openly and respectfully by individuals who participated in protests against the WTO in Seattle, Washington, portending a hopeful sign of things to come.

Fourth, we must help to foster international alliances among working-class, environmental, and human rights organizations and movements. Projects that remain restricted to improving life, labor, and leisure within one nation are, especially in the light of transnational capitalist realities, less likely to succeed than are those that coordinate their efforts with progressive projects in other nations. Encouraging workers to identify first with their nation undermines the kind of transnational solidarity that is needed to combat transnational capital. Although West's post-*Evasion* politics focus on the United States, as chapter 6 indicates, West was correct when he suggested in *Prophesy Deliverance* and *Prophetic Fragments* that liberation depends on building an international working-class movement. Nation-states, the principal regulatory agencies during previous periods of capitalist development, are being practically, albeit unevenly and contradictorily, superseded by transnational regulatory agencies (see Yaghmaian 1998-99; Burbach and Robinson 1999). Transnational capital is reducing even the most powerful nation-states to the role of administrating their own labor and resource markets and, in the case of the NATO allies, to protecting the transnational system of capitalist exploitation. To the extent that productive relations reach across regional, state, national, and continental lines and stand above the specific laws governing these territories, opposition to international capitalist domination—that is, opposition of the living against the rule of the dead—is best advanced through coordinated international organizations and movements.

Fifth and finally, we ought to reimagine our present position and projected future in relation to the struggle to abolish capitalism and create a global society based on universally life-enhancing social, political, economic, and environmental relations. I am fully cognizant that for many who identify themselves as left, socialism is dead. It appears that only a severe case of historical amnesia or ideological dogmatism can explain those who, like myself and the early West, argue that building a socialist society offers the best hope for humanizing our relationships with one another and with nature. Those who believe otherwise are just not willing to face the facts. They cling to yesterday's dreams because they cannot confront today's realities.

Nevertheless, for those on the left who, along with the secular and religious right, believe that socialism is dead forever, it is worth recalling that capitalism did not come into the world fully formed. It took centuries of colonizing, pillaging, plundering, enslaving, and murdering, as well as centuries of rebellions and revolutions and scientific and technological developments, before capitalism became the globally dominant mode of socioeconomic organization. Until the end of the eighteenth century, many would have argued that the capitalist "experiment" had "failed," a failure the Catholic clergy and feudal nobility celebrated until the eve of their beheading. When the bourgeoisie did finally obtain political power, their apologists wasted no time before they began to argue that their new world order was, in the speculative discourse of Hegel, the absolute realization of absolute spirit or, in the discourse of social Darwinists, the expression of humanity's natural disposition to acquire, accumulate, possess, and control. Humanity, they maintained, had reached the end of history.

But there is nothing natural about capitalist relations of production. They are humanly created relations, and the creation of a more life-enhancing mode of human existence begins with the recognition that what is need not be and that something better can be made in its place. And so I propose, to conclude this work, the necessity for adopting a point of view that reorients our labor in relation to the task of building a life-enhancing mode of being and becoming. We are, then, laboring after the end of what might be described as the first international attempt to create a postcapitalist society and on the eve of a second international movement to accomplish the same. Our guiding goal ought to be that of fostering working-class solidarity and building international organizations that are capable of challenging the dictatorship of capital. In this way our work might become a real force in the human struggle to build a democratic, peaceful, life-enhancing, humane, and environmentally responsible society, a society in which "our gifts and resources are held not for ourselves alone but as instruments of service for the rest of humanity" (King 1986:206).

Notes

Introduction

1. In *One World, Ready or Not,* William Greider notes that the "economics of globalization relies upon a barbaric transaction—the denial of individual rights—as a vital element of profitability. The fact that this practice is widely accepted and commercially efficient or that it has a long, notorious history from earlier industrial eras does not remove the moral stain. Exploitation involves extracting profit from the inherent weakness of other human beings—people who are unable, for whatever reason, to defend themselves against domination. The presence of exploitative conditions is usually reflected in two complementary facts: First, the industrial wage is so low that it cannot sustain a minimal livelihood, even for young single workers in very poor countries. Second, the power of the state is actively employed to prevent workers from overcoming their [position of] weakness" (1997:388).

2. In *Prophesy Deliverance* West goes so far as to claim that "an alliance of prophetic Christianity and progressive Marxism" represents "a last humane hope for humankind" (1982:95). The classic elaboration of contemporary post-Marxist politics is *Hegemony and Socialist Strategy: Towards a Radical Democratic Politics* (1985) by Ernesto Laclau and Chantal Mouffe. Two useful elaborations of post-Marxist discourses are Aronson 1994 and Sherman 1995. For productive critiques of post-Marxist theory and politics, see Targ 1996 and Eagleton 1996.

3. When Eva L. Corredor asked him about the value of Marxism, West responded: "Marx was fundamentally concerned about the interlocking relation between corporate, financial and political elites who had access to a disproportionate amount of resources, power, prestige and status in society. Certainly, that is a starting point for understanding any society that we know of today, especially in the United States. Once we lose sight of the very complex relations between those three sets of elites, corporate, financial-banking and political elites, and the reasons why the working people, the working poor and the very poor, find themselves with very little access to resources—once we lose sight of that, which the Marxist tradition, which was not the only but the primary tradition which would analyze this, once we lose sight of this, then we have little or no analytical tools in our freedom fight" (West 1993c:59).

4. For more on U.S. race and labor relations see Foner and Lewis 1989; Davis 1981; and Jones 1998.

5. Royal Plankenhorn, a process operator for the A.E. Staley Manufacturing Company, clarified the social work at hand when he stated: "We have to break down the walls that divide us because his battle is my battle, my battle is his battle, and your battle is my battle. We can't succeed any other way" (in Brecher 1998:363).

6. In *The Promise of Pragmatism: Modernism and the Crisis of Knowledge and Authority* (1994), John Patrick Diggins offers an illuminating account of the history of twentieth-century pragmatism and, in particular, the ways in which postmodernist and poststructuralist arguments and concepts regarding knowledge, power, society, self, politics, freedom, history, and being are prefigured in the work of American pragmatists from James to Rorty. *Deconstruction and Pragmatism* (1996), edited by Simon Critchley and Chantal Mouffe, contains essays by Critchley, Jacques Derrida, Ernesto Laclau, Chantal Mouffe, and Richard Rorty on the philosophical, sociological, and political similarities and differences between pragmatism, poststructuralism, and postmodernism.

7. In *Late Capitalism* Ernest Mandel notes that "the fate of the semi-colonies assumes its most tragic form in the growing under-nourishment of these nations. In the 30's they were still able to export 14 million tons of grain products annually. By the 60's they had to import 10 million tons of grain-products annually, and the volume of these imports risks becoming much larger during the second half of the 70's [and beyond]. This is due neither to demographic explosion nor lack of foresight, but to the socio-economic structures imposed by imperialism. Increasing areas of land are being converted to export crops, catering to the needs of the metropolitan countries and not those of the local populations: in Africa alone, coffee output increased by 300% between 1959 and 1967" (1975:375). In *The Hunger Machine* (1987), Jon Bennet and Susan George note that there is enough grain produced annually to feed over six billion people, yet millions of tons are burned in order to sustain artificially high market prices. In addition, recent decades have seen not only mass starvation but also a dramatic and horrifying resurgence of slavery, in which women and children are sold on the world capitalist market as wage laborers and slaves. For more on women and children see Mies 1986 (esp. 112–44); L. Robinson 1993; and Brock and Thistlethwaite 1996.

8. The World Wildlife Fund estimated that more tropical forests were burned in 1997 than at any other time this century. More than 80 percent of these fires were set deliberately by multinational companies seeking to clear land to raise cattle or grow crops for export to First World nations.

9. The "important goal of U.S. policy is to make the world safe for the *Fortune 500* and its global system of capital accumulation. Governments that strive for any kind of economic independence or any sort of populist redistributive politics, that attempt to take some of their economic surplus and apply it to not-for-profit services that benefit the people—such governments are the ones most likely to feel the wrath of U.S. intervention or invasion" (Parenti 1995:39); examples include Guatemala under Arbenz, Chile under Allende, and Nicaragua under the Sandinistas. In "various fundamental ways, the United States promotes and props up the global trading system, allowing it to evade many of its gathering contradictions and instabilities. An economic crisis will likely be joined when the United States is no longer able to do this—a climactic moment that is fast approaching" (Greider 1997:192).

10. For more on the theoretical and political history of the Marxist-pragmatist exchange, see Novack 1975; Kloppenberg 1986; Livingston 1991; and Westbrook 1991.

Chapter 1: The Christian-Marxist Dialogue and the End of Liberation Theology

1. Interestingly, if not ironically, much of this ideology uncritically drew from and reproduced Stalinist propaganda, claiming that the Soviet Union was a communist coun-

try, just as Stalin declared it to be, and that Stalin's policies and practices were a necessary consequence of policies and practices elaborated by Lenin (if not also Marx and Engels, leading to the ahistorical, idealist, and totalizing claim that "Marxism equals Stalinism"). In fact, West himself does not avoid circulating a variation of this cold war equation, for in the concluding chapter of *Prophesy Deliverance* he contends that Leninism and Trotskyism, though slightly more progressive than Stalinism, remain, like Stalinism, part of what he calls "regressive, or right-wing Marxism" (1982:131). Both are marked by "rigidity, dogmatism, and elitism" (ibid.). The claim that Stalin represented the revolutionary tradition articulated by Lenin and others would have appeared to Trotsky and other members of what became known as the Left Opposition—that is, if they had not been imprisoned or murdered—as another example of Stalinist "pravda." Trotsky's *Revolution Betrayed* (1972), completed just prior to his assassination by Stalin's thugs in 1940, remains an indispensable critique of the politically reactionary nature of Stalin's "socialism in one country" by a major leader of the Bolshevik Revolution and member of the Left Opposition.

2. The political nature of the construction and reconstruction of historical memory is especially evident in the case of King. "What is often not discussed—and perhaps deliberately ignored—is how King dramatically revised his views, glimpsed most eloquently in his Vietnam-era antiwar rhetoric and in his War-on-Poverty social activism" (Dyson 1995:27). King came to more openly and directly support a redistribution of power, property, and wealth.

3. Malcolm X's post-Mecca philosophical and political changes were largely unaddressed and unexamined in Spike Lee's film tribute (see Dyson 1995:129–44; Marable 1995:137–41).

4. For more on North American liberation theology, see Cone 1984, 1986b; Grant 1989, 1993; Beverly Harrison 1985; King, Maynard, and Woodyard 1988; Ruether 1975, 1983, 1989, 1992; Brown 1990; Wilmore and Cone 1993; Wallis 1994; and King and Woodyard 1999.

5. Although Marxists have not by and large focused their attention on questions of culture as much as on politics and economics, it does not follow, as many post-Marxists contend, that Marxism is *theoretically* incapable of addressing such questions and providing productive interpretations of them. In fact there is a rich body of Marxist work that has engaged primarily in questions of culture. The theoretical outline for a historical materialist analysis of culture was sketched out by Marx and Engels in, among other works, Marx's *Class Struggles in France* and *The Eighteenth Brumaire of Louis Bonaparte,* and Engels's *Peasant War in Germany.* These works focus on the role of *noneconomic* factors in the development of social, political, and economic reality. Following Marx and Engels, there are, among other works, Kautsky's study of early Christianity, Gramsci's work on popular religion, Jean-Paul Sartre's study of psychoanalysis, and Stanley Aronowitz's study of the making of the American working class. In a letter to Joseph Bloch, Engels contested the vulgarization of historical materialism: "According to the materialist conception of history the *ultimately* determining element in history is the production and reproduction of real life. More than this neither Marx nor I have ever asserted. Hence if somebody twists this into saying that the economic element is the *only* determining one, he transforms that proposition into a meaningless, abstract, senseless phrase. The economic situation is the basis, but the various elements of the superstructure: political forms of the class struggle and its results, to wit: constitutions established by the victorious class after a successful battle, etc., juridical forms, and then even the reflexes of all these actual struggles in the brains of the participants, political, juristic, philosophical theories, religious views and their further development into systems of dogmas, also exercise their influence upon the course of the historical struggles and in many cases preponderate in determining their *form.* . . . In the second place, however, history is made in such a way that the final result always arises from conflicts between many individual wills, of which each again has been made what it is by a host of particular conditions of life. Thus, there

are innumerable intersecting forces, an infinite series of parallelograms of forces which give rise to one resultant—the historical event" (in Tucker 1978:760–61).

6. Although Christian theologians have posited the ideal equality of human beings before God, Christianity has supported the subordination of human beings to diverse forms of exploitative social relations. Orthodox Christian theology's dualistic anthropology has made it possible to affirm the spiritual equality of human beings before God and to accept the material inequality of human beings within social organizations. All may be equal before the eyes of God, but all are not equal in the eyes of human beings. At the same time, however, Christians have opposed existing social relations and those who benefit from these relations by insisting that spiritual equality necessarily demands material equality. The history of black resistance to slavery and segregation was in large measure inspired by this claim.

7. In *The Invisible Religion* Thomas Luckmann argues that it "is in keeping with an elementary sense of the concept of religion to call the transcendence of biological nature by the human organism a religious phenomenon" (1967:49). Luckmann's comments echo the gloss on religion in *The German Ideology* when Marx writes, "Religion is from the outset consciousness of the transcendental arising from actually existing forces" (in Kee 1990:283).

8. For an especially illuminating and sobering analysis of the state of the Earth, see Athanasiou 1996. Athanasiou examines the relationship between economics and ecology and argues that ecological well-being depends on closing the division between rich and poor and establishing democratic modes of authority over economic institutions and societal planning. Also see King and Woodyard 1999.

9. Gramsci elaborates on the politics of metaphysical materialism: "This is why it is essential at all times to demonstrate the futility of mechanical determinism: for, although it is explicable as naive philosophy of the mass and as such, but only as such, can be an intrinsic element of strength, nevertheless when it is adopted as a thought-out and coherent philosophy on the part of the intellectuals, it becomes the cause of passivity, of idiotic self-sufficiency" (1971:337).

10. I am paraphrasing the ex-slave, abolitionist, and spokesperson for women's rights Frederick Douglass, who, in the process of determining why "some people are slaves, and others masters," was, as he put it, "not very long in finding out the true solution of the matter. It was not color, but crime, not God, but man, that afforded the true explanation of the existence of slavery; nor was I long in finding out another important truth, viz.: what man can make, man can unmake" (in Zinn 1980:176). Although theologians may describe slavery as evil and explain its existence as a manifestation of sin, these categories remain, from Douglass's point of view, discursive mystifications of its nonmetaphysical, this-worldly causes. In short, the categories of evil, sin, and tragedy are theological "translations" or linguistic "transubstantiations" of humanly manufactured and transformable conditions of existence (see Genovese and Fox-Genovese 1987).

11. In an interview published in *The Harvard Review of Philosophy,* West explains: "I've always been obsessed with the problem of evil and I wrestle with various forms of unjustified suffering, unmerited pain, and unnecessary social misery" (1999a:45).

12. Coming to terms with "the dark side of modernity" has become a prominent task for West (1999b:562). "My view of what it means to be human," says West in the introduction to *The Cornel West Reader,* "is preeminently existential—a focus on particular, singular, flesh-and-blood persons grappling with dire issues of death, dread, despair, disease, and disappointment" (xvii).

13. "Sin," says Gutiérrez, "appears, therefore, as the fundamental alienation, the root of a situation of injustice and exploitation" (1973:175).

14. In "The Market as God" (1999) Harvey Cox argues that the market now constitutes God within the everyday metaphysical psychology of capitalist society. The free market, says Cox, "is fast becoming a postmodern deity—believed despite the evidence" (18)—

that is, believed in even though the empirical evidence does not support bourgeois ideological fantasies that it can and will shepherd humanity into the land of milk and honey. On the global theological movement for a truly new international socioeconomic order and what this movement portends for North Americans, especially U.S. Christians, see Brown 1990.

15. See Barber 1995 for an interesting discussion of the ways in which fundamentalism constitutes a nostalgic, often antidemocratic response to the exploitative forces of capitalism.

16. Moreover, recall that Catholicism not only provided the ideological and institutional infrastructure of the feudal mode of social organization; in addition, along with Protestantism, it constituted the religion of the European colonizers, slave traders, and slave masters and was quite deliberately mobilized as a mechanism for maintaining blacks in a state of subjection. Slave traders and slave masters prohibited slaves from practicing their own religious traditions and subjected them to Christian education in the hope that it would increase their willingness to accept slavery as ontologically necessitated by God. Both "ecclesiastical and temporal masters hoped that what the cowhides of mortals did not achieve, the lash of God would accomplish," writes historian Norrece T. Jones Jr. in *Born a Child of Freedom, Yet a Slave* (1990:132). "By stressing the brevity of life on earth and the impartiality of the Judgment in determining one's *eternal* state, both the temporal power elite and its holy cohorts sought to merge the interests of the enslaved with the enslaver. Every person, regardless of rank, was a child of God held accountable equally for [his or her] deeds" (ibid.). According to Jones, Christianity typically supported the interests of the southern slaveholding class, just as it has so far supported all ruling classes. Of course, whereas proslavery Christianity as expressed by white and black preachers alike promoted submissiveness to both earthly and heavenly masters, promising pie in the sky as compensation for crumbs here on Earth, some blacks refashioned the Christian ideal of universal brotherhood and sisterhood into a spiritual weapon of struggle against slavery. Slave masters depended on the dissemination of quietistic, otherworldly Christian metaphysics among their "human capital," a Christianity that offered eternal life in Heaven in exchange for obedience here on Earth. Yet there was always the frequently realized possibility that slaves might interpret the gospel message of Christianity as one of liberation from bondage, God as the God of the oppressed, and the life of Jesus as prophetically challenging the misuse of Christianity by whites to protect slavery and the slave-owning class by insisting that slavery contradicted the will of God and the ethic of love. Even among those who saw God as being "on their side," however, many remained convinced, as Christianity taught, that whenever and "wherever liberation did occur, God would be the primary actor and instigator" (152). Alternatively, as West concludes in *Prophesy Deliverance,* since we are fundamentally fallen and yet dignified creatures, we should "approximate as close as is humanly possible the precious values of individuality and democracy," that is, "as soon as God's will be done" (1982:146).

17. Yet the "battle for socialism," says Marable, "will force the Black Church to place the collective needs of Black humanity ahead of the narrow individual needs of any single person. Whether the Black Church, and those courageous ministers who embody the militant tradition of Blackwater [the tradition of black resistance to slavery, segregation, and discrimination], can face this test remains to be seen. . . . If they succeed, they have the potential to spark anew moral and ethical commitment that remains essential within the struggle against racism and capitalist exploitation" (1983:214).

Chapter 2: Race, Class, Power

1. West's essay was originally published in *Year Left,* ed. Michael Sprinker, 74–90 (London: Verso, 1985), and republished in West's collection *Keeping Faith: Race and Faith in America* (1993d).

2. It is perhaps useful to bear in mind that Foucault's own project largely derives from Nietzsche. Foucault explains: "If I wanted to be pretentious, I would use 'the genealogy of morals' as the general title of what I am doing. It was Nietzsche who specified the power relation as the general focus, shall we say, of philosophical discourse—whereas for Marx it was the production relation. Nietzsche is the philosopher of power, a philosopher who managed to think of power without having to confine himself within a political theory in order to do so" (1980:53). In *Racist Culture* (1993) and *Racial Subjects* (1997), David Theo Goldberg offers a carefully detailed description and critical analysis of the discursive generation of racialized identities and inequalities. In *Race in North America* (1998), Audrey Smedley offers an illuminating analysis of the particular role of English chauvinism in the articulation of racist ideologies and practices.

3. Regrettably such theories remain alive, even if not well, in the work of contemporary scientists such as William Cockily, Arthur Jenson, Richard Herrnstein, and Charles Murray, who provide "proof" that racists are correct: "The National Front in Britain and the Nouvelle Droite in France argue that racism and anti-Semitism are natural and cannot be eliminated, citing as their authority E. O. Wilson of Harvard, who claims that territoriality, tribalism, and xenophobia are indeed part of the human genetic constitution, having been built into it by millions of years of evolution" (Lewontin, Rose, and Kamin 1984:27). More recently, Herrnstein and Murray advanced the argument that socioeconomic inequalities between racial groups result from inequalities in the average intelligence of the members of these groups. For a critique of their work, see Fraser 1995.

4. Perhaps not by whites. Many blacks, however, and perhaps most notably black abolitionist David Walker, challenged precisely this assumption. In his *Appeal to the Colored Citizens of the World* (1965), originally published in 1829, Walker advances a prophetically eloquent and intellectually rigorous critique of racist ideology, including a critique of Thomas Jefferson's "naturalistic" justification of slavery, the slave system, and various Christian explanations (justifications) of slavery (see "Article One"). Also see Benjamin Banneker's letter to Thomas Jefferson in which he critiques Jefferson claims regarding the purported "natural" inequality of the "races" (Banneker 1993:48–50).

5. In *Black Looks: Race and Representation* (1992) and *Killing Rage: Ending Racism* (1995) bell hooks elaborates on this issue.

6. Jacqueline Jones notes that the "price and availability of various groups of laborers, rather than any ideology of 'racial' inferiority, determined the extent of slavery in specific cities and regions" (1998:127). When white workers in the city of Richmond struck against the Tredegar Iron Works in 1847 for higher wages and in protest of the employment of "highly skilled slave puddlers," they were dismissed and replaced with an all-black workforce. "To drive home his point, [the manager] Anderson sued his former employees, charging that they had conspired to deprive him of his slave labor," and reminded "all white workmen that their labor was more often valued according to its price than the color of its skin" (217). Whites who today celebrate their "Confederate heritage" mistakenly assume what was never true, namely, that the slaveholding, plantation-owning class maintained anything other than an interest in exploiting workers regardless of color.

7. Du Bois writes that "the income-bearing value of race prejudice was the cause and not the result of theories of race inferiority; that particularly in the United States the income of the Cotton Kingdom based on Black slavery caused the passionate belief in Negro inferiority and the determination to enforce it even by arms" (1940:129). As James Freeman Clarke, a white abolitionist, remarked, "We dislike them [blacks] because we are unjust to them" (in J. Jones 1998:20).

8. Interestingly, the very system that has perpetuated racial divisions is increasingly dissolving them and thus is fostering increased recognition of the artificial nature of these divisions. In this way, the same motive that compels capitalists to invade every corner of

the world in search of higher rates of return on investments generates social circumstances that render, again unevenly, claims regarding the supposed superiority or inferiority of different "races" increasingly difficult to support empirically and, as important, incompatible with forms of production that depend on cooperation among individuals of different "races." In the light of these transformations, which have been made possible by the abolition of Jim Crow, the passage of civil rights legislation, and the affirmation of diversity, it should come as no surprise that the frequency of sexual relations between persons ascribed to different "races" has dramatically increased over the past twenty years. In this regard it is worth quoting Marx, who wrote that "capitalist production only really begins . . . when each individual capital simultaneously employs a comparatively large number of workers, and when, as a result, the labour-process is carried on on an extensive scale, and yields relatively large quantities of products. A large number of workers working together, at the same time, in one place (or, if you like, in the same field of labour), in order to produce the same sort of commodity, under the command of the same capitalist, constitutes the starting-point of capitalist production" (1977:439)—not to mention the starting point for the organization of resistance to capitalist rule.

9. See Marx's critique of machinery in *Capital,* vol. 1, and Georg Lukács's of Taylorism, the application of scientific engineering to the physical motions and movements of workers, in *History and Class Consciousness: Studies in Marxist Dialectics* (1971). "Like every other instrument for increasing the productivity of labour," said Marx, "machinery is intended to cheapen commodities and, by shortening the part of the working day in which the worker works for himself, to lengthen the other part, the part he gives to the capitalist for nothing" (1977:492). Manufacturing under capitalism "seizes labour-power by its roots. It converts the worker into a crippled monstrosity by furthering his particular skill as in a forcing-house, through the suppression of a whole world of productive drives and inclinations, just as in the states of La Plata [Argentina, Paraguay, and Uruguay] they butcher a whole beast for the sake of his hide or his tallow" (481). Marx's discussion of the capitalist development of machines in *Capital* remains invaluable for understanding the development and deployment of science and technology in the contemporary period.

10. It is far from accidental that Heidegger ascribed so much philosophical importance to Heraclitus's fragment 53, which was pivotal to Nietzsche's own articulation of the will to power, during those years in which he gave his most "unconcealed" and "resolute" support to Hitler and National Socialism. "The Führer has awakened this will in the entire people and has welded it into *one* single resolve," said Heidegger in 1933 while serving as rector of Freiburg University (in Wolin 1991:52). For a defense of Heidegger in full recognition of his affiliation with the Nazis and total silence regarding the Jewish question, see J. Young 1997.

11. In addition to the denial of food, clean water, housing, health care, education, and employment to hundreds of millions of human beings, perhaps the most horrific recent example of development driven by profits is the emerging story regarding the development, use, and sale of depleted uranium (DU) weapons. According to a report issued by the National Gulf War Veterans Resource Center, "696,628 U.S. troops served in the Gulf War between August 2, 1990, and July 31, 1991—these are considered 'Gulf War Conflict' veterans by the VA. Of the 696,628, 575,978 (83%) are eligible for benefits through the VA." As of October 15, 1999, "of the 575,978, more than 263,000 (45%) [have] sought medical care at the VA. . . . 183,629 (32%) [have] filed claims against the VA for service-related medical disabilities [and out] of the 183,629 VA claims filed, 136,031 (74%) [have so far been] approved in whole or in part . . . 136,031 (24%) are now considered disabled by the VA less than ten years since the start of the Gulf War. . . . Another 27,622 claims against the VA [are] still pending [and] more than 9,600 Gulf War veterans have died" (1999:1). Although the exact causes of the illnesses suffered by Gulf War veterans remain undeter-

mined, the Department of Defense has revealed that "as many as 100,000 U.S. troops were exposed to repeated low-levels of chemical warfare agents, including sarin, cyclosarin, and mustard gases; more than 250,000 received the investigational new drug pyridostigmine bromide (PB pills) . . . [;] 8,000 received the investigational new botulinum toxoid (Bot Tox) vaccine; 150,000 received the hotly debated anthrax vaccine; [and] 436,000 entered into or lived for months within areas contaminated by more than 315 tons of depleted uranium radioactive toxic waste possibly laced with trace amounts of highly radioactive Plutonium and Neptunium, almost all without any awareness, training, protective equipment, or medical evaluations" (ibid.). A policy report issued by Dan Fahey on December 15, 1999, suggests that "during and after the Gulf War, thousands of American and coalition soldiers and local civilians may have inhaled or ingested DU dust while climbing on and entering contaminated equipment" (1999). Although the exact health risks from exposure to depleted uranium weapons remain unknown, "those who profit from the manufacture and sale of depleted uranium ammunition, and those who desire to use it, are maneuvering to ensure the unrestricted future use of DU munitions. Among the parties with an economic stake in the continued use of DU ammunition are the US Department of Energy, US Department of Defense, US ammunition manufacturers such as Primex Technologies and Aerojet Corp., and arms merchants in Russia, Pakistan and other countries" (ibid.). See Mesler 1997.

12. In the past twenty-five years, U.S. pharmaceutical companies, helped by political representatives, have been able to include strict patent rights regarding the production of drugs, so that they are able to exercise monopoly control over their distribution and maintain "acceptable" rates of profit on their sale. In 1998 Clinton administration officials were able to undermine a World Health Organization (WHO) proposal to adopt the principle that people's well-being ought to assume priority over corporate profits when it comes to providing medicine. Representing the special interests of the Pharmaceutical Research and Manufacturers Association (PhRMA), an organization that represents such companies as Johnson and Johnson, Bristol Myers Squib, and Eli Lilly, the trade representatives were able to block ratification of this proposal. In addition, the U.S. pharmaceutical representatives were able to strong-arm other nations into accepting stricter regulations on intellectual property rights by threatening trade sanctions and harsh tariffs. Although these "rights" mean higher profits for drug companies, they also mean that millions of people around the world who need but cannot afford to buy these drugs will suffer and die needlessly.

13. In *Gaia and God* (1992) Rosemary Ruether indicates that "total American military spending over the forty-five years since 1945 has topped $4,400 billion; $1,500 billion from 1945 to 1975; $1,500 billion from 1976 to 1985 and $1,400 billion from 1986 to 1990"; in addition, the military budget has remained between $250 and $275 billion since 1990 (103). There is of course no way to estimate precisely how much better the quality of life in the United States would be if even half of this money had been invested in the development of education, transportation, health care, child care, and the environment, although it is reasonable to assume that everyday living conditions for the majority of citizens would be vastly improved.

Chapter 3: Racism and the Struggle for Working-Class Democracy

1. It is important to point out that many North American liberation theologians have begun to move beyond the race-based analyses and identity politics that informed their initial works. In *My Soul Looks Back* James Cone remarks: "[As] with feminism, my first response [to racism] was to ignore the problem of class, because race appeared to be the most dominant manifestation of injustice in the United States" (1986b:123). Critiques by

Latin American and feminist theologians later enabled Cone to recognize the relationship between sexism and racism and, more important, the role of class: "We cannot continue to speak against racism without any reference to a radical change in the economic order. I do not think that racism can be eliminated as long as capitalism remains intact. It is time for us to investigate socialism as an alternative to capitalism" (130). In fact, black feminist theologians have led the way beyond the theoretical, patriarchal, and practical limitations of earlier attempts to articulate a theology of black liberation. See, for example, Grant 1989; Townes 1997; D. Williams 1993.

2. See Brouwer 1998 and Mishel, Bernstein, and Schmitt 1999 for more on how the pie is cut.

3. Asked in 1965 about Elijah Muhammad's race-based theology, Malcolm X responded "that an objective analysis of events that are taking place on this earth today points toward some type of ultimate showdown. You can call it a political showdown, or even a showdown between the economic systems that exist on the earth which almost boil down to along racial lines" (1965:216). And in his last formal speech, "The Black Revolution and Its Effect upon the Negroes of the Western Hemisphere," delivered on February 18, 1965, Malcolm X argued that "it is incorrect to classify the revolt of the Negro as simply a racial conflict of black against white, or as a purely American problem. Rather, we are today seeing a global rebellion of oppressed against oppressor, the exploited against the exploiter. The Negro revolution is not a racial revolt" (217).

4. In 1970 Kwame Nkrumah wrote that "the dramatic exposure in recent years of the nature and extent of the class struggle in Africa, through the succession of reactionary military coups and the outbreak of civil wars, particularly in West and Central Africa, has demonstrated the unity between the interests of neo-colonialism and the indigenous bourgeoisie. . . . For the African bourgeoisie, the class which thrived under colonialism, is the same class which is benefiting under the post-independence, neocolonial period. Its basic interest lies in preserving capitalist social and economic structures. It is therefore, in alliance with international monopoly finance capital" (1970:9, 10).

5. Jack Nelson-Pallmeyer's *Brave New World Order: Can We Pledge Allegiance?* (1994) exposes the elite global interests served by what former U.S. president George Bush, borrowing from fascist rhetoric, called the "New World Order." Paul Vallely's *Bad Samaritans: First World Ethics and Third World Debt* (1991) examines the role of transnational institutions, especially the International Monetary Fund, World Bank, and World Trade Organization, in transferring value from Third to First World nations and the devastating consequences this transfer exacts on people living, laboring, and dying for corporations in the fields, factories, and mines of Third World nations.

6. At the time this book was being written, Senator Joseph Kennedy Jr. had placed before the U.S. Senate a new bill, the third of its kind, calling on Congress to shut down the U.S. Army School of the Americas, located at Fort Benning, Georgia. In its fifty-year history the school has trained over 60,000 military personnel, who constitute a "who's who" among Latin American military dictators and death-squad leaders. For a critique of the school, see Nelson-Pallmeyer 1997.

7. The extent to which the international system of capitalist exploitation remains a system of global *white* supremacy is provocatively presented by Charles W. Mills in *Blackness Visible: Essays on Philosophy and Race* (1998). In chapter 5, "Revisionist Ontologies: Theorizing White Supremacy," Mills argues that to the extent that the dominant classes are "white," this system is most accurately described as a white supremacist system. The "larger world—the global economy, the international financial institutions—is dominated by First World powers, which (except for Japan), are themselves white and are linked by various political, economic, and cultural ties to local whites, thus differentially privileged" (103). I find much of Mills's argument compelling. Nevertheless, I still believe that the socioeconomic system is, at the highest level of abstraction, best understood as a "capi-

talist" system characterized by private ownership of the means of production, organization of production for the purpose of producing capital, and competition among property owners to increase their respective shares of the total available productive properties, labor markets, and commodity markets internationally. At a slightly lower level of abstraction, with slightly less conceptual applicability to existing empirical realities, it is a system in which the majority of individuals who constitute the dominant economic class and control the dominant financial, political, social, and economic institutions are racially coded as "white." What is key, however, is that their interests are primarily financial, not racial. The color of their interest, as with the interest of capitalists defined as "nonwhite," is the color of money.

8. Here, at Virginia Commonwealth University, the proposal to create an undergraduate major in African American studies was twice unanimously affirmed by the Board of Visitors, only to be voted down by the Virginia State Council of Higher Education after Jeff Brown, the only African American whom former governor George Allen Jr. appointed to the council, argued vociferously against the proposal. Brown's qualifications to oversee higher education in Virginia officially rested in the fact that he had graduated from the Naval Academy and had worked as a jet pilot and a manager for Circuit City, a company with a history of racist hiring and promotion practices. His unofficial qualification seems to be, as Adolph Reed notes, that "he is black, and his militant ideological commitment to a simple-minded notion of 'colorblindedness' comforts the conservative orthodoxy. That orthodoxy insists that any attempts to do anything specifically in behalf of nonwhites or women are self-defeating, debilitating, and unjust" (1997c:18). The "VCU African American Studies controversy speaks of the breadth of the right's combativeness, and its eagerness to employ any black conservative to carry its water" (ibid.).

9. For a wide range of selections by the new black conservatives on a variety of topics, see Conti, Faryna, and Stetson 1997.

10. See Herrnstein and Murray 1994. For a critical assessment of their work, see Fraser 1995; Hadjor 1995; and Steinberg 1995. For a discussion of welfare policy and the conditions of life for the poor and working poor, see Gans 1995 and Handler and Hasenfeld 1997. For a discussion of residential and employment discrimination, see Massey and Denton 1993; Chideya 1995; Oliver and Shapiro 1995; and Marable 1997a.

11. According "to the Southern Poverty Law Center's project Klan Watch, in 1989 there were 7 cross burnings, 34 instances of vandalism, and 125 hate-crime related murders. By 1992, those numbers had risen to 31 cross burnings, 117 instances of vandalism, and 3222 murders" (Chideya 1995:187). On right-wing religious movements, see Diamond 1995, 1996; Abanes 1996; and Dyer 1997. On race war, see Delgaldo 1996.

12. Dalton Conley writes that black infants "are much more likely than white infants to be born with a low (under 2,500 grams) or a very low (under 1,500 grams) birth weight. In 1994, medical complications associated with low birth weight were the primary cause of death among black infants and the third leading cause for white infants. Correspondingly, the mortality rate among black infants that year (15.8 per thousand) was well over twice that among white and Hispanic babies (6.6 and 6.5 per thousand, respectively)" (1999:10).

13. Seymour Melman, "chairperson of the National Commission for Economic Conversion and Disarmament, observes that 750,00 additional jobs would be created 'if $165 billion were transferred from the military to education, transportation, environment, housing, etc. If an additional $80 billion, raised by restoring 1980 tax levels on the superrich, were spent on conversion, an additional 2.5 million jobs could be created'" (Marable 1997a:50–51).

14. Since 1980 the prison population in the United States has almost tripled, reaching 1.6 million persons in 1996, the highest rate of incarceration of any nation in the world. In California the prison population increased fivefold between 1977 and 1992. At present

growth rates, the prison population is doubling every seven years. Prison construction is one of the most lucrative and fastest-growing industries in the United States. Although blacks constitute 12 percent of the total population, nearly half of all state and federal inmates are African Americans. By "1995, 30 percent of all black males in their 20s nationwide were either in prison or jail, on probation or parole, or awaiting trial" (Marable 1997a:214). Thirty years after civil rights legislation, there are more black men in prison than there are in university graduate programs in the United States.

15. In *Seeing a Color-Blind Future* Harvard law professor Patricia Williams describes her own experience of applying for a home loan and how the bank changed the terms of her loan (e.g., raising the interest rate) once they discovered that she is black (1998:38–39).

16. The percentage of white children under eighteen living in poverty increased from 11.8 percent in 1979 to 16.1 percent in 1997, while the percentage of black children living in poverty decreased from 41.2 percent to 37.2 percent. Finally, the proportion of white families living in poverty increased from 6.9 percent in 1979 to 8.4 percent in 1997, while that of black families living in poverty decreased from 27.8 percent to 23.6 percent (Mishel, Bernstein, and Schmitt 1999:280–81).

17. The question of the extent to which black labor has been rendered expendable in the United States is highly debated. Michael Goldfield argues that those who make this claim fail to appreciate the extent that black workers remain "vital to the operation of the economy," in large measure by continuing to fill the most dehumanizing and least remunerative jobs (1997:354). In "U.S.: The Black Poor and the Politics of Expendability," Barbara Ransby emphasizes the possibility that a sizable portion of the black population is being made expendable. Although I would not minimize the genocidal potentials of capitalist development, potentials presently being realized around the world, the question of whether blacks have become expendable or simply remain lodged on the lowest rung of the social ladder should not distract us from the unquestionable fact that for most blacks in the United States and elsewhere, life is miserable.

18. In *Reflecting Black* cultural critic Michael Eric Dyson notes that it "is the lack of acknowledgment of the underside of the American Dream, the avoidance of its division of blacks by class, that is the most unfortunate feature of the Huxtable opulence. Cosby defends against linking the authenticity of the Huxtable representation of black life to the apparently contradictory luxury and comfort the family lives in when he says, 'To say that [the Huxtables] are not black enough is a denial of the American dream and the American way of life. My point is that this is an American family—an *American* family—and if you want to live like they do, and you're willing to work, the opportunity is there'" (1993:85). To this affirmation Dyson replies, "But surely Cosby knows better than this" (ibid.). Perhaps in his heart of hearts he does. But this has not prevented him from acting, along with Michael Jordan and others, as a "quintessential pitchman in American society" (69).

19. Mike Davis notes that "stratifications rooted in the differential positions in the social process have been reinforced by deep-seated ethnic, religious, racial, and sexual antagonisms within the working class. In different periods these divisions have fused together as definite intra-class hierarchies (for example, 'native + skilled + Protestant' versus 'immigrant + unskilled + Catholic') representing unequal access to employment, consumption, legal rights, and trade-union organization. The political power of the working class within American 'democracy' has always been greatly diluted by the effective disfranchisement of large sectors of labor: blacks, immigrants, women, migrant workers, among others" (1986:16). This is why black, feminist, immigrant, environmental, and gay and lesbian struggles remain integral to the development of a truly anticapitalist political movement for working-class democracy.

20. The strategy of divide and rule has been mobilized for as long as societies have been divided into classes. Michael Parenti points out that some "Greek and Roman writers,

including Plato and Aristotle, stressed the desirability of importing slaves of different nationalities and languages as a necessary means of preventing them from coalescing in rebellion. Aristotle writes: 'The husbandmen should by all means be slaves, not of the same nation, or men of any spirit; for thus they would be laborious in their business, and safe from attempting any novelties'" (1994:128). Referring to Reconstruction, Du Bois writes: "The theory of labouring class unity . . . failed to work in the South . . . because the theory of race was supplemented by a carefully planned and slowly evolved method, which drove such a wedge between white and black workers that there probably are not today in the world two groups of workers with practically identical interests who hate and fear each other so deeply and persistently and who are kept so far apart that neither sees anything of common interests. It must be remembered that the white group of labourers, while they received a low wage, were compensated for by a sort of public and psychological wage. They were given public deference and titles of courtesy because they were white. They were admitted freely with all classes of white people to public functions, public parks, and public schools. The police were drawn from their ranks, and the courts, dependent upon their votes, treated them with leniency as to encourage lawlessness. Their vote selected public officials, and while this had small effect upon the economic situation, it had great effect upon their personal treatment and the deference shown them. White schoolhouses were the best in the community, and conspicuously placed, and they cost anywhere from twice to ten times as much per capita as the coloured schools. The newspapers specialized in news that flattered the poor whites and almost utterly ignored the Negro except in crime and ridicule. . . . On the other hand, in the same way, the Negro was subject to public insult; was afraid of mobs; was liable to the jibes of children and the unreasoning fears of white women; and compelled almost continuously to submit to various badges of inferiority. The result of this was that the wages of both classes could be kept low, the whites fearing to be supplanted by the Negro labour, the Negroes always being threatened by the substitution of white labour" (in Callinicos 1992:19–20).

Chapter 4: The Pragmatic Concepts of Truth, Reality, and Politics

1. Brazilian liberation theologian Leonardo Boff explains: "You can jump into a river to save your drowning friend, and this shows your good will. In fact, it shows your love. But if you have never learned to swim, you do not save your friend. On the contrary, the two of you die together. Love you certainly had. But it was not a very intelligent love, and it was totally inefficacious, ineffective" (Boff and Boff 1984:4–5).

2. In an interview with Anders Stephanson, West argued that the category of totality is necessary to grasp "the mediations, interrelations, interdependencies, [the] totalizing forces in the world," adding that without this category "our politics become emaciated, our politics become dispersed, our politics become nothing but existential rebellion" (1988b:270).

3. In *Prophesy Deliverance* West posited the existence of class divisions "in light of the overwhelming evidence for their existence," adding that "only class divisions can explain the gross disparity between rich and poor, the immense benefits accruing to the former and the depravity of the latter" (1982:116). In view of this analysis West argued that workers must organize to fight capital's assault. After ten years of massive wealth redistribution from working-class to wealthy citizens, West became less certain about the need for class struggle. Following a lecture at Le Moyne College in Syracuse, New York, on February 17, 1993, entitled "Race Matters," in response to a question concerning his position on the relationship between race and class, West said that the most important concern for freedom fighters is to remain "attuned to the complexities of the past," adding that "this may not necessarily result in class struggle or allow one to infer given the evidence

that class struggle is a valid conclusion that one makes. It might or it might not" (1993e:n.p.). Why did West hesitate to take a position on a question he was absolutely clear about in *Prophesy Deliverance* and *Prophetic Fragments*? Said West: "I want to be open minded about this. I affirm the Peircean ideal that we must never block the road to inquiry. And then I add, if one wants to travel that road then all travelers must be willing to put their naked power and ignorance under the spotlight. Come to the conversation. Become self-critical in a self-righteous way" (ibid.). What remains to be explained is why being "self-critical in a self-righteous way" is more important than taking a stance on the question of the class.

4. In "Left Feminism and the Return to Class," Joanne Naiman writes that "the 'oppression theorists' quickly came to criticize what they felt was the economic determinism of traditional Marxism, and its limited view of the working class as the most revolutionary force in history. These theorists focused on oppressed groups distinct from the working class as central to social transformation" (1996:13).

5. In *Science, Class, and Society,* Goran Therborn notes that the tendency "to turn economic and political struggles and transformations into questions of culture and morality . . . is rather common among both liberal and radical American intellectuals" (1976:31–32).

6. Postmodern critiques of foundationalist and realist presuppositions have in the main had less to do with philosophy and more with supporting liberal-pluralist politics. Robert B. Westbrook notes that many who reject the quest for metaphysical foundations "adopt pragmatism as their 'anti-foundationalist' epistemological theory of choice and then couple it with a variety of moral and political commitments which owe more or less of a debt to Peirce, James and Dewey" and that seldom, if ever, include a commitment to socialist politics (1993:2, 11).

7. I would argue the opposite. As a mode of knowledge production, the "scientific method" involves subjecting all truth claims to critical analysis, empirical verification, rational argumentation, and public scrutiny. Inasmuch as it does these things, scientific method resists the dogmatism inherent in other modes of knowledge production, such as religion, that demonstrate the truth of their claims on the authority of tradition (e.g., "Men should rule because they have always ruled") and revelation (e.g., "The Scriptures say that men shall rule and the scriptures are the word of God"). Scientific method breaks with the closed circle of metaphysical systems by insisting that all claims be verified through empirical research, experimentation, and observation. Although scientists have been influenced deeply by ideological prejudices, institutional barriers, and socioeconomic interests, science nevertheless provides a way to question claims that have been made to justify oppressive social relations (e.g., demonstrating the groundlessness of race as a biological concept). In other words, the fact that scientists have supported racist, sexist, and classist social relations does not mean that we should abandon the claim that empirical research and inductive reasoning are key to discerning how the world works and what can be done to improve our circumstances.

8. West's position on truth and reality and on the relationship between the two is similar to Dewey's when Dewey argues in *The Quest for Certainty: A Study of the Relation of Knowledge and Action* that "when the physical sciences describe objects and the world as being such and such, it is thought that the description is of reality as it exists in itself" (1960:136–37; in West 1989:191). Nevertheless, Dewey continues, the "business of thought is not to conform to or reproduce the characters already possessed by objects but to judge them as potentialities of what they become through an indicated operation" (137). The object of knowledge is not "that which has being prior to and wholly independent of the operations of knowing" (196). It is rather partly constituted (discursively, linguistically, conceptually, etc.) by the subject in the act of knowing.

9. West argues that "Dewey considered Marx's magnum opus *Capital* as the most influential book of the half-century preceding 1930 . . . not because he believed Marx had

laid bare the iron laws of capitalism but rather because the book had such impact on political movements in the world" (1989:109). Dewey thought *Capital* was influential because, tautologically, it had so much influence. Given that, as West writes, "in regard to Marxism, Dewey remained a stranger, a novice, [and yet] an extreme critic" (107), perhaps it is no surprise that Dewey did not consider the possibility that *Capital* enjoyed its influence precisely because it explained capitalism, that is, because Marx expressed theoretically the particular characteristics of the capitalist mode of social production.

10. In the first preface to *Capital,* vol. 1, Marx indicates that his "standpoint, from which the development of the economic formation of society is viewed as a process of natural history, can less than any other make the individual responsible for relations whose creature he remains, socially speaking, however much he may subjectively raise himself above them" (1997:92). We are, especially as individuals, more products of than producers of our conditions of self-realization.

11. In "Democratic Evasions: Cornel West and the Politics of Pragmatism," Robert B. Westbrook argues that West's claim regarding the relationship between pragmatism and democratic politics is at least questionable. Westbrook points out that Max Otto was himself troubled by "Dewey's 'contention that Emerson is the philosopher of democracy.' No one, Otto ventured to say, who had as little to say as Emerson did about the practice of democracy could lay claim to that title" (1993:9). In fact, Dewey himself wrote that "he had forgotten he had ever said Emerson was the philosopher of democracy, and this was certainly not something he would say in 1941" (ibid.). "Despite the impression West sometimes leaves, the connections between the pragmatic evasion of philosophy and Emersonian democracy are contingent, not necessary. . . . This contingency also explains why so many of West's evaders prove disappointing democrats," as West's own genealogy of American pragmatism indicates (5–6).

12. Recall President Reagan's manic obsession with the Sandinistas and his hysterical (though not very humorous) political geography lesson in which he sought to help Americans fully appreciate the impending threat of being dominated by a foreign power by informing them that Managua, Nicaragua, is only one day's drive from Brownsville, Texas. For an "entertaining" history of U.S. relations with Latin American nations during the twentieth century, see Black 1988.

13. For more on Reagan's lies, see Chomsky 1987, 1991, 1993; Parenti 1988, 1995.

14. In *Divided Planet: The Ecology of Rich and Poor* Tom Athanasiou devotes an extended discussion to "greenwashing," that is, the corporate manipulation of public representations to give the appearance of being environmentally responsible without changing destructive policies. The "basis of the greenwashing industry is the slippage between reality and images of reality" (1996:230). Criticizing greenwashing depends above all else on our ability to discern, via research, analysis, and evaluation, the difference between the two.

15. This is precisely Marx's critique of Feuerbach's ahistorical and mechanical materialism. "The chief defect of all hitherto existing materialism," writes Marx in the first of his eleven theses on Feuerbach, "is that the thing, reality, sensuousness, is conceived only in the form of the object or of *contemplation,* but not as *human sensuous activity, practice,* not subjectively. Hence it happened that the *active side,* in contradistinction to materialism, was developed by idealism—but only abstractly, since, of course, idealism does not know real, sensuous activity as such. Feuerbach wants sensuous objects, really distinct from the thought objects, but he does not conceive human activity itself as *objective* activity" (in Tucker 1978:143).

16. In "The Use and Abuse of Modernity: Postmodernism and the American Philosophic Tradition," John Ryder suggests that there is no logical connection between the claim that "the cognitive process is necessarily perspectival and inherently creative" and the putatively consequent claim that objective knowledge of nature and society is impossible: "From the claim that objective knowledge, knowledge derived from no perspec-

tive or point of view, is impossible, it does not follow that knowledge of the objectively determinate traits of nature is impossible" (1993:100). What is missing from most antifoundationalist, antirealist arguments (though not from pragmatism) and absolutely crucial to "confirm theoretic, including philosophic, knowledge of objectively determined traits" is the category of *sensuous activity, human practice* or, as Hegel indicated, *labor* (ibid.).

17. I am deeply indebted to John Rosenthal for my understanding of the nature of Marx's object of investigation, the value form, especially as manifest in the money commodity; see his *The Myth of Dialectics: Reinterpreting the Marx-Hegel Relation*. Marx repeatedly criticized political economists, says Rosenthal, "for having confused the material 'content' of capital, understood in this context simply as produced means of production, with the 'form-determination' which first converts this material 'content' *into* capital, viz. the application of such means of production within those determinate relations of production which allow them to function simultaneously as *means of valorization*" (1998a:43).

18. West cites Marx from the preface to the first German edition of *Capital*, vol. 1: "It is the ultimate aim of this work, to lay bare the economic laws of motion of modern society" (in West 1991b:96).

19. Given his antirealist, antifoundationalist perspective, it perhaps should come as no surprise that Pascal is a significant figure for West. In an interview with Eva L. Corredor entitled "On the Influence of Lukács," West says: "[There is] one fundamental divergence between my own view and that of Lukács: for me there is always a dialectic of doubt and faith, of skepticism and leap of faith, so that I am much more influenced by Pascal or Montaigne, who is part of a particular tradition that understands that the doubt is inscribed within that faith" (1993c:50). He adds, "Pascalian sensibility is probably my central sensibility" (67).

20. Along these lines, Roy Bhaskar argues that "the crucial questions in philosophy are not whether to be a realist or an anti-realist, but *what sort* of realist to be (an empirical, conceptual, transcendental or whatever realist); whether one explicitly theorizes or merely implicitly secretes one's realism; and whether and how one decided, arrives at or absorbs one's realism. While arguing that we never encounter reality *except under a chosen description* (*Consequences of Pragmatism* p. xxxix), Rorty unwittingly imbibes and inherits Hume's and Kant's chosen descriptions of the reality known by the sciences" (1989:153)—as well as descriptions of capitalism known by liberal theorists.

21. Rosenthal usefully explains that "social relations as such always *concern* material things, since in all their various configurations they form the framework for the commerce of human beings with their natural environment, making the satisfaction of the individual's wants and needs a function of his or her subordination to the collective. Inasmuch as it is supposed to represent a principle of socio-historical research and in its most lucid formulations at any rate, this pre-eminent materiality of social life is the very point of Marx's materialism. ('One thing is clear,' Marx writes bluntly in *Capital*, 'the Middle Ages could not live on Catholicism, nor could the ancient world on politics' . . .)" (1998a:61).

22. The introductory chapter of *Race Matters* was first published in the August 2, 1992, *New York Times Magazine* by the title "Learning to Talk about Race."

23. In response to growing international economic crises, President Clinton has been hinting about the possibility of something like a global New Deal social contract. Whether he will find support for such a "revolutionary" proposal remains to be seen. What is noteworthy, however, is that Clinton, unlike West, argues that a social contract among business, labor, and government must be international, rather than merely national. In this way Clinton's vision differs significantly from West's vision in *Race Matters, The War against Parents,* and *The Future of American Progressivism,* exceeding it by almost an entire planet.

24. Based on this formulation gay men are not males; in fact, Hewlett and West come close to arguing as much in *The War against Parents,* a work I examine at length in chapter 7.

Chapter 5: The Past, Present, and Future of American Pragmatism

1. In *Lies My Teacher Told Me* the educator and social historian James W. Loewen relates that "Keller's commitment to socialism stemmed from her experience as a disabled person and from her sympathy for others with handicaps. She began by working to simplify the alphabet for the blind, but soon came to realize that to deal solely with blindness was to treat symptom, not cause. Through research she learned that blindness was not distributed randomly throughout the population but was concentrated in the lower class. Men who were poor might be blinded in industrial accidents or by inadequate medical care; poor women who became prostitutes faced the additional danger of syphilitic blindness. Thus Keller learned how the social class system controls people's opportunities in life, sometimes determining even whether they can see. Keller's research was not just book-learning. 'I have visited sweatshops, factories, and crowded slums. If I could not see it, I could smell it'" (1995:11–12).

2. Pragmatists have not been alone among post-Enlightenment philosophers in failing to address the problem of racism and especially in failing to develop explicitly antiracist philosophical arguments and ethics. As West notes in his "Genealogy of Modern Racism" and as Charles W. Mills elaborates in *The Racial Contract* (1997), the majority of post-Enlightenment Western philosophers have participated in what Mills calls a "racial contract" that reinforces white privilege by explicitly defending exclusions based on race or by avoiding the matter of race altogether through a failure to connect the problem of racism to that of socioeconomic opportunity.

3. Throughout this work I distinguish between "established" and "contingent" professors. The former category includes those professors who occupy tenured positions that offer relatively high wages, health and retirement benefits, and some degree of power to shape educational policy, curriculum development, and faculty employment. The latter includes professors who are paid relatively low wages, enjoy little or none of the benefits and securities offered to tenured professors, and work in positions based on temporary—that is, seasonal—contracts. At my own institution, Virginia Commonwealth University (VCU), 41 percent of the faculty are hired on this basis; half of all faculty members at the state's community colleges are part-timers. Average wages received by adjuncts for each course taught range from $1,206 at the community colleges to $2,070 at VCU and a high of $4,000 at the University of Virginia (*Richmond Times-Dispatch,* Oct. 19, 1998:A1, A12). Virginia figures parallel national averages both in terms of faculty composition and pay scales. The educational, social, and political implications of these numbers are becoming more evident as struggles over wages, benefits, job security, and the kind and quality of education become more frequent and more intense (e.g., the graduate student strikes at Yale and U.C. Berkeley).

4. In *Killing Rage* hooks writes that "opportunistic longings for fame, wealth, and power now lead many black critical thinkers, writers, academics, and/or intellectuals to participate in the production and marketing of black culture in ways that are complicit with the existing oppressive-exploitative structure" (1995:176). Referring to the work of the film director Spike Lee as emblematic of the conflict-ridden position of relatively well paid, privileged, and powerful black intellectuals, hooks contends that his "work cannot be revolutionary and generate wealth at the same time. Yet it is in his class interest to make it seem as though he, and his work, embodies the 'throw down ghetto' militant blackness that is the desired product. Not only must his middle-class origins be down-played,

so must his newfound wealth" (179), all of which makes exploring the impact of class on the content and character of intellectuals and their work challenging and troubling. It is not accidental that almost all the most visible and vocal black public intellectuals in America are grappling with the question of class. Inasmuch as they have been charged with representing "their race," the growing class gap that separates academic intellectuals from the reality of life for the majority of blacks becomes a problem that cannot be easily ignored.

Chapter 6: Saving the Nation in the Era of Transnational Capitalism

1. See Stephanie Coontz, *The Way We Never Were: American Families and the Nostalgia Trap* (1992) for an entertaining look at the myth of the "Good Old Days" that informs contemporary policy debates. Also see, by the same author, *The Way We Really Are: Coming to Terms with America's Changing Families* (1997).

2. King clarified the connections between the U.S. imperialism, racism, and poverty: "Here we spend thirty-five billion dollars a year to fight this terrible war in Vietnam and just the other day the Congress refused to vote forty-four million to get rid of rats in the slums and the ghettos of our country" (in Cone 1991:240); needless to say, the same dynamic is played out every day in a nation that spends fortunes on weapons of mass destruction and yet will not spend enough to ensure that all citizens have access to health care, quality education, and housing.

3. UNICEF's 1998 report indicates that the rate of infant mortality in Cuba is now 7.1 per 1,000.

4. In "U.S. Blockade Harmful to Health of Cuban People," Julia Lutsky quotes the American Association for World Health (AAWH) report entitled "Denial of Food and Medicine: The Impact of the U.S. Embargo on Health and Nutrition in Cuba," which reports that "researchers encountered numerous cases where individual children were suffering needlessly with terrible pain merely because some drugs are unavailable due to the embargo" (*People's Weekly World,* June 21, 1997:9). The embargo has inflicted undue suffering not only on the citizens of Cuba but also on U.S. citizens, for "many drugs and medical techniques developed by Cuban medical research are unavailable here, viz., Meningitis B vaccine, cheaply produced interferon and streptokinase, and an AIDS vaccine currently under test on the island" (16). Increasing numbers of U.S. religious organizations (some of which are critical of Castro) are defying what they, along with the pope, the United Nations, and most "developed" capitalist nations, hold to be an illegal, unjust, and immoral policy by sending medical aid and food supplies to the Cuban people.

5. Greider points out that even when evidence overwhelmingly supports claims regarding the systemic causes of hard times, "the culture of individualism [does] not prepare people to understand the failure as systemic, not personal" (1997:383). The "self-help" businesses, which constitute a multibillion-dollar industry, are predicated on this misunderstanding.

6. Louis Althusser's theory of ideology is heavily indebted to Lacan's post-Saussurian formulation of Freud's concept of the unconscious. In his seminal essay "Ideology and Ideological State Apparatuses," Althusser argues that the reproduction of capitalist relations of production depends on the production of individuals who "accept" their place within these relations and, even more, work vigorously and proudly to defend and expand them. One of the primary means by which bourgeois subjects are produced is through ideology. Althusser assumes, in other words, as "St. Paul admirably put it, [that] it is in the 'Logos,' meaning in ideology, that we 'live, move and have our being.' It follows that, for you and for me, the category of the subject is a primary 'obviousness' (obviousnesses are always primary): it is clear that you and I are subjects (free, ethical, etc. . . .). Like all

obviousness, including those that make a word 'name a thing' or 'have a meaning' (therefore including the obviousness of the 'transparency' of language), the 'obviousness' that you and I are subjects—and that does not cause any problems is an ideological effect, the elementary ideological effect. It is indeed a peculiarity of ideology that it imposes (without appearing to do so, since these are 'obviousnesses') obviousness as obviousness, which we cannot *fail to recognize* and before which we have the inevitable and natural reaction of crying out (aloud or in the 'still, small voice of conscience'): 'That's obvious! That's right! That's true!' . . . I shall then suggest that ideology 'acts' or 'functions' in such a way that it 'recruits' subjects among individuals (it recruits them all), or 'transforms' the individuals into subjects (it transforms them all) by that very precise operation which I have called *interpellation* of hailing, and which can be imagined along the lines of the most commonplace everyday police (or other) hailing: 'Hey, you there!'" (1971:171–72, 174).

7. For an excellent discussion of the historical development and politics of the concept of the juridical subject, see Rosenthal, *The Myth of Dialectics* (1998a), chapter 5, "Property and Person (or the Birth of the Juridical Subject)," pp. 60–65.

8. In *Sharing the Pie: A Citizen's Guide to Wealth and Power in America* (1998), Steve Brouwer points out that "during the era of the Robber Barons, the Courts made use of the 14th Amendment, which, ironically, had originally been written to guarantee citizenship and equal civil rights to ex-slaves at the end of the Civil War. The Court invoked the amendment to define the corporation as a 'person' under the law. This meant that government could not interfere with the activities of this corporate 'person' lest it be guilty of abridging citizens' rights" (125).

9. The irrationality of capitalism is nowhere more evident than in production to meet basic needs. In *The Hunger Machine* (1987) Jon Bennet and Susan George point out that enough grain was produced in 1986 to feed more than six billion people (the number projected to inhabit the planet in the year 2000). However, millions of tons of grain were burned that same year to raise the price of wheat so that agribusinesses might "reap" a hearty return (12). Also see Lappe, Collins, and Rosset 1998.

10. In "Sweatshop Blues" Charles Kernaghan notes that garment workers in El Salvador (almost all of whom are women who often work seven days a week, sometimes fifteen hours a day, and in extreme cases twenty-two hours straight) are pressured to produce through verbal and physical threats; have limited access to bathrooms; are tested for pregnancy, with those found to be pregnant being fired on the spot; and are paid on average 60 cents per hour, which meets about one-third of the cost of living (1999:18). When Kernaghan asked workers to name the company whose clothes they made, they "reached into their pockets and took out a label, Liz Claiborne. The jacket cost $198 and the women in El Salvador were paid 84 cents to sew it. . . . As for the factory that the clothing was produced in, the cinderblock walls are ten feet high, topped by barbed wire, and there are locked metal gates. It's the same everywhere you go in Central America. There are teenagers going in to work. When the door opens, there are goons—armed guards—carrying pistols and sawed-off shotguns" (ibid.). Kernaghan also notes that "for the last two years the Liz Claiborne company has co-chaired the White House Task Force to eliminate sweatshop abuses. It says a lot about how far we have to move from the theory of ending sweatshop labor to the reality. El Salvador is now the eighth-largest exporter worldwide of apparel to the United States. This year it will send us 288 million garments. There are 60,000 to 65,000 *maquiladora* workers, and not one union—they are not allowed" (ibid.). In fact, for all the Kathie Lee Gifford–led public relations hoopla about corporate commitments to ending sweatshop labor, most companies have simply found alternative means for disguising their ongoing exploitation of workers around the world. Wal-Mart, for example, which publicly declares its commitment to stock its shelves with goods primarily made in the United States, sells goods that are mostly made outside the United States: 99.9 percent of its shoes, 89 percent of its Kathie Lee Gifford handbags, 96 percent

of its McKids children's clothes, 87 percent of its Faded Glory men's clothing, and 83 percent of all other goods surveyed (20). According to Kernaghan, Mexican and Indonesian workers still produce most of the Kathie Lee Gifford line. Meanwhile, electronics workers in the thousands of free-trade zones that dot the peripheral nations of the world suffer working conditions and wages similar to those of garment workers. "Aside from low wages," notes Gerald Sussman as he describes the situation of electronic workers in a Malaysian factory, "one of [the] biggest 'rents' paid by electronics workers for the privilege of being exploited is the damage done to their health. Workers interviewed by several Malaysian scholars have reported high rates of lung cancer deaths among otherwise healthy women working in the mold rooms where inhalation of toxic particles is common" (in Sussman and Lent 1998:133). Brouwer notes that "among the products Americans purchase in great quantity from factories operated abroad are athletic shoes, first and foremost those with the Nike label" (1998:75). And although Phil Knight, the owner of Nike, claims he is committed to ensuring that workers who produce its shoes are paid a living wage, evidence suggests that workers are still paid what amounts to starvation wages: "Nike produces sneakers at a cost of about $6.50, materials and labor combined, then sells them for $73 to $135 per pair all over the world. Nike, based in Oregon, has no U.S. production facilities and depends entirely on fast, high-dexterity, low-pay labor abroad. The company scours the world to find subcontractors who pay the lowest possible wages" (ibid.). In 1996, when Nike came under fire for its poor treatment of workers in Thailand and Indonesia, it began to pursue "cheaper options with its subcontractors in China, which now produces almost one half of all the world's shoes" (ibid.). Human rights violations are more difficult to document in China, thereby ensuring Nike's protection from being publicly embarrassed for its exploitation of labor. Moreover, the U.S. government has made it clear that it conceives of progress on human rights and profits made from property rights to be separate, if not unrelated, concerns—a conception that the Chinese government obviously shares, for it surrenders Chinese workers to foreign investors while it busily suppresses struggles for democracy, social justice, and workers' rights. The Chinese workers assembling "Nike, Reebok, Adidas, [and] L.A. Gear" are quite often overseen by "foreign managers, brought in from Taiwan (where many were once officers in the Taiwanese army), [who] scream out orders and march new recruits around in military formation. Workers live in newly constructed barracks—ten to a room is considered relatively low-density housing—and perform twelve hour shifts. The workplaces resemble prisons" (ibid.). A "shoe worker in Indonesia, for instance," writes Greider, "would have to work three or four months to earn enough cash to buy the sports shoes she assembles (though of course, she would never be able to save her earnings for such luxury). Typically, she lives in the company dormitory or perhaps in a settlement of bamboo-covered huts near the factory, sharing a tiny living space with five or six other workers who sleep in shifts on humble pallets" (1997:390). The compulsion of global capitalist competition produces "grotesque convergences between great wealth and great poverty. The most famous shoe producer, Nike, was said to pay more in one year's promotional fees to one American basketball star, Michael Jordan, than the entire workforce earned in the Indonesian shoe industry—the 25,000 workers who made Nike, Reebok, L.A. Gear, Adidas and other famous brands" (ibid.). It is easy to appreciate the incredible difference it makes to move production to nations where the price of labor is cheap and why, given the intensity of global competition, companies cannot afford to consider principles other than the bottom line. It is worth considering that Third World export-processing zones constitute the primary model for the creation of inner-city "domestic enterprise zones," a model that amounts to little more than a labor camp. Indeed, "we can now find the same sorts of abuses here at home. Some of the worst examples have been found in the sweatshops that employ legal and illegal immigrants and flourish in the New York and Los Angeles metropolitan areas. The most infamous of these was the 'slave labor' compound set up in 1988 by Thai and Chinese emigres in El Monte, California. When labor inspectors finally investigated in 1995 after seven years of operation, they found seventy-two Thai workers in a small compound of houses surrounded by a ten-foot wall topped with barbed wire. The immigrants were required to work seventeen-hour days for as little as 60 cents an hour. The clothing they sewed was routinely sold by wholesalers to premier department stores such as Neiman Marcus, Dayton Hudson, and Hecht's. The company, called D&R Fashions, was able to do business until 1995 because most garment workers in the United States now work in small establishments which are seldom ever seen by U.S. Department of Labor inspectors, who are overworked and understaffed due to government cutbacks" (Brouwer 1998:77).

11. Brecher and Costello note that "exclusive focus on national interests distorts people's understandings of what is really going on in the global economy. During the 1980s, as U.S. manufacturers deliberately disinvested in U.S. industry and moved their operations 'offshore,' many U.S. workers directed their hostility to Japanese workers; 'Toyota-bashing' became a highly publicized national sport. Corporations cannily exploited this attitude: at the very time it was abandoning steel plants instead of modernizing them, the U.S. Steel Corporation showed its workers a movie called 'Where's Joe?' blaming job loss on Japanese competition and asking for protection against Japanese steel imports" (1998:76).

12. In "Race, Riots, and Clouds of Ideological Smoke," the sociologist Kofi Buenor Hadjor notes that "Clinton signed the death warrant of traditional liberal Democratic Party politics at the end of July 1996, when he finally signed the Republican Personal Responsibility and Work Opportunity Act—a measure through which, as the not normally melodramatic *Newsweek* noted, 'the 60-year-old New Deal system established by Franklin Roosevelt to protect poor children and their mothers was simply abolished'" (1997:29).

13. This force, as I have noted, cost U.S. taxpayers more than 4 trillion dollars since 1980; that is, it cost them the possibility of raising the quality of life in United States for all citizens by spending this money on, for example, education, health care, child care, and the environment (see Glasberg 1997; Gottlieb 1997). For more on corporate welfare, see C. Collins 1997.

14. It is interesting to note the similarity of West's project to the platform articulated at the black convention held in Syracuse, New York, on the eve of presidential elections in 1864. Delegates formed the National Equal Rights League, which attacked the Republican Party for, as historian Vincent Harding relates, "even considering a truce with slavery, and for excluding blacks from their planning for the nation's future, [yet the league still] relied on the party. . . . More tragically, the staunch black men and women at Syracuse plunged even deeper into the heart of the contradiction, declaring: 'That we hereby assert our full confidence in the fundamental principles of this Government, the forces of acknowledged American ideas, the Christian spirit of the age, and the justice of our cause; and we believe that the generosity and sense of honor inherent in the great heart of this nation will ultimately concede us our just claims, accord us our rights, and grant us our full measure of citizenship under the broad shield of the Constitution'" (Harding 1981:248).

15. The "Wobblies were the early homegrown radicals of the American labor movement, formally organized as Industrial Workers of the World and proclaiming an all-encompassing, transnational challenge to corporate power" (Greider 1997:77).

Chapter 7: Prophetic Pragmatism and the American Evasion of Class Struggle

1. In this regard, it is worth recalling that Athens's "Golden Age" was built on the back of slave labor. For a Marxist interpretation of the causes, nature, and outcome of World War II, see Mandel 1986 and Parenti 1997.

2. "Why did I write that this [family breakdown] was the result of poverty? Why did I not write that poverty was the result of THIS? Ignorance. . . . I was surely no Marxist . . . Yet I thought, as a good Madisonian, that the 'various and unequal distribution of property' accounted for many social phenomena. What I had not adequately grasped was the degree to which these unequal distributions of property were in turn dependent upon a still more powerful agent—the behavior of individuals and communities" (in Hadjor 1995:152).

3. Kofi Buenor Hadjor points out that "a fashionable solution for the inner cities put forward by business and political commentators has been to argue that the ghettos can be revitalized by creating more of a business culture there. . . . One proposal that has come to the fore since the 1992 Los Angeles riots is for the extension of enterprise zones in the inner city," a proposal once popular with conservatives that has become popular with liberals and "figures prominently in the Democrats' agenda too" (1995:82). Both conservative and liberal politicians encourage tax-paying citizens to support giving "tax-breaks to companies that start up in desolate areas [because their investments] can help to kick-start the inner-city economies back to life" and thereby help to create a more democratic and prosperous America (ibid.). In fact, politicians and business leaders around the country have been remarkably successful in their efforts to enlist public support for such programs; over "the past decade or so, 38 states have created more than 600 enterprise zones in their inner cities" (83). Nevertheless, adds Hadjor, "the zones have made little discernible difference to the people of the blighted areas they encompass" (ibid.). This failure rests on a principle I have been arguing throughout this work: "companies will only move to an inner-city area if it makes sense according to the same criterion by which they judge everything—the drive to maximize profits" (ibid.). Inner-city enterprise zones function similarly to the *maquiladora* system in Mexico, where American corporations have managed, with the aid of the political leaders and the strong arm of the World Bank and International Monetary Fund, to set up a string of factories in which they are able to employ workers to produce goods at a fraction of what it would cost to produce these goods in the United States. So, for example, "in the aftermath of the 1992 riots, Disney said that it might build a factory in South Central LA—and might pay the California minimum wage of $4.25 an hour. That generous offer would instantly place a full-time worker at a level 25 percent below the official poverty line" (84). Enterprise zones offer generous tax breaks, subsidized power, and cheap labor to businesses seeking, as all businesses are, to reduce their production costs and thus increase the rate of surplus-value production and profits. Although enterprise zones represent "a mixture of government, business, and labor" and "do not follow any existing blueprint," they do not "invigorate the common good"; rather, they further only the good of corporations. The "proposal for more enterprise zones typifies the official response to the latest crisis in the American inner city," but they are not a "practical solution to the economic plight of the inner cities" (84, 85). However, "as a political device to strengthen the post-liberal consensus about the causes of Black poverty and reinforce the trend to scapegoat the ghetto, the calls for more enterprise zones can be seen as another useful message on behalf of the powerful and propertied elites" (85). Although enterprise zones may put many folks "back to work," this generally means back to work at poverty-level wages and in conditions not unlike those found in "deregulated" Bantustans such as Mexico, Indonesia, and Taiwan, where there are few, if any, environmental or workplace health and safety regulations to ensure the well-being of their citizens. Without articulating the class interests that inform all policy discussions, workers are left extremely vulnerable to politicians who claim their interests will be served by creating such zones, that they are in the best interest of everyone. A class analysis is necessary to expose the hidden interests that structure the public space and, in particular, the special corporate interests that exercise control of consciousness production, political discussion, and legislative action, and in so doing exercise enormous control over which policies will be given serious public consideration.

4. In *Another America* Hadjor points out that "the Clinton administration has tried to take up the Republican law-and-order mantel and to pursue the crusade against inner-city youth. The effect has been to reinforce all of the elite notions about the criminal tendencies of Black men from the inner city" (1995:117). At the time of this writing, Clinton has pursued a policy of continuous bombing of Iraq and military intervention in the former Yugoslavia. Of course these policies do nothing to advance the cause of democracy and in fact signal the United States' renewed commitment not only to being the global capitalist cop but also to using weapons of mass destruction in pursuit of profit.

5. It "is a just animosity that underpaid and overworked employees might feel toward those who squeeze as much profit from their labor as possible, who deny them the right to collective bargaining, who use repressive laws against unions, who oppose and ignore occupational safety codes, who refuse to negotiate contracts and violate the contracts that are negotiated, who raid employee pension funds, who force workers to take cuts in pay while awarding themselves lavish dividends and bonuses, and who live in utter opulence while their employees are deprived of minimum amenities. The hatred that the poor might feel toward their politico-economic oppressors has a basis in reality and is correctly directed. The hatred that the owning class feels toward organized workers is anchored in their fear of losing their privileged way of life" (Parenti 1994:134–35).

Works Consulted

Abanes, Richard. 1996. *American Militias: Rebellion, Racism, and Religion.* Downers Grove, Ill.: Intervarsity.

Ahmad, Aijaz. 1992. *In Theory: Classes, Nations and Literatures.* London: Verso.

———. 1996. "Issues of Class and Culture: An Interview with Aijaz Ahmad." *Monthly Review* 48, no. 5 (Oct.): 10–28.

Ake, Claude. 1994. "The African Context of Human Rights." In *Applied Ethics: A Multicultural Approach,* ed. Larry May and Shari Collins Sharratt, 35–40. Englewood Cliffs, N.J.: Prentice-Hall.

Alexander, Peter. 1987. *Racism, Resistance and Revolution.* London: Bookmarks.

Allen, Norm R., Jr. 1994. "The Crisis of the Black Religious Intellectual." *Free Inquiry* (Summer): 9–10.

Allen, Theodore William. 1994. *The Invention of the White Race.* New York: Verso.

Althusser, Louis. 1971. *Lenin and Philosophy.* Trans. Ben Brewster. New York: New Left Books.

Amin, Samir. 1993. "Historical and Ethical Materialism." *Monthly Review* 45, no. 2 (June): 44–56.

Anderson, Jervis. 1994. "The Public Intellectual." *The New Yorker,* Jan. 17, p. 40.

Aptheker, Herbert. 1992. *Anti-Racism in U.S. History: The First Two Hundred Years.* Westport, Conn.: Greenwood.

Aronson, Ronald. 1994. *After Marxism.* New York: Guilford.

Athanasiou, Tom. 1996. *Divided Planet: The Ecology of Rich and Poor.* Boston: Little, Brown.

Baldwin, James. 1962. *The Fire Next Time.* New York: Dell.

Banneker, Benjamin. 1993. "Letter to Thomas Jefferson." In *Crossing the Danger Water: Three Hundred Years of African-American Writing,* ed. Deirdre Mulane, 47–50. New York: Doubleday.

Barber, Benjamin. 1995. *Jihad vs. McWorld.* New York: Times Books.

Bell, Derek A. 1992. *Faces at the Bottom of the Well.* New York: Basic Books.

Bello, Walden F., Shea Cunningham, and Bill Rau. 1994. *Dark Victory: The United States, Structural Adjustment, and Global Poverty.* London: Pluto.

Bennet, Jon, and Susan George. 1987. *The Hunger Machine.* Cambridge, Mass.: Polity.

Bhaskar, Roy. 1989. *Reclaiming Reality: A Critical Introduction to Contemporary Philosophy.* London: Verso.

Black, George. 1988. *The Good Neighbor.* New York: Pantheon.
Boff, Clodovis. 1987. *Theology and Praxis.* Trans. Robert R. Barr. Maryknoll, N.Y.: Orbis Books.
Boff, Leonardo, and Clodovis Boff. 1984. *Salvation and Liberation: In Search of a Balance between Faith and Politics.* Trans. Robert R. Barr. Maryknoll, N.Y.: Orbis Books.
Bonino, José Míguez. 1974. *Marxists and Christians.* Grand Rapids, Mich.: William Eerdmans.
Bowman, Jim. 1994. "A Conference on Racism." *Commonweal* 121, no. 4 (Feb. 25): 6–9.
Boynton, Robert S. 1991. "Princeton's Public Intellectual." *New York Times Magazine,* Sept. 15, p. 39.
Brecher, Jeremy. 1998. *Strike!* Rev. ed. Boston: South End.
Brecher, Jeremy, and Tim Costello. 1998. *Global Village vs. Global Pillage: Economic Reconstruction from the Bottom Up.* 2d ed. Boston: South End.
Brock, Rita Nakashima, and Susan Thistlethwaite. 1996. *Casting Stones: Prostitution and Liberation in Asia and the United States.* Minneapolis, Minn.: Fortress.
Brouwer, Steve. 1998. *Sharing the Pie: A Citizen's Guide to Wealth and Power in America.* New York: Henry Holt.
Brown, Robert McAfee, ed. 1990. *Kairos: Three Prophetic Challenges to the Church.* Grand Rapids, Mich.: William Eerdmans.
Buchanan, Patrick J. 1998. *The Great Betrayal.* Boston: Little, Brown.
Bullard, Robert D., and Beverly Wright, eds. 1992. *Confronting Environmental Racism: Voices from the Grassroots.* Boston: South End.
Burbach, Roger, and William I. Robinson. 1999. "The Fin de Siècle Debate: Globalization as Epochal Shift." *Science and Technology* 63, no. 1 (Spring): 10–39.
Bushart, Howard L., John R. Craig, and Myra Barnes, eds. 1998. *Soldiers of God: White Supremacists and Their Holy War for America.* New York: Kensington.
Callinicos, Alex. 1992. "Race and Class." *International Socialism* 55 (Summer): 3–39.
———. 1993. *Race and Class.* London: Bookmarks.
Carré, François J. 1992. "Temporary Employment in the Eighties." In *New Policies for the Part-Time and Contingent Labor Force,* ed. Virginia L. duRivage, 1–14. Armonk, N.Y.: M. E. Sharpe.
Carter, Stephen L. 1991. *Reflections on an Affirmative Action Baby.* New York: Basic Books.
Chideya, Farai. 1995. *Don't Believe the Hype: Fighting Cultural Misinformation about African-Americans.* New York: Plume.
Chomsky, Noam. 1987. *The Chomsky Reader.* New York: Pantheon.
———. 1991. *Deterring Democracy.* London: Verso.
———. 1993. *What Uncle Sam Really Wants.* Berkeley, Calif.: Odonian.
Churchill, Ward. 1996. *From a Native Son: Selected Essays on Indigenism, 1985–1995.* Boston: South End.
———. 1997. *A Little Matter of Genocide: Holocaust and Denial in the Americas, 1492 to the Present.* San Francisco: City Lights Books.
Cleaver, Kathleen. 1998. "Interview." *Frontline: The Two Nations of Black America.* Television program broadcast Feb. 13. Text available at <www.pbs.org/wgbh/pages/fron_shows/race/interviews/kcleaver.html>.
Clorfene-Casten, Liane. 1996. *Breast Cancer: Poisons, Profits, and Prevention.* Monroe, Me.: Common Courage.
Colletti, Lucio. 1973. *Marxism and Hegel.* Trans. Lawrence Garner. London: Verso.
Collins, Chuck. 1997. "Aid to Dependent Corporations: Exposing Federal Handouts to the Wealthy." In *Current Economic Issues: Progressive Perspectives from Dollars and Sense,* ed. Marc Breslow, Abby Scher, and the *Dollars and Sense* Collective, 23–25. 2d ed. Somerville, Mass.: Dollars and Sense.

Cone, James. 1984. *For My People: Black Theology and the Black Church.* Maryknoll, N.Y.: Orbis Books.
———. 1986a. *A Black Theology of Liberation.* 2d ed. Maryknoll, N.Y.: Orbis Books.
———. 1986b. *My Soul Looks Back.* Maryknoll, N.Y.: Orbis Books.
———. 1991. *Martin and Malcolm: A Dream or a Nightmare.* Maryknoll, N.Y.: Orbis Books.
Conley, Dalton. 1999. *Being Black, Living in the Red.* Berkeley: University of California Press.
Conti, Joseph G., Stan Faryna, and Brad Stetson, eds. 1997. *Black and Right: The Bold New Voice of Black Conservatives in America.* Westport, Conn.: Praeger.
Cook, Blanche Wiesen. 1989. "The Impact of Anti-Communism in American Life." *Science and Society* 53, no. 4 (Winter): 470–75.
Coontz, Stephanie. 1992. *The Way We Never Were: American Families and the Nostalgia Trap.* New York: Basic Books,
———. 1997. *The Way We Really Are: Coming to Terms with America's Changing Families.* New York: Basic Books,
Coughlin, Ellen. 1993. "Cornel West Matters: The Celebrity Philosopher." *The Chronicle of Higher Education,* Sept. 22, p. A8–10.
Cox, Harvey. 1999. "The Market as God." *Atlantic Monthly,* Mar., p. 18–23.
Critchley, Simon, and Chantal Mouffe, eds. 1996. *Deconstruction and Pragmatism.* New York: Routledge.
Davis, Mike. 1986. *Prisoners of the American Dream.* London: Verso.
Delgado, Richard. 1996. *The Coming Race War?: And Other Apocalyptic Tales of America after Affirmative Action and Welfare.* New York: New York University Press.
Deloria, Vine. 1973. *God Is Red: A Native American View of Religion.* New York: Dell.
———. 1998. *For This Land: Writings on Religion in America.* New York: Routledge.
Depew, David, and Robert Hollinger, eds. 1995. *Pragmatism: From Progressivism to Postmodernism.* Westport, Conn.: Praeger.
Dewey, John. 1960. *The Quest for Certainty: A Study of the Relation of Knowledge and Action.* New York: Putnam's.
Diamond, Sara. 1995. *Roads to Dominion: Right-Wing Movements and Political Power in the United States.* New York: Guilford.
———. 1996. *Facing the Wrath: Confronting the Right in Dangerous Times.* Monroe, Me.: Common Courage.
Diggins, John Patrick. 1994. *The Promise of Pragmatism: Modernism and the Crisis of Knowledge and Authority.* Chicago: University of Chicago Press.
Du Bois, W. E. B. 1940. *Dusk of Dawn: An Essay Toward an Autobiography of a Race.* New York: Schocken Books.
———. 1969. *An A.B.C. of Color.* New York: International/Seven Seas Books.
———. 1976. *Black Reconstruction.* Millwood, N.Y.: Kraus-Thomson.
duRivage, Virginia L., ed. 1992. *New Policies for the Part-Time and Contingent Work Force.* Armonk, N.Y.: M. E. Sharpe.
Dyer, Joel. 1997. *Harvest of Rage: Why Oklahoma City Is Only the Beginning.* Boulder, Colo.: Westview.
Dyson, Eric Michael. 1993. *Reflecting Black: African-American Cultural Criticism.* Minneapolis: University of Minnesota Press.
———. 1995. *Making Malcolm: The Myth and Meaning of Malcolm X.* New York: Oxford University Press.
Eagleton, Terry. 1996. *The Illusions of Postmodernism.* Cambridge, Mass.: Blackwell.
Engels, Frederick. 1970 [1878]. *Anti-Dühring.* Trans. Emile Burns; ed. C. P. Dutt. New York: International.

Engels, Frederick, and Karl Marx. 1975. *On Religion.* Moscow: Progress.

Epstein, Barbara. 1996. "Radical Democracy and Cultural Politics." In *Radical Democracy: Identity, Citizenship, and the State,* ed. David Trend, 127–39. New York: Routledge.

Fahey, Dan. 1999. "Depleted Uranium Ammunition." Text available at the National Gulf War Resource Center website, <www.ngwrc.org>.

Farley, Reynolds. 1997. "Racial Trends and Differences in the United States 30 Years after the Civil Rights Decade." *Social Science Research* 26, no. 3 (Sept.): 235–62.

Farrakhan, Louis. 1993. *A Torchlight for America.* Chicago: FCN.

Foner, Philip. 1974. *Organized Labor and the Black Worker.* New York: International.

Foner, Philip, and Ronald L. Lewis, eds. 1989. *Black Workers: A Documentary History from Colonial Times to the Present.* Temple University Press.

Foster, John Bellamy. 1993. "Introduction to a Symposium on *The Ethical Dimensions of Marxist Thought.*" *Monthly Review* 45, no. 2 (June): 8–16.

Foucault, Michel. 1977. *Language, Counter-Memory, Practice: Selected Essays and Interviews.* Ed. Donald F. Bouchard; trans. Donald F. Bouchard and Sherry Simon. Ithaca, N.Y.: Cornell University Press.

———. 1980. *Power/Knowledge: Selected Interviews and Essays: 1972–1977.* Ed. Colin Gordon; trans. Colin Gordon, Leo Marshall, John Mepham, and Kate Soper. New York: Pantheon Books/Harvester.

Fraser, Steven, ed. 1995. *The Bell Curve Wars: Race, Intelligence, and the Future of America.* New York: Basic Books.

Gans, Herbert J. 1995. *The War against the Poor: The Underclass and Antipoverty Policy.* New York: Basic Books.

Gapasin, Fernando, and Michael Yates. 1997. "Organizing the Unorganized: Will Promises Become Practices?" *Monthly Review* 49, no. 3 (July-Aug.): 46–62.

Gates, Henry Louis, Jr. 1996. "Parable of the Talents." In Henry Louis Gates Jr. and Cornel West, *The Future of the Race.* New York: Knopf.

———. 1998. "Henry Louis Gates, Jr.: Interview with June Cross." *Frontline: The Two Nations of Black America.* Television program broadcast Feb. 13. Text available at <www.pbs.org/wgbh/pages/fron_shows/race/interviews/kcleaver.html>.

Genovese, Eugene D., and Elizabeth Fox-Genovese. 1987. "The Divine Sanction of Social Order: Religious Foundations of the Southern Slaveholders' World View." *Journal of the American Academy of Religion* 55, no. 2 (Summer): 211–29.

Glasberg, Davita Silfen. 1997. *Corporate Welfare Policy and the Welfare State.* New York: Aldine de Gruyter.

Goldberg, Carey. 2000. "Bradley and Gore Campaigns Split Harvard's Top Black Scholars." *New York Times,* Jan. 15, p. A7.

Goldberg, David Theo. 1993. *Racist Culture: Philosophy and the Politics of Meaning.* Cambridge, Mass.: Blackwell.

———. 1997. *Racial Subjects: Writing on Race in America.* New York: Routledge.

Goldfield, Michael. 1997. *The Color of Politics.* New York: New Press.

Gottlieb, Sanford. 1997. *Defense Addiction: Can America Kick the Habit?* Boulder, Colo.: Westview.

Gramsci, Antonio. 1971. *Selections from the Prison Notebooks.* Ed. and trans. Quintin Hoare and Geoffrey Nowell Smith. New York: International.

Grant, Jacquelyn. 1989. *White Women's Christ and Black Women's Jesus: Feminist Christology and Womanist Response.* Atlanta, Ga.: Scholars.

———. 1993. "Black Theology and the Black Woman." In *Black Theology: A Documentary History,* ed. Gayraud Wilmore and James H. Cone, 323–38. Rev. ed. Maryknoll, N.Y.: Orbis Books.

Greider, William. 1997. *One World, Ready or Not: The Manic Logic of Global Capitalism.* New York: Simon and Schuster.

———. 1998. "Global Roulette: In a Volatile World Economy, Can Everyone Lose?: A Colloquy with William Greider, Jeffrey E. Garten, and Ted C. Fishman." *Harpers,* June, pp. 39–50.

Gutiérrez, Gustavo. 1973. *A Theology of Liberation: History, Politics, and Salvation.* Trans. and ed. Sister Caridad Inda and John Eagleson. Maryknoll, N.Y.: Orbis.

Hacker, Andrew. 1992. *Two Nations: Black and White, Separate, Hostile, Unequal.* New York: Ballantine Books.

Hadjor, Kofi Buenor. 1995. *Another America: The Politics of Race and Blame.* Boston: South End.

———. 1997. "Race, Riots, and Clouds of Ideological Smoke." *Race and Class* 38, no. 4 (Apr.-June): 15–31.

Handler, Joel F., and Yeheskel Hasenfeld. 1997. *We the Poor People: Work, Poverty, and Welfare.* New Haven, Conn.: Yale University Press.

Harding, Vincent. 1981. *There Is a River.* New York: Vintage.

Harrison, Beverly. 1985. *Making the Connections: Essays in Feminist Social Ethics.* Ed. Carol S. Robb. Boston: Beacon.

Heidegger, Martin. 1969. *On the Question Concerning Technology and Other Essays.* Trans. William Lovitt. New York: Harper.

Hewlett, Sylvia Anne, and Cornel West. 1998. *The War against Parents: What We Can Do for America's Beleaguered Moms and Dads.* New York: Houghton Mifflin.

Hoecklin, Lisa. 1995. *Managing Cultural Differences: Strategies for Competitive Advantage.* Workingham, U.K.: Addison-Wesley/Economist Intelligence Unit.

Hollinger, David A. 1995. "The Problem of Pragmatism in American History: A Look Back and a Look Ahead." In *Pragmatism: From Progressivism to Postmodernism,* ed. David Depew and Robert Hollinger, 13–37. Westport, Conn.: Praeger.

hooks, bell. 1992. *Black Looks: Race and Representation.* Boston: South End.

———. 1995. *Killing Rage: Ending Racism.* New York: Henry Holt.

International Action Center. 1997. *Metal of Dishonor: The Pentagon's Secret Weapon.* New York: International Action Center.

Ireland, Paddy. 1997. "Corporations and Citizenship." *Monthly Review* 49, no. 1 (May): 10–27.

Isasi-Díaz, Ada María. 1993. *En la lucha/In the Struggle: Elaborating a Mujerista Theology.* Minneapolis, Minn.: Fortress.

Jackson, Njeri. 1998–99. "Race and Racism: One Down, One to Go." In *Perspectives on Multiculturalism and Cultural Diversity,* ed. Napoleon L. Peoples, 2–3. Richmond: Virginia Commonwealth University.

Jameson, Fredric. 1981. *The Political Unconscious: Narrative as a Socially Symbolic Act.* Ithaca, N.Y.: Cornell University Press.

Jones, Jacqueline. 1998. *American Work: Four Centuries of Black and White Labor.* New York: W. W. Norton.

Jones, Norrece T., Jr. 1990. *Born a Child of Freedom, Yet a Slave: Mechanisms of Control and Strategies of Resistance in Antebellum South Carolina.* Middletown, Conn.: Wesleyan University Press; Hanover, N.H.: University Press of New England.

Kaplan, Jeffrey, and Tore Bjorgo, eds. 1998. *Nation and Race: The Developing Euro-American Racist Subculture.* Boston: Northeastern University Press.

Kee, Alistair. 1990. *Marx and the Failure of Liberation Theology.* Philadelphia: Trinity International.

Kenney, Martin. 1986. *Biotechnology: The University Industrial Complex.* New Haven, Conn.: Yale University Press.

Kernaghan, Charles. 1999. "Sweatshop Blues." *Dollars and Sense,* Mar.-Apr., pp. 18–21.

King, Martin Luther, Jr. 1958. *Stride toward Freedom.* New York: Harper and Row.

———. 1967a. *Where Do We Go from Here: Chaos or Community?* Boston: Beacon.

———. 1967b. *The Trumpet of Conscience.* New York: Harper and Row.
———. 1981. *Strength to Love.* Philadelphia: Fortress.
———. 1986. *A Testament of Hope: The Essential Writings and Speeches of Martin Luther King, Jr.* Ed. James Melvin Washington. San Francisco: Harper San Francisco.
King, Paul G., Kent Maynard, and David O. Woodyard. 1988. *Risking Liberation: Middle Class Powerlessness and Social Heroism.* Atlanta, Ga.: John Knox Press.
King, Paul G., and David O. Woodyard. 1999. *Liberating Nature: Theology and Economics in a New Order.* Cleveland, Ohio: Pilgrim.
Kloppenberg, James T. 1986. *Uncertain Victory: Social Democracy and Progressivism in European and American Thought, 1870–1920.* New York: Oxford University Press.
Kovel, Joel. 1997. "Cuba and South Africa: The Fate of the Revolution." *Z Magazine,* June. Text available at <www.zmag.org>.
Laclau, Ernesto, and Chantal Mouffe. 1985. *Hegemony and Socialist Strategy: Towards a Radical Democratic Politics.* Trans. Winston Moore and Paul Cammack. London: Verso.
Landau, Saul. 1999. "The Revolution Turns Forty." *The Progressive,* Apr., pp. 24–30.
Lappe, Francis Moore, Joseph Collins, and Peter Rosset. 1998. *World Hunger: Twelve Myths.* 2d ed. New York: Grove.
Lappe, Marc, Britt Bailey, and John Lauritsen. 1998. *Against the Grain: Biotechnology and the Corporate Takeover of Your Food.* Monroe, Me.: Common Courage.
Larudee, Mehrene. 1997. "Who Gains from Trade?" In *Real World International: A Reader in Economics, Business, and Politics,* ed. Marc Breslow, David Levy, and Abby Scher, 2–3. Somerville, Mass.: Dollars and Sense.
Lauritsen, John. 1993. *The AIDS War: Propaganda, Profiteering, and Genocide from the Medical Industrial Complex.* New York: Asklepios.
Lerner, Richard M. 1992. *Final Solution: Biology, Prejudice, and Genocide.* University Park: Pennsylvania State University Press.
Lewis, Charles. 2000. "The Buying of the Presidency 2000." The Center for Public Integrity. Text available at <www.public-i.org/story_01_010400.htm>.
Lewontin, R. C. 1991. *Biology as Ideology: The Doctrine of DNA.* New York: HarperPerennial.
Lewontin, R. C., Steven Rose, and Leon J. Kamin. 1984. *Not in Our Genes.* New York: Pantheon.
Lilla, Mark. 1998. "Derrida's Politics." *New York Review of Books,* June 25, pp. 36–41.
Livingston, James. 1991. *Pragmatism and the Political Economy of Cultural Revolution.* Chapel Hill: University of North Carolina Press.
Lloyd, Brian. 1997. *Left Out: Pragmatism, Exceptionalism, and the Poverty of American Marxism, 1890–1922.* Baltimore, Md.: Johns Hopkins University Press.
Loewen, James W. 1995. *Lies My Teacher Told Me.* New York: New Press.
Long, Charles H. 1986. *Significations: Signs, Symbols, and Images in the Interpretation of Religion.* Philadelphia: Fortress.
Loy, David R. 1997. "The Religion of the Market." *Journal of the American Academy of Religion* 65, no. 2 (Summer): 275–90.
Luckmann, Thomas. 1967. *The Invisible Religion.* New York: Macmillan.
Lukács, Georg. 1971. *History and Class Consciousness: Studies in Marxist Dialectics.* Trans. Rodney Livingstone. Cambridge, Mass.: MIT Press.
———. 1981. *The Destruction of Reason.* Trans. Peter Palmer. Atlantic Highlands, N.J.: Humanities.
Malik, Kenan. 1996. "Universalism and Difference: Race and the Postmodernists." *Race and Class* 37, no. 3 (Jan.-Mar.): 1–17.
Mandel, Ernest. 1975. *Late Capitalism.* Trans. Joris de Bres. London: Verso.
———. 1986. *The Meaning of the Second World War.* London: Verso.

Marable, Manning. 1981. *Blackwater: Historical Studies in Race, Class Consciousness, and Revolution.* Niwot: University Press of Colorado.
———. 1983. *How Capitalism Underdeveloped Black America.* Boston: South End.
———. 1991. *Race, Reform, and Rebellion.* 2d ed. Jackson: University Press of Mississippi.
———. 1992. *The Crisis of Color and Democracy: Essays on Race, Class, and Power.* Monroe, Me.: Common Courage.
———. 1995. *Beyond Black and White.* New York: Verso.
———. 1997a. *Black Liberation in Conservative America.* Boston: South End.
———. 1997b. "Black Leadership and the Labor Movement." *Working USA,* Sept.-Oct., pp. 39–48.
———. 1998. "Louis Farrakhan and the Radical Right." *Dissent,* Spring, pp. 69–76.
Marsa, Linda. 1997. *Prescription for Profits: How the Pharmaceutical Industry Bankrolled the Unholy Marriage between Science and Business.* New York: Scribner's.
Marx, Karl. 1963 [1847]. *The Poverty of Philosophy.* New York: International.
———. 1977. *Capital: A Critique of Political Economy.* Vol. 1. Trans. Ben Fowkes. New York: Vintage.
Marx, Karl, and Frederick Engels. 1970 [1845–46]. *The German Ideology.* New York: International.
———. 1975. *On Religion.* Moscow: Progress.
Marx, Karl, Frederick Engels, and Vladimir Lenin. 1977. *Dialectical Materialism.* Moscow: Progress.
Massey, Douglas S., and Nancy A. Denton. 1993. *American Apartheid: Segregation and the Making of the Underclass.* Cambridge, Mass.: Harvard University Press.
McGarrity, Gayle. 1992. "Race, Culture, and Social Change." In *Cuba in Transition: Crisis and Transformation,* ed. Sandor Halebsky and John M. Kirk, with Carolle Bengelsorf, et al., 193–205. Boulder, Colo.: Westview.
McMurtry, John. 1995. "The Social Immune System and the Cancer Stage of Capitalism." *Social Justice: A Journal of Crime, Conflict, and World Order* 22, no. 4 (Winter): 1–25.
Meltzer, Milton. 1994. *Cheap Raw Material: How Our Youngest Workers Are Exploited and Abused.* New York: Viking.
Mesler, Bill. 1997. "Pentagon Poison: The Great Radioactive Ammo Cover Up." *The Nation* 264, no. 20 (May 26): 17–20.
Mészáros, István. 1993. "Marxism—Politics—Morality." *Monthly Review* 45, no. 2 (June): 28–36.
Mies, Maria. 1986. *Patriarchy and Accumulation on a World Scale.* Atlantic Highlands, N.J.: Zed.
Mills, Charles W. 1997. *The Racial Contract.* Ithaca, N.Y.: Cornell University Press.
———. 1998. *Blackness Visible: Essays on Philosophy and Race.* Ithaca, N.Y.: Cornell University Press.
Mishel, Lawrence, Jared Bernstein, and John Schmitt. 1999. *The State of Working America: 1998–99.* Ithaca, N.Y.: Cornell University Press.
Mitter, Swasti. 1986. *Common Fate, Common Bond.* London: Pluto.
Moody, Kim. 1997. *Workers in a Lean World: Unions in the International Economy.* London: Verso.
Moody, Kim, and Mary McGinn. 1992. *Unions and Free Trade: Solidarity vs. Competition.* Detroit, Mich.: Labor Notes.
Morris, Lloyd R. 1950. *William James: The Message of a Modern Mind.* New York: Scribner and Sons.
Naiman, Joanne. 1996. "Left Feminism and the Return to Class." *Monthly Review* 48, no. 2 (June): 12–28.
National Gulf War Resource Center. 1999. "1999 Gulf War Statistics." Text available at <www.ngwrc.org>.

Nelson-Pallmeyer, Jack. 1989. *War against the Poor: Low Intensity Conflict and Christian Faith.* Maryknoll, N.Y.: Orbis Books.

———. 1994. *Brave New World Order: Can We Pledge Allegiance?* Maryknoll, N.Y.: Orbis Books.

———. 1997. *School of Assassins: The Case for Closing the School of the Americas and for Fundamentally Changing U.S. Foreign Policy.* Maryknoll, N.Y.: Orbis Books.

Nielsen, Kai. 1989. "The Concept of Ideology: Some Marxist and Non-Marxist Conceptualizations." *Rethinking Marxism* 2, no. 4 (Winter): 146–73.

Nietzsche, Friedrich. 1977. *A Nietzsche Reader.* Trans. R. J. Hollingdale. New York: Penguin.

Nkrumah, Kwame. 1970. *Class Struggle in Africa.* New York: International.

Novack, George. 1975. *Pragmatism versus Marxism: An Appraisal of John Dewey's Philosophy.* New York: Pathfinder.

Oliver, Melvin L., and Thomas M. Shapiro. 1995. *Black Wealth/White Wealth: A New Perspective on Racial Inequality.* New York: Routledge.

Parenti, Michael. 1988. *The Sword and the Dollar.* New York: St. Martin's.

———. 1994. *Land of the Idols: Political Mythology in America.* New York: St. Martin's.

———. 1995. *Against Empire.* San Francisco: City Lights.

———. 1997. *Blackshirts and Reds: Rational Fascism and the Overthrow of Communism.* San Francisco: City Lights.

Parker, Mike, and Jane Slaughter. 1988. *Choosing Sides: Unions and the Team Concept.* Detroit, Mich.: Labor Notes.

Popkin, Richard H. 1977–78. "Hume's Racism." *Philosophical Forum* 9, nos. 2–3 (Winter-Spring): 211–26.

Pringle, Rosemary, and Sophie Watson. 1992. "'Women's Interests' and the Post-Structuralist State." In *Destabilizing Theory: Contemporary Feminist Debates,* ed. Michèle Barrett and Anne Phillips, 53–73. Cambridge, Mass.: Polity.

Quammen, David. 1998. "Planet of Weeds: Tallying the Losses of Earth's Animals and Plants." *Harpers,* Oct., pp. 57–69.

Ransby, Barbara. 1996. "U.S.: The Black Poor and the Politics of Expendability." *Race and Class* 38, no. 2 (Oct.-Dec.): 1–11.

Reed, Adolph. 1991a. "The Rise of Louis Farrakhan." *The Nation* 252, no. 2 (Jan. 21).

———. 1991b. "All for One and None for All." *The Nation* 252, no. 3 (Jan. 28).

———. 1995. "What Are the Drums Saying, Booker? The Current Crisis of the Black Intellectual." *Village Voice,* Apr. 11, pp. 31–36.

———. 1997a. "Token Equality." *The Progressive,* Feb., pp. 18–19.

———. 1997b. "A New Minimum: $10 an Hour." *The Progressive,* Apr., pp. 16–12.

———. 1997c. "The Descent of Black Conservatism." *The Progressive,* Oct., pp. 18–20.

———. 1997d. "Yackety-Yak about Race." *The Progressive,* Dec., pp. 18–19.

Reich, Robert. 1984. *The Next American Frontier: A Provocative Program for Economic Renewal.* New York: Viking/Penguin.

———. 1991. *The Work of Nations.* New York: Knopf.

Reiman, Jeffrey H. 1996. *The Rich Get Richer and the Poor Get Prison: Economic Bias in American Criminal Justice.* Boston: Allyn and Bacon.

Robinson, Cedric J. 1983. *Black Marxism: The Making of the Black Radical Tradition.* London: Zed.

Robinson, Lillian. 1993. "Touring Thailand's Sex Industry." *The Nation* 257, no. 14 (Nov. 1): 492–97.

Roediger, David. 1994. *Towards the Abolition of Whiteness: Essays on Race, Class, Politics, and Working Class History.* London: Verso.

Rorty, Richard. 1982. *The Consequences of Pragmatism.* Minneapolis: University of Minnesota Press.

———. 1991. "The Professor and the Prophet." *Transition: An International Review* 52:78.

Rosenthal, John. 1998a. *The Myth of Dialectics: Reinterpreting the Marx-Hegel Relation.* New York: St. Martin's.

———. 1998b. "Hitler or Malthus? On Two 'Models' of Capitalism." Unpublished manuscript. Colorado College, Colorado Springs.

Ross, Andrew, ed. 1988. *Universal Abandon? The Politics of Postmodernism.* Minneapolis: University of Minnesota Press.

———, ed. 1997. *No Sweat: Fashion, Free Trade, and the Rights of Garment Workers.* New York: Verso.

Ross, Robert J. S., and Kent C. Trachte. 1990. *Global Capitalism: The New Leviathan.* Albany: State University of New York Press.

Ruether, Rosemary Radford. 1975. *New Woman, New Earth: Sexist Ideologies and Human Liberation.* New York: Seabury.

———. 1983. *Sexism and God-Talk: Toward a Feminist Theology.* Boston: Beacon.

———. 1989. *Disputed Questions: On Being a Christian.* Maryknoll, N.Y.: Orbis Books.

———. 1992. *Gaia and God: An Ecofeminist Theology of Earth Healing.* San Francisco: Harper.

Ryder, John. 1993. "The Use and Abuse of Modernity: Postmodernism and the American Philosophic Tradition." *Journal of Speculative Philosophy* 7, no. 2:92–102.

Sanders, Mark A. 1994. "Race Matters." *Callaloo* 17, no. 2 (Spring): 645–50.

Sanoff, Alvin P. 1992–93. "Cornel West: A Theology for the Streets." *U.S. News and World Report,* Dec. 28–Jan. 4, p. 94.

Schwarz, John E. 1998. "The Hidden Side of the Clinton Economy." *Atlantic Monthly,* Oct., pp. 18–21.

Sciacchitano, Katherine. 1999. "Welfare Reform in the Global Economy." *Z Magazine,* Mar., pp. 26–31.

Scott, Robert E., Thea Lee, and John Schmitt. 1997. "Trading away Good Jobs: An Examination of Employment and Wages in the U.S., 1979–94." *Economic Policy Institute.* Text available at <epinet.org/bptrade.html>.

Segundo, Juan Luis, S.J. 1976. *The Liberation of Theology.* Trans. John Drury. Maryknoll, N.Y.: Orbis Books.

Selsam, Howard, David Goldway, and Harry Martel, eds. 1970. *Dynamics of Social Change.* New York: International.

Seymour, Gene. 1994. "The Fresh Prince of Ideas." *Newsday,* Jan. 17, p. 33.

Sherman, Howard, J. 1995. *Reinventing Marxism.* Baltimore, Md.: Johns Hopkins University Press.

Silk, Mark. 1988. *Spiritual Politics: Religion and America since World War II.* New York: Simon and Schuster.

Simpson, Lorenzo C. 1993. "Evading Theory and Tragedy?: Reading Cornel West." *Praxis International* 13, no. 1 (Apr.): 31–44.

Smedley, Audrey. 1998. *Race in North America.* Boulder, Colo.: Westview.

Smith, Sharon. 1994. "Mistaken Identity—or Can Identity Politics Liberate the Oppressed?" *International Socialism,* no. 62 (Spring): 3–50.

Soley, Lawrence C. 1995. *Leasing the Ivory Tower: The Corporate Takeover of Academia.* Boston: South End.

Steinberg, Stephen. 1995. *Turning Back: The Retreat from Racial Justice in American Thought and Policy.* Boston: Beacon.

Sussman, Gerald, and John A. Lent. eds. 1998. *Global Productions: Labor in the Making of the "Information Society."* Cresskill, N.J.: Hampton.

Tabb, William K. 1999. "Progressive Globalism: Challenging the Audacity of Capital." *Monthly Review* 50, no. 9 (Feb): 1–10.

Targ, Harry R., ed. 1996. *Marxism Today: Essays on Capitalism, Socialism, and Strategies for Social Change.* Westport, Conn.: Praeger.

Therborn, Goran. 1976. *Science, Class, and Society.* London: Verso.
Townes, Emilie M. 1997. *Embracing the Spirit: Womanist Perspectives on Hope, Salvation, and Transformation.* Maryknoll, N.Y.: Orbis Books.
Trotsky, Leon. 1972. *The Revolution Betrayed: What Is the Soviet Union and Where Is It Going?* Trans. Max Eastman. New York: Pathfinder.
Tucker, Robert C., ed. 1978. *The Marx-Engels Reader.* 2d ed. New York: Norton.
Unger, Roberto Mangabeira, and Cornel West. 1998. *The Future of American Progressivism.* Boston: Beacon.
Vallely, Paul. 1991. *Bad Samaritans: First World Ethics and Third World Debt.* Maryknoll, N.Y.: Orbis Books.
Walker, David. 1965. *Appeal to the Coloured Citizens of the World and Very Expressly to Those of the United States of America.* New York: Hill and Wang.
Wallis, Jim. 1994. *The Soul of Politics: Beyond the "Religious Right" and the "Secular Left."* San Diego: Harcourt, Brace.
Walsh, Joan. 1998. "America's War on Children." *Salon.* Internet journal. <www.salon1999.com/mwt/feature/1998/04/cov_23feature.html>.
West, Cornel. 1982. *Prophesy Deliverance!* Philadelphia: Westminster.
———. 1988a. *Prophetic Fragments.* Grand Rapids, Mich.: William Eerdmans.
———. 1988b. "Interview with Cornel West." Interview with Anders Stephanson. In *Universal Abandon,* ed. Andrew Ross, 269–86. Minneapolis: University of Minnesota Press.
———. 1989. *The American Evasion of Philosophy: A Genealogy of Pragmatism.* Madison: University of Wisconsin Press.
———. 1991. *The Ethical Dimensions of Marxist Thought.* New York: Monthly Review Press.
———. 1993a. *Race Matters.* Boston: Beacon.
———. 1993b. *Prophetic Thought in Postmodern Times: Beyond Eurocentrism and Multiculturalism.* Monroe, Me.: Common Courage.
———. 1993c. *Prophetic Reflections: Notes on Race and Power in America.* Monroe, Me.: Common Courage.
———. 1993d. *Keeping Faith: Philosophy and Race in America.* New York: Routledge.
———. 1993e. "Race Matters." Lecture delivered at Le Moyne College, Syracuse, New York, Feb. 17.
———. 1994. "West of Righteous." Interview with Anders Stephanson. *Art Forum* 32, no. 6 (Feb.).
———. 1996. "Black Strivings in a Twilight Civilization." In Henry Louis Gates Jr. and Cornel West, *The Future of the Race,* 53–112. New York: Knopf.
———. 1996–97. "The Talented Two." *Smith Alumnae Quarterly,* Winter, pp. 14–18.
———. 1997a. "Cornel West: Interview with John Nichols." *The Progressive* 61, no. 1 (Jan.): 26–29.
———. 1997b. Foreword. In Mumia Abu-Jamal, *Death Blossoms: Reflections from a Prisoner of Conscience,* xi–xii. Farmington, Pa.: Plough Publishing House of the Brunderhof Foundation.
———. 1998. "Cornel West: Interview with Henry Louis Gates Jr." *Frontline: The Two Nations of Black America.* Television program broadcast Feb. 13. Text available at <www.pbs.org/wgbh/pages/frontline/shows/race/interviews/west.html>.
———. 1999a. "Philosophical Faith in Action." Interview. *Harvard Review of Philosophy* 7 (Spring): 45–55.
———, ed. 1999b. *The Cornel West Reader.* New York: Basic Civitas Books.
West, Cornel, and bell hooks. 1991. *Breaking Bread: Insurgent Black Intellectual Life.* Boston: South End.

Westbrook, Robert C. 1991. *John Dewey and American Democracy.* Ithaca, N.Y.: Cornell University Press.

———. 1993. "Democratic Evasions: Cornel West and the Politics of Pragmatism." *Praxis International* 13, no. 1 (Apr.): 1–13.

Westra, Laura, and Peter S. Wenz, eds. 1995. *Faces of Environmental Racism: Confronting Issues of Global Justice.* Lanham, Md.: Rowman and Littlefield.

White, Jack E. 1993. "Philosopher with a Mission." *Time,* June 7, pp. 60–62.

Wieseltier, Leon. 1995. "All and Nothing at All: The Unreal World of Cornel West." *New Republic* 212, no. 10 (Mar. 6): 31–36.

Wilkinson, Richard G. 1996. *Unhealthy Societies: The Afflictions of Inequality.* London: Routledge.

Williams, Delores S. 1993. *Sisters in the Wilderness: The Challenge of Womanist God-Talk.* Maryknoll, N.Y.: Orbis Books.

Williams, Eric. 1944. *Capitalism and Slavery.* New York: Putnam.

Wilmore, Gayraud S. 1983. *Black Religion and Black Radicalism: An Interpretation of the Religious History of Afro-American People.* Maryknoll, N.Y.: Orbis Books.

Wilmore, Gayraud S., and James H. Cone, eds. 1993. *Black Theology: A Documentary History.* Rev. ed. Maryknoll, N.Y.: Orbis Books.

Wolfe, Edward N. 1996. *Top Heavy: The Increasing Inequality of Wealth in America and What Can Be Done about It.* New York: New Press.

Wolin, Richard, ed. 1991. *The Heidegger Controversy.* New York: Columbia University Press.

Wood, Ellen Meiksins. 1986. *The Retreat from Class: A New "True" Socialism.* London: Verso.

———. 1997a. "Back to Marx." *Monthly Review* 49, no. 2 (June): 1–9.

———. 1997b. "Labor, the State, and Class Struggle." *Monthly Review* 49, no. 3 (July-Aug.): 1–17.

X, Malcolm. 1964. *The Autobiography of Malcolm X.* New York: Ballantine Books.

———. 1965. *Malcolm X Speaks.* New York: Grove Weidenfeld.

Yaghmaian, Behzad. 1998–99. "Globalization and the State: The Political Economy of Global Accumulation and Its Emerging Mode of Regulation." *Science and Society* 62, no. 2 (Summer): 241–65.

Yancy, George. 1998. *African-American Philosophers: 17 Conversations.* New York: Routledge.

Yates, Michael D. 1999. "Braverman and the Class Struggle." *Monthly Review* 50, no. 8 (Jan.): 2–11.

Young, Julian. 1997. *Heidegger, Philosophy, Nazism.* New York: Cambridge University Press.

Young, Liz. 1997. *World Hunger.* New York: Routledge.

Zinn, Howard. 1980. *A People's History of the United States.* New York: Harper and Row.

Index

MARK DAVID WOOD is an assistant professor jointly appointed in religious studies and African American studies at Virginia Commonwealth University.

Typeset in 10.5/12.5 Adobe Minion
Composed by Jim Proefrock
at the University of Illinois Press
Manufactured by Thomson-Shore, Inc.

University of Illinois Press
1325 South Oak Street
Champaign, IL 61820-6903
www.press.uillinois.edu